Built in Texas

BENBROOK PUBLIC LIBRARY

3426700103 0274

Built in Texas

PUBLICATIONS OF THE TEXAS FOLKLORE SOCIETY NUMBER XLII

Copyright © 1979 The Texas Folklore Society

Second edition 2000

Printed in the United States of America

Requests for Permission to reproduce material from this work
should be sent to:

Permissions
University of North Texas Press
PO Box 311336
Denton TX 76203-1336
940-565-2142

The paper in this book meets the minimum requirements of the
American National Standard for Permanence of Paper for Printed
Library materials, Z39.48.1984

Library of Congress Cataloging-in-Publication Data

Built in Texas / edited by Francis Edward Abernethy ; line drawings
by Reese Kennedy.—2nd ed.
       p.   cm.—(Publications of the Texas Folklore Society ; no. 42)
    ISBN 1-57441-092-X (pbk. : alk. paper)
    1. Vernacular architecture—Texas. I. Abernethy, Francis Edward. II.
Series.

GR1 .T4 no. 42 2000
[NA730.T5]
390 s—dc21
[720'.9764]   00-029877

Design by Roger Lindstrom

Built in Texas

edited by
FRANCIS EDWARD ABERNETHY

Line drawings by
REESE KENNEDY

University of North Texas Press
Denton, Texas

Preface (In which the editor reflects upon his perambulations and peregrinations)

He was right, you know. You must be born again—and again and again, *ad infinitum,* or at least *ad cemeterium.* Those who aren't periodically reborn are like the snake who fails to shed his skin and is eventually squeezed to death by the narrowness of his old confines. Archer Fullingim, the ex-editor of *The Kountze News,* is a professed born-again Big Thicketite. Periodically he flings himself off into the wilderness of the Big Thicket and splashes around in Village Creek and wades through bay galls and pin-oak flats, and the Holy Ghost of the Big Thicket (and elsewhere, of course) takes a Pentecostal possession of him. He is born again and he talks in tongues that are almost as strange as some of his brass-collar-Democrat ravings. He rolls hollily in the Thicket grasses and leaves, and he shakes and quakes through spasms of love and communion until he sheds his old, city skin and is born again to a new identification with the Thicket and the Great Spirit that it is a part of. Then he goes contentedly back into town to grow gourds and make mayhaw jelly, agitate the political conservatives of Hardin County, and wait for his next call to the wilderness.

Driving around Texas looking at gates and windmills and adobe houses was an experience for me similar to Archer's periodic assumption of the Holy Ghost of the Big Thicket. I have a visceral need to make seasonal pilgrimages about the state, to touch it and taste it and smell it, to see that the sage and prairie grass and the water that flows through the sandy creek beds and the winds that blow through the rock hills are still there. And they always are, no matter what

the season. The leaves wither and fall or they turn glassy green—the water freezes in the stock ponds, or spills over under the watchful eye of a dragonfly, or settles down to a warm brown as the cows chug down the mud slope to drink—and nothing really changes. Archer's Holy Ghost is there too, in different, ever shifting shapes perhaps but always blessing the earth with its presence. It broods with warm breast and ah! bright wings over Texas (and, granted, elsewhere) and when you are close enough to it you feel that you can almost wrap the good earth around you like a great soft steer hide and feel its love and comfort.

I camped one night in the Palo Duro and awoke the next morning swallowed by a fog which filled the canyon so thick you could see it move, and every boulder and tourist and roadrunner became an ingredient in the thick, grey soup. I spent a bright night with a sweet moon behind a cotton gin on the Trinity and watched an old mammy coon and her young'un stroll by about a nickel's flip away. The old mammy waddled on down into the cotton rows barely acknowledging my presence, while the coon-child skipped and nosed the air and looked back over his shoulder. "Hey, Mama, I think there was somebody in that sleeping bag!" I trespassed one night in the mesquite and tall grass north of Ozona and figured I was about to get my plough cleaned by the ranch foreman, who relented and took me where the grass was shorter and less combustible, and who later, around midnight, rousted me out to help him fix a float valve on a water trough in the next pasture.

My best camp was in those rocky hills south of Marfa, just before they drop off into the Rio Grande valley and Presidio. I pulled in around sundown, pitched camp, fixed an ailing clutch spring, and then poked along the trails for a while looking for snakes. I got back to the pickup at good dark and stirred around considerably fixing supper, which consisted of frying a steak I had picked up at Alpine and opening a can of fruit cocktail. After supper I cleaned up meticulously, wiping out the skillet with a Scott Towel, burning my paper plate, lipping my fork, and cleaning my pocket knife on my boot. But with all this activity I still wasn't tired enough to relax and go to bed, and I recognized that I was feeling lonesome and bored. The radio didn't help and neither did several cigarettes and an Old Charter nightcap. I glumped around, sitting on the tailgate, then lying on my bed roll, till I finally gave up, put on my headlight, and started walking along the ridge road. I guess I walked a mile, stopping to look at crawling things, seeing a baby diamondback coiled in a circle no bigger than a silver dollar, before I finally got to the edge of the hill, where it falls off into the valley below. I found a throne rock there, where somebody put it so that you could sit and lean back and look down at the lights of Presidio and Ojinaga and at the little yellow lights shining from the people of the long river valley and watch the lights from the cars and trucks as they rolled off the high places and sailed almost silently down the long road to the bottom. I sat and watched and breathed in all the sounds and sights, and soon everything went easy, and I wasn't lonesome or bored or anything that you sometimes are when you are feeling alone. There are rare and magic times when the distractions of the flesh fade and the body relaxes enough for the soul to slip out and take communion with whatever broods over the bent world with its bright and silent wings.

I wrapped around me all those rocks and chiming stars and the sounds of trucks whining down the mountains—and all those night walkers that start little rock slides and rustle through yucca stumps and dead bear grass—I wrapped all this gentle pulse around me and walked back to camp to lie down and thread my eyebeams with the stars.

The next day at Presidio the temperature was 108°, and I damn near fried.

I bathed in rivers and stock ponds, usually well off the road, but once in sweaty desperation and the heat of mid-August afternoon I performed my ablutions in Live Oak Creek near Fort Lancaster while traffic sped over me on the highway bridge. Now I can't drive over a highway bridge without wondering what's going on underneath. One evening south of Blanco a bunch of old nosey mama cows came to watch me as I lay immersed in a spring pool trying to bring down the body's temperature and to flush off the dust of the road. Much refreshed, I arose like a skinny Proteus from the sea, and off they ran, tails lofted indignantly in the air, shrieking, "Run away, run away—it's a nekkid man!" They eyed me from the security of a patch of live oak, still wary of my intentions, as I dried off in the sun and put on my clothes. By the time I got back to the road they had walked to the pool and were looking suspiciously around to see what else might come out of the water.

I drove through Hale Center when the sirens and radios were screaming the town's population into their storm cellars, and rain poured out of an angry cloud that sat down over us like a black-iron skillet lid. Little tails funneled down out of the dark clouds to the west, and there wasn't ditch number-one to get into in case one of the twisters had gotten serious and cut off my retreat to the south.

On my first trip, up through the blacklands and the Cross

Timbers to the Panhandle, I carried enough camping gear to support a safari. Thereafter I cut down to essentials and during the day grazed on cheese, milk, and oatmeal cookies. Most of the time I had a cot to sleep on, but I enjoyed the ground when I wasn't in rocks. The one night I got caught in the rain, I tied my lariat to the front bumper, ran it over the cab and back past the tailgate to a mesquite tree. Then I hung the tarpaulin over the rope, letting it hang down on both sides of the truck bed. That makes a good tent. By the time I got it up I was wet and the rain had begun to slacken and soon stopped. I went to bed under the tarp anyway and got hot and hoped it would start raining again to justify my discomfort. Buzzing and whirring things flew out of the prickly pear and into the tent and couldn't find their ways out. I finally roused myself enough to gamble that the rain was over and to strip back the tarp. Breathing came easier under the open sky, and it didn't rain.

I saw a world of barns and fences and bump gates, I mean really saw them with fresh eyes, and looked at worn wood grain and saddle-notches and rubble and specks of shiny gravel in adobe, and saw how stone fences have thin shims between the big rocks on both sides of the fence so the rocks will slope into the middle and support each other. I admired the good standing houses built in the traditional style and ways, but I learned more from the old-timers that were crippled over to one side with their ribs showing and their blank eyes staring. They were houses unadulterated, with all their sins and blemishes apparent, showing how the maker put them together in the beginning. Sometimes the chinking still showed the marks of fingers and palms, and old worried boards revealed bent square nails with cuss words still on them.

Old houses—decayed, crumbling, propped—are not dead things when you sit down and visit with them. Their lives might be over as far as providing comfort and cover, but their past is rich in all the life and living and sinning and dying that they had sheltered. They've seen the elephant and heard the owl. When they finally do go, the old chimney stands for a while like a tombstone over the house place till time and vines drag it, too, into the dust from whence it came.

Deep East Texas and the Hill Country were the richest in traditional houses. I could have worn my camera out taking pictures of East Texas log barns. That part of the state still has a lot of traditional building, because people were still building with logs and in the old styles through the 1930's and 1940's. And those log buildings that were built in the nineteenth century out of fat pine will be there till somebody pushes them over. The Germans of the Hill Country built the best and sturdiest houses, mostly rock, some out of cedar logs, and one could spend a lifetime savoring the work of those master builders. I didn't find many old houses and farm buildings in the Panhandle. They were probably used up during the Depression and the Dust Bowl. While I was there I wound my way through pastures to our old ranch house on the Washita, and all that was left was the blacksmith shop, the concrete horse trough, and my grandmother's Great Majestic wood cook stove. I looked for a piece of myself among the debris, but nothing was there except the sound of the wind that dusted the old place out in the thirties.

The old things are usually kept where land and property are handed down. People that belong to an area keep the things of their families' and their culture's past; new people clean out for a fresh start.

A preface should be placed at the end of the book rather than at the first because the editor writes the preface after he's built the book, and he's usually mulling over the whole job to see what he learned and whether it was worth all the fuss. It was worth it. I discovered the new and revisited the old and learned again the deep love I have for this land and the life upon it. I'm too much in love with the present to worship the past, but I do respect it mightily. The old folks have planted the vines from which we gather the grapes, and the stock is still strong and the fruit is sweet.

The Texas Folklore Society got a lot of help from its friends with this volume. The contributors, of course, are the stars of the production and we genuinely appreciate their labors.

Because of the size of this book and the ever increasing production costs, we had to have financial assistance from the outside. We thank the following foundations and individuals for their help, and we want them to know that we couldn't have made it without them: the Moody Foundation, the George and Mary Josephine Hamman Foundation, Southland Paper Mill Foundation, The Harris and Eliza Kempner Fund, Buddy and Ellen Temple, Time Incorporated, and a generous Society member. And I could not have run all over the state looking and taking pictures without a much appreciated faculty research grant from Stephen F. Austin State University. The Society is ever in debt to those foundations and individuals who have come to its aid and made its spending less deficital.

For their continuing support of the Texas Folklore Society on the Stephen F. Austin State University campus, the Society thanks President William R. Johnson and Roy E. Cain, head of the department of English. And may the sun and moon shine ever brightly on the Society's secretary and assistant editor, Mrs. Martha Dickson, who does the hard work that turns ideas into realities.

Francis Edward Abernethy
Nacogdoches, Texas
April 19, 1979

Table of Contents

Texas Folk Building:
an introduction

Folk building is opportunistic and it is traditional. A man takes whatever materials he has at hand—logs, rocks, sometimes the very earth itself—and he builds with those materials whatever it takes to survive. The methods he uses to shape his log or thatch his roof are those he learned from his forefathers or from the people he has lived among. The forms that he shapes, whether they are barns or fences or stock tanks, are those that satisfy not only the immediate needs for which they are built, but also satisfy what the eye has been conditioned by his culture to see as beautiful. Folk building is a part of the landscape from which it is made, and it accommodates the land and people equally.

Texas is peculiarly suited for the invasion of immigrants from all directions. From the northeast came the Scotch-Irish. Across the Southern states came the English, Scots, and Irish who had earlier left Virginia and the Carolinas after completing their indentures. Into Galveston and Indianola came Germanic and Slavic people from Europe. And from the south across the Rio Grande came the Mexicans, many of whom were on Texas soil before the outlanders even thought of coming to the state. Each group brought its own styles and methods of building, and each adapted the styles to the material at hand and began building to keep off the rain and to cope with the wild, new land.

1

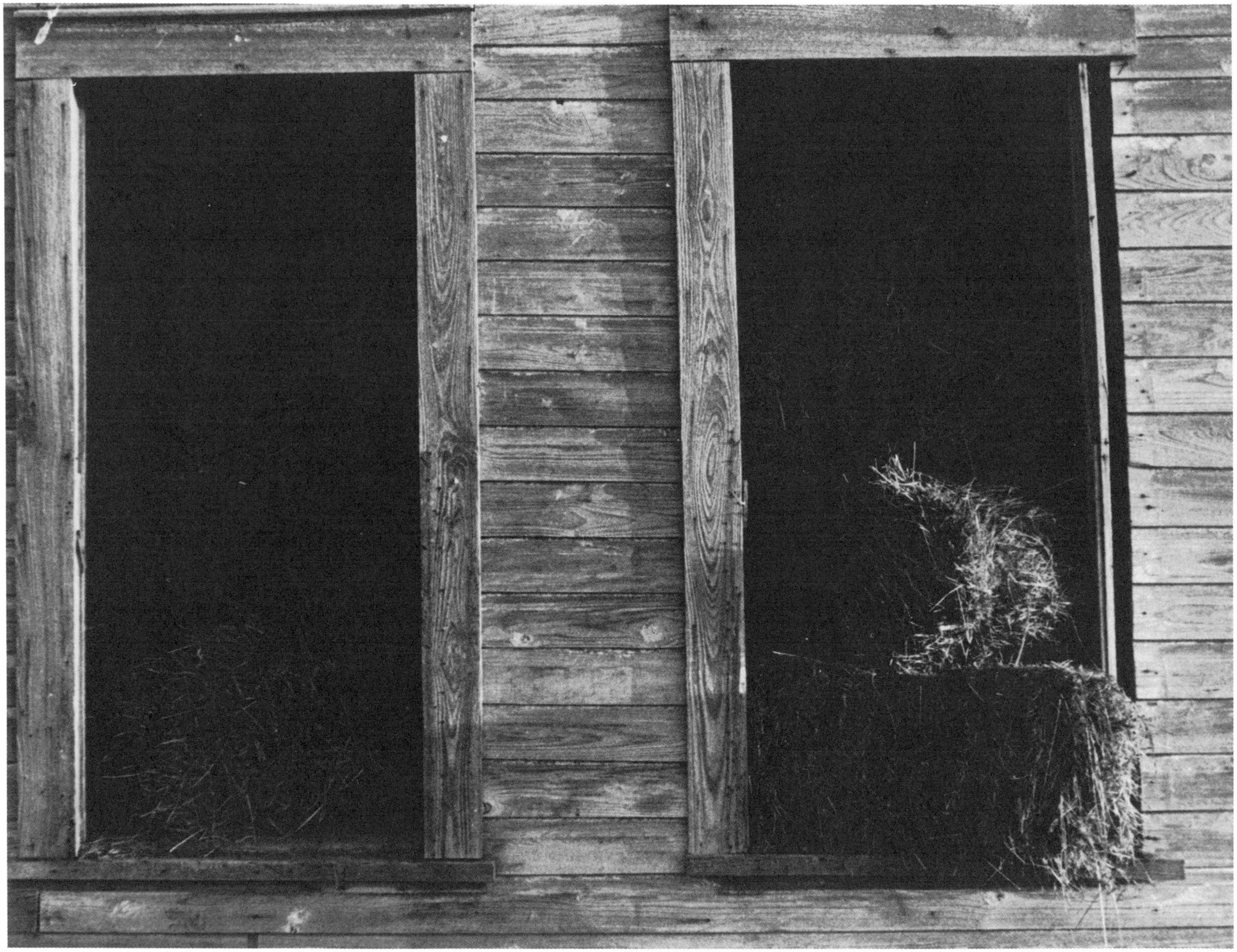

A house becomes a barn

Built in Texas

F. E. Abernethy

Man is naturally and genetically a builder, continually struggling to plumb and square life into an order that he can cope with. He builds books out of words, songs out of sounds, and he goes into the big woods of his old beliefs, cuts and dresses the logs, and dovetails them together into new religions. He takes whatever is in the lumber pile of his culture and shapes it into traditional forms. His folk art and philosophies and religions are shelters he has constructed to protect himself from the harsher elements of life and from the slings and arrows of the fortune that rages out about him. He builds his barns and bungalows and material needs for survival from the same sorts of sources and for the same reason, for protection from the disorder that nature and life subject him to. Walling, fencing, and impounding are fundamental to life and fundamental to preserving the order that is necessary for survival. The walls might be individual or social, chain-linkly literal or morally figurative, but they constitute bounds within which life began and within which society was able to continue. And they are our folklore.

Everything begins with walls. The nervous, throbbing life that we evolved from and still relate to began with a walled-off cell of impounded protoplasm, fenced in so that it could not escape. Then the cell wall became a wall of cells and later a chitin-plastered house sheltering a family of cooperating cells. As life became more affluent it shingled the roof and walls with scales and later thatched the house with feathers or finished it with fur. And there we stood

and still stand, unadulterated and slightly embarrassed, before our bathroom mirrors in a house fine enough for a god. The modesty imposed by our culture and the raw sport of nature require that we cover one wall with another; so, like the old German that sophisticatedly plastered over the original limestone rock of his house or the Anglo that framed his log cabin in with more fashionable board and batten, we veneer our originality with Hart, Schafner and Marx.

The lower animals are the primal "folk builders," instinctively rather than traditionally using the materials and methods and following the forms of their ancestors. Like the folk, they build utilitarian structures of naturally available materials to provide a place to produce and protect their young and to shelter them from the elements. The dirt dauber builds his neat little house out of mud. Beavers cut and stack sticks and logs into island huts. Roadrunners throw a stick nest together like the poorest type of white trash, while the fashionable oriole meticulously hangs and weaves its scrotum-like home out of the finest sorts of horse hair, moss, and leaves. That which the animal builds is purely functional, every angle and corner of roof and wall and floor. This satisfies a basic characteristic of folk architecture.

Man in his dim beginnings lived in much the same way as did his animal kinsmen, crawling into holes and caves for shelter, stacking rocks across a cave entrance for protection, burrowing down in the deep grass like deer, living as a part of his environment, sometimes barely softening it with walls. But he became what sociologists refer to as the folk and became a folk builder, constructing his walls with what was at hand, rocks into huts, skins and hides into teepees, posting logs side by side, like trees growing, to make a palisade wall, and covering all with palmetto leaves. The Bushmen of the Kalihari have a way of teepeeing a clump of tall grass by twisting it together at the top that will wall out some of the night's cold. A Mexican with a machete can quickly build a shelter out of a few sticks and banana leaves that will roof out the rain. And an Eskimo, almost as quickly, can cut and stack blocks of ice, sealed with snow, into an igloo that will keep out some of the bone-chilling cold.

The early builders in Texas followed the same patterns of living and building. The Morrises, moving from Mississippi to Fisher County in the 1860's spent their first winter in a cave on the bluffs of the Clear Fork of the Brazos. Ben Abernethy proved his claim in Old Greer County living in a dugout. Those settlers who tarried on the timbered lands of East Texas built with the readily available pine logs in the traditions of their fathers; those in the Western Cross Timbers used oak. European migrants into central Texas stacked rocks into houses in the fashions learned in the Old Country. West Texans of the Pecos, who had neither rocks nor logs to build with, mixed mud and grass, made adobe brick, and built in traditions borrowed from the Mexican-Indian population already settled there. These were the folk, building out of the environment, wasting nothing, building forms to suit their needs.

This purest type of folk building blends with its surrounding as closely as the homes of the animals the folk lived among. The log house with stick-and-mud chimney and puncheon floor was as natural to the forest world that

it was a part of as the nest of a bird. The sod shanties and dugouts of the plains were as much a part of the landscape as prairie dog mounds, and both men and dog shared his home with the rattlesnakes and spiders and centipedes of the prairie.

Those early Texas settlers were conscious of their primitive homes and their vulnerability to nature, and they certainly were not living in the primitive manner just to be colorful. If given a choice between a log house and an aluminum-sided trailer house, they would probably have chosen the latter. They planned to do better as soon as possible. They left us some of their reflections in the folk music they sang about themselves and their surroundings. The legendary Tom Hight sings about his home in Old Greer County, Texas, in a traveling folk song sung to the tune of "The Irish Washerwoman." Tom reportedly went to Greer County in the 1880's, suffered much under trying circumstances, and then resigned his claim and returned to civilization. Tom probably lived in a half-dugout. That is, he dug a room down about four feet, built walls from ground level up two or three more feet, covered it with boards or logs, and sodded it over with turf.

My house is built out of natural soil,
The wall are erected according to Hoyle,
The roof has no pitch but is level and plane,
And I always get wet if it happens to rain.

Tom also commented on his closeness to nature and to the creatures of nature that he shared his home with.

How happy am I when I lay down to bed,
A rattlesnake hisses a tune at my head,
A gay little centipede all without fear
Crawls over my pillow and into my ear.

Primal buildings — a crawdad chimney and a spider's web

Rocks and logs (*Hays Co.*)

6

Present-day tool house made of old logs and modern telephone poles *(Hays Co.)*

7

Hinges

One particular city-bred Easterner who came west in search of fame, fortune, and adventure sang his song about "The Little Old Sod Shanty" to the tune of "Little Old Log Cabin in the Lane," a popular minstrel song of the 1880's and '90's. The distance that lay between the dream and the reality was emphasized by the contrast between the pastoral and ideal Log Cabin in the Lane and the starkly uncomfortable and lonesome sod shanty on the claim on the Texas frontier.

> I'm getting mighty weary now just holding
> down my claim.
> My vittles are not always of the best.
> The mice creep shyly round me as I lay me
> down to rest
> In my little old sod shanty on my claim.
> The hinges are of leather and the windows have
> no glass,
> And the board roof lets the howling blizzard in.
> I can see the hungry coyote as he creeps up
> through the grass
> In my little old sod shanty on my claim.

Housing was easier to come by in East Texas where tall, straight, rich pine grew, ready for hacking and hewing and being laid into walls. But the log house, as romantic as it might seem to be now, was not so to the people of the settled and civilized South who had graduated to houses of brick and milled lumber. A come-all-ye that had as its burden a warning to all young ladies who were considering going west with a Texan is called "Louisiana Girls." The song begins with a warning about Texans generally, about their uncouth manners and dress, and then describes the living conditions.

> They'll take you to a house with hewed log walls,
> And it ain't got no windows at all,
> An old board roof and a puncheon floor,

It's that way all Texas o'er.
It's that way all Texas o'er.

The journals of early Texans give an even more graphic description of the folk building of the early settlers, many of whom had never built any kind of housing before. They were able to get help and do better or, discouraged, return to the Old Country.

One group of Polish settlers who came directly from their homes in Upper Silesia to Texas arrived in December, 1854, and during that first winter, as one settler put it, "We lived in burrows covered with brush and stalks."[1] The Poles continued to live close to nature and the wild life that they shared it with even after they built their first year's huts in Panna Maria. Father Leopold Moczygemba tells about entertaining friends in his home and a rattlesnake falling through the grass roof and landing on the dinner table.[2]

Caroline von Hinuber tells about her first home in Industry, which her German family occupied through the winter of 1831-32:

After we had lived on Fordtran's place for six months [Charles Fordtran, a tanner from Westphalia], we moved into our own house. This was a miserable little hut, covered with straw and having six sides, which were made out of moss. The roof was by no means water-proof, and we often held an umbrella over our bed when it rained at night, while the cows came and ate the moss. Of course, we suffered a great deal in the winter. My father had tried to build a chimney and fireplace out of logs and clay, but we were afraid to light a fire because of the extreme combustibility of our dwelling. So we had to shiver.[3]

Ferdinand Roemer described the first houses of the New Braunfels Germans in 1846 as hovels made of cedar posts set side by side, palisade style, and roofed with tent cloth or buffalo hides.[4] Fredrick Olmsted described the German-Alsatian settlement of D'Hanis in Medina County as a most singular spectacle upon the verge of the great American wilderness. It is like one of the smallest and meanest of European peasant hamlets. There are about twenty cottages and hovels, all built in much the same style, the walls being made of poles and logs placed together vertically and made tight with clay mortar, the floors of beaten earth, the windows without glass, and roofs built so as to overhang the four sides and deeply shade them, and covered with thatch of fine brown grass laid in a peculiar manner, the ridge-line and apexes being ornamented with knots, tufts, crosses or weathercocks.[5]

Father Claude-Marie Dubuis, a Catholic missionary came to Castroville in 1847, and wrote a letter home describing his first rectory.

...I was solemnly installed in the house set apart for the Missionary. Without delay I will describe it to you. The walls consist of several stakes driven into the ground and the little grass thrown above formed the roof. No need of doors or windows, the whole building was pervaded by daylight. A few dozen scorpions mingled with myriads of insects had been domiciled there and formed the only furnishings, with the exception of a cowhide on which I could expect the repose of a sybarite.[6]

Life and building methods improved, and Carl Urbantke tells about building a house in later, more settled times. He built his first Texas home near Millheim, Washington County, in the mid-1850's.

At last everything was prepared for the building of a house. Logs, rafters, boards, all dressed with the ax; also several thousand shingles, made from logs of the Spanish oak. My friend Wilm let me use his wagon and mules, with which I hauled it all to my building site. In the erecting of the house we helped each other. Logs, sixteen feet long, were notched at the ends and joined together. In this manner the four walls were made, into which openings were cut for the doors and windows. The cracks between the logs were filled with a mixture of clay and dry grass. The floor was two feet above the ground and was built, like the walls, of wood and clay. In this manner a strong log house was

erected, sixteen by sixteen feet, with a porch on the south side, and I had no expense whatsoever except what I paid for the nails I used on the roof.[7]

The first houses, especially of the European settlers, were poorly primitive because the people had neither the skills nor the individual traditions to build with. They soon were able to adapt to their new environment, use the traditional forms and building methods from some of their own craftsmen, blend with the Anglo and Mexican traditions which they encountered, and establish ways of building that provided comfortable and enduring shelters.

Man builds because he has to. He has to have a den to protect him from the elements and from predators, a warren in which he feeds and breeds and shelters his family. Like the lower animals, he requires order. His order, however, is not just a familiar place to flee to, but one that reflects and satisfies his culture's traditional forms and fashions. His house must be comfortable to the eye as well as to the body. He also has a need for symmetry. Balance of form, whether round or rectangular, satisfies this need for order. This drive, or instinct, is stronger in some than it is in others, but in the true builder a violation of plumbness and squareness, of straight, true, and round in his own work is a continuing aggravation, like an old sin committed but never paid for.

Folk building is still going on, though not always in the ways of our ancestors. Early Texans lived in dugouts only as long as they had to. When lumber became available they moved out of the ground and into houses with floors and shingle roofs, still built, however, in a traditional style. The old log and rock houses became barns when people could afford something better or when transportation facilities allowed them to move into towns. As the old slipped or

Alsatian house now used as a barn *(Medina Co.)*

11

Rock fence (Mason Co.)

Interior of rock house at Terlingua

12

began to decay, the useable materials were used to build other outbuildings. The Texas countryside is covered with homes that were demoted from housing people to housing hay. As the buildings deteriorated further they were patched with whatever tin was handy (Old Prince Albert cans and license plates are considered to be the best patches for rat holes.), with parts of other buildings, or shored against further decay with asbestos shingles or composition siding. The owner does whatever is necessary to keep a shelter in service a few more years. When the building finally groans and falls under the weight of ice or snow or the force of a strong wind, the useable material is pulled to make hog pens and chicken houses or to make patching for other buildings suffering the inevitable vicissitudes of old age. A man keeps buildng with old materials just as rats and mice take parts of old nests to make new ones.

Folk building is primarily utilitarian, and keeping a building functional as long as possible is as much a part of the folk building process as hewing the logs or quarrying the stone for the original structure. Sealing wall cracks with split-out cardboard boxes and papering the walls with newspapers is part of the continual building process that is done in a traditional manner. Door hinges made from the leather of old shoes and porch posts wired at a crack with baling wire is a part of the continuous process of folk building. A home is never finished. Like the body, it starts breaking down almost as soon as it is born, and the responsibility of the man of the house is to keep it wired, propped, and patched as long as it is useful. The folk process is in operation as long as he is using available materials. This doesn't mean available from the hardware store, lumber yard, or mail-order catalog, but from the materials that naturally accumulate around a house place: old telephone poles and railroad ties—cables, chains, and

baling wire—combine belts, binder twine, and tin.

People know about building things from tradition and experience. They know to put the wire on the inside of a fence post so that an old cow leaning through to graze on the other side won't spring out the staples. They know, because their elders told them, to put the boards on the inside of a crib's stud wall so that the weight of the corn or the grain won't pop the walls off. They know by observation to put the fireplace on the north wall so winter's norther will ease the heat south through the house. And experience taught them to build their outhouses far enough from the house—but not too far—and to station the wood pile by the well-worn path so that one trip could serve two purposes.

Most folk building is found in the country and in small towns or on the urban margins, because that is where a person can build without reference to his peers. There he does not have to conform to building codes, zoning laws, or the tastes, standards, and styles set by urban neighbors. Plastic urbanity limits traditional building not only by style and space but by economics. The urbanite works steadily so that he can hire somebody to house him with newly purchased and pre-fabricated materials. The rural or outskirts man with no regular income or time-limiting occupation builds and maintains because he has to.

Deciding who the folk are sometimes poses a problem and the term "folk" is often used with condescension. But more likely, they are those who are tossed into nature and can survive, those who can cope and make do with what they have to live and build with. They are those who don't have to send out for a plumber or electrician or carpenter everytime something breaks down. They are those who never throw away a piece of Strong Barn or a 2 x 4 because they know they will need it and use it eventually. The folk are also those who are kin to the land both in sympathy and ancestry, and they use the products of the land and the remnants of its past uses as naturally and comfortably as they use their hands.

A man knows that those things which he does for himself provide him with the richest rewards and the most satisfaction. The food he raises, the game he hunts and kills, the barn he designs and builds with his own hands—the products of these occupations are the offspring of his energy and his imagination. They are parts of his life and of his and his forefathers' traditions and are continuing proofs of his ability to survive. His building is a result of his own conception and is a tangible result of himself. And a shed that he builds for himself will always mean more to him and to his people than the prefabricated aluminum garage hauled in and jointed together by strangers.

Noah must have been mighty proud of the Ark.

NOTES:

¹T. Lindsay Baker, "Panna Maria and Pluznica: A Study in Comparative Folk Culture," *The Folklore of Texan Cultures*, PTFS XXXVIII (Austin: Encino Press, 1974), 206.

²Ann Carpenter, "O Ty Polshi!," *The Folklore of Texan Cultures*, PTFS XXXVIII (Austin: Encino Press, 1974), 206.

³Caroline von Hinuber, "Life of German Pioneers in Early Texas," *Texas State Historical Association Quarterly*, II, No. 3 (Jan., 1899), 229.

⁴Ferdinand Roemer, *Texas*, Oswald Mueller, trans. (San Antonio: Standard Printing Co., 1935), p. 93.

⁵Fredrick Law Olmsted, *Journey Through Texas* (Austin: Von Boeckmann-Jones Press, 1962), p. 170.

⁶Claude M. Dubuis, "Texas Recollections: A Letter from Castroville: 1847," *The Kountze News* (March 1, 1978), p. 6.

⁷Carl Urbantke, *Texas Is the Place for Me* (Austin: The Pemberton Press, 1970), p. 24.

Details of a stone wall (*Medina Co.*)

Alsatian rock house near Quihi (*Medina Co.*)

Cedar post barn (*Blanco Co.*)

15

Last stages of rock house with outdoor stairs to sleeping loft (*Medina Co.*)

Last stages of a log house (*Robertson Co.*)

A caboose that became a house and then a barn (*Hamilton Co.*)

16

Plaster over rock (*Hays Co.*)

Log house interior with stripping to hold inner wall

Patched screen door

17

Grain chute

Chicken nests

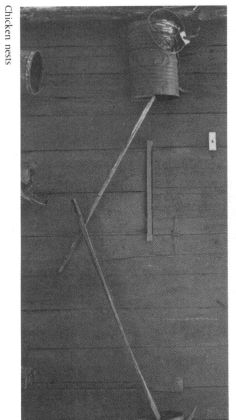

Guinea nest

Hay ramp

18

Chicken trough

Hanger

Matched corners in tie barn

19

TRAILS TO TEXAS

By
G. Loyd Collier

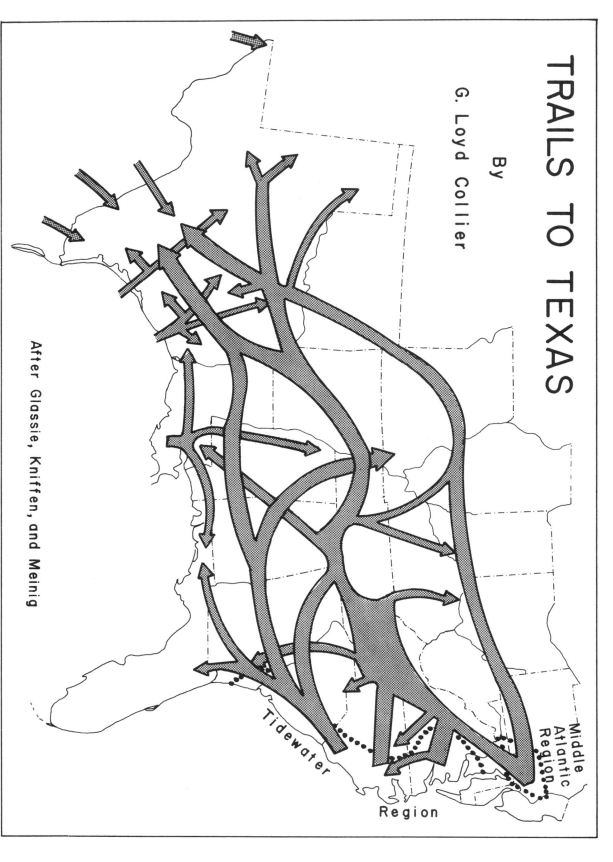

After Glassie, Kniffen, and Meinig

The arrows on the map are intended to suggest more the general direction of flow of people and building ideas than specific routes. Rarely did routes with identifiable paths extend very far in the eastern United States, at least as compared to those in the west. The arrows do reflect the effect of topography on the flow, for instance, the avoidance of the Ozarks as the settlers chose the lower and smoother lands both to the north and the south. The great broadening of the arrow in southwestern Virginia and adjacent states is to suggest the great amount of blending of traditions from the various source regions in that locale.

Middle Atlantic Region

Tidewater Region

20

The Cultural Geography of Folk Building Forms in Texas

G. Loyd Collier

The urge to preserve one's lifestyle in familiar surroundings is a powerful force. When people move to a new region, they seek out locales like the ones they left. Even when the new locations are not identical with the old, the migrants perpetuate the form and arrangement of their homes, barns and other outbuildings, fences, fields, and towns. In time the culture elements so carefully implanted may undergo modification in the new physical and social environment but rarely are they eliminated entirely.

The conservation of lifestyle is particularly meaningful in the study of folk building forms in Texas because of the state's unique settlement history. Texas received settlers from both the upper and lower South, and it received more direct migrants from Europe than any southern or southwestern state. In the Texas setting each group worked with the available building materials and familiar construction techniques and styles.

For Anglo-American settlers, one important source region which contributed folk building forms to Texas was the Tidewater region from Chesapeake Bay southward to about Cape Hatteras in North Carolina and from the coast westward to the Blue Ridge. In this, the area of the earliest English settlement in the New World, one of the common house forms was a single room (also called a bay or pen) about sixteen feet square. This room served all family activities except sleeping. The house characteristically had a very steep gable roof enclosing a loft space used for sleeping. If there were windows in the loft, they were small and near the loft floor. The front door normally was the only entrance and was either centered or displaced away from the gabled chimney wall. Sometimes the chimney protruded into the room, but most often it did not because of its large size. In part this was because the English chimney was large enough to contain a bake oven, and in part it was because of the bulky building materials used (stone or clay and sticks).

In the construction of the house, first a load-bearing frame of thick timbers was built, using mortise-and-tenon joints pegged together with cross braces between the vertical studs to provide lateral stability. The spaces between the timbers were filled with wattle and daub or with stone, brick, or clay "cat" nogging.[1] For wattle-and-daub construction the space was filled with a lattice of interwoven withes or small sticks which was then covered with clay and smoothed both inside and out. The clay "cats" were merely wads of mud mixed with grass and given shape by being wrapped around a stick.[2] To protect the clay, or simply to hide the bricks or stones, the outer surface of the wall was covered with overlapping horizontal weatherboarding (also called clapboarding or merely siding). Houses built in this style are known as covered frame houses. When the framing timbers were left exposed to be a part of the wall's decoration and only the nogging covered with stucco, the result is known as half-timbering (*Fachwerk* in German).[3]

Cats also could be used to make a chimney. The use of

cats in nogging did not extend very far west of the Mississippi Valley but catted chimneys persisted well into Texas. The form was degenerating by the time it reached Texas as is evidenced by abandonment of the stick to give form and strength to each cat. A wooden framework to provide general shape to the structure was retained.[4] Some decomposed catted chimneys examined by this author in East Texas are nothing but rained-smoothed mounds of clay.

When the Tidewater family found itself in need of more space another room was added to the basic square house on the end opposite the chimney. The new room, normally smaller than the other, was designated the "parlor," while the large room continued to be called the "hall" as it had been ever since medieval times. The front entrance usually was off center, for it gave access to the hall rather than the parlor. Each room had only one window on the front wall.

The next logical step was to partition off part of the larger room to make a central passageway from which access to either the parlor or the hall could be obtained. The central passageway enabled the creation of symmetry in the placement of doors and windows. When the room size was increased, the front wall could support two windows on either side of the door, making an "advanced" form of hall-and-parlor house. A derivative of the hall-and-parlor form, containing two equal rooms and without the central passageway, is the double-pen house. There may be separate outside entrances to each of the rooms but normally only one room has a chimney.

When buildings larger than the one-story hall-and-parlor house were needed, builders generally followed one of two plans. One option was to add another story, creating a house two stories tall but only one room deep. The form is well represented in the Tidewater region and in England.

Because it was first identified in the states of Indiana, Illinois, and Iowa and because of its resemblance to the capital letter "I," this house form has come to be called the I house.[5]

The other option was to build on the back of the house, making it two rooms deep. The roof line was continued, but at a flatter angle from the top of the wall, making the familiar "saltbox" form of New England; it was also well known in colonial Virginia where it was called a "catslide" house. A good example of the westward migration of the type is found at Washington-on-the-Brazos in the house in which the Texas Declaration of Independence was signed.

After bricks became more plentiful and cheap, Tidewater settlers built both chimneys and entire homes of brick. To cut down on the amount of masonry work in the chimney, the size was sharply reduced above the top of the firebox. The outer line of the chimney was kept straight and the upper section pulled several inches away from the wall. This tradition of chimney making is well represented in many homes in eastern Texas.

For reasons which are not yet completely clear, even before the American Revolution some Tidewater homes were raised above ground on stone or brick piers; sometimes the elevation amounted to a full story. "Raised houses" are to be found scattered all across the South and into Texas and are one of the contributions of the Tidewater region.[6]

To summarize, the Tidewater region was the source of the square, single-room house, and the rectangular hall-and-parlor house as well as the tall, thin I house. These forms spread into the Appalachians with only minor changes. There they were to encounter the stream of settlers coming from southeastern Pennsylvania with other house forms, and the two streams were to blend and carry

Log house with extra loft space and attached barn (*Rusk Co.*)

23

One-room stone house built in 1870's *(Hamilton Co.)*

24

Log I-house with siding (Cherokee Co.)

25

Norse home also served as barn. *(Bosque Co.)*

Wagon drive through center of house

Stairs leading to sleeping loft and hay loft

27

the combined forms on south and westward.[7]

The second of the major source regions for "Southern" building techniques and styles is the Middle Atlantic region centered in southeastern Pennsylvania and secondarily in adjacent Maryland. This region was settled by two distinctly different cultural groups. Great numbers of Scotch-Irish came to Pennsylvania in the middle of the eighteenth century and settled just west of the English. Arriving at about the same time, and generally settling among the Scotch-Irish, were the Germans.

The Scotch-Irish, from the timber-poor provinces of northern and western Ireland, brought with them their tradition of building with stone and mud. Their rectangular houses were frequently divided into two unequal rooms very much like the English hall-and-parlor house. The front door was either centered or displaced toward the chimney end, and characteristically there was a rear door in line with the front door. Rear shed additions were common and gabled rear ells and front porches were more common than on the English square cabin or hall-and-parlor house. The chimney on one gable wall was much smaller than the English chimney because the Irish and Scots traditionally baked beside the fire rather than in an oven in the chimney.

The Germans came from the heavily forested regions of eastern Germany and what is today central and western Czechoslovakia and adjacent Poland. It is only among these people, both in their European homeland and their American settlements, that is found the type of horizontal log construction which has come to be the stereotype of pioneer construction in America.[8]

In timber-rich America, the Scotch-Irish dropped their stone-and-mud construction technique for the log technique of their German neighbors. The Germans, in turn, dropped their three-room log house with central chimney for the two-room, end-chimney form of their Scotch-Irish neighbors.

Two main streams of migration originated in the Middle Atlantic source region and swept across the U.S. to contribute building styles and techniques to Texas. One stream extended across Pennsylvania and then broadly along the route marked by the Ohio River into Missouri, Arkansas, and Texas. Moving westward along this stream were two main types of houses. One was the English I house. The earlier I houses were usually built of brick but later ones were frame or log with a large limestone chimney at each end.[9] By the late nineteenth century the front wall was decorated with a portico or porch. Although sometimes two stories high in the beginning, the later and more common form of front porch was only one story high and only slightly wider than the enclosed central hallway. One- or two-storied gabled ells were often added to the back, giving floor plans resembling the letters "L" or "T" depending on where the ells were attached to the front unit. This form is frequently referred to as the Midwestern I house because it was first identified in that region, but it also occurs in the Middle Atlantic source region and in Texas.

Wherever it was built, the I house became the symbol of stability and wealth, especially wealth derived from agriculture.[10] Settlers of lesser status constructed a log cabin or house using the Germanic construction technique and a form inspired by the Scotch-Irish. Two-room log houses commonly featured the extra room on the chimney end of the original house, creating what has been designated a "saddlebag" house. The central chimney suggests something of the original German tradition. The saddlebag log house lent itself to conversion to an I form with the addition of the second story, perhaps with an ell added to the back. The central chimney rather than one at a gable may be the only outer indication that the house was not built in I form in the beginning.

Another characteristic transmitted along this route was the custom of increasing the loft space by carrying the log wall three feet or so higher than the plate at the top of the ground floor wall. In this way the loft space was enlarged to provide what was in effect another story.

The other migration stream out of southeastern Pennsylvania moved southward along the Appalachians and carried the merged German and Scotch-Irish building styles deep into the heart of the South. While the Tidewater English culture was being carried westward to the Middle Atlantic region were moving southward along the Ridge and Valley province of the Appalachians (locally called the Valley of Virginia), west of the Blue Ridge. In the Valley of Virginia the two streams of migrants from the two source regions began to merge. The old English square frame-and-weather-board house with stone or brick chimney easily kept the form in logs cut German style. The rectangular Scotch-Irish cabin, now also built in log, met the English hall-and-parlor and I-house forms and each found the other compatible. Horizontal weatherboards under the eaves of the gable ends of Texas log cabins are in the English tradition.; vertical boards, however, are in the German tradition. Both may be found widely and freely intermixed in Texas.

Even the barns transmitted along this stream are both English and German. The small English one-crib barn, often with flanking sheds, is to be contrasted with the large transverse two-or four-crib barn which evolved from German antecedents from southeastern Pennsylvania before the settlers left the southernmost part of the Valley

of Virginia for the lowland South.

Still something of a mystery is the time and place of derivation of the house form which perhaps more than any other means Southern folk housing to the cultural geographer and the culture historian—the open centrl passageway or "dogtrot" house. It is such a practical solution to a number of conditions that it probably was invented several times individually. In any event, it is to be found across the South and throughout much of Texas.

The dogtrot house form is an excellent adaptation to the climate and to available materials and techniques because it permits the use of short logs which were both abundant and easily maneuvered. It was not easy to find logs some forty feet long, without too much taper, to permit building a single two-room log house, and handling logs of this size was also a major task. Two symmetrical smaller units connected by a common roof and with the space between made useful by a floor could be built either all at once or half at a time as the need arose.

The dogtrot form captures the symmetry of the old English hall-and-parlor house with central passageway.; the passage is merely left open rather than enclosed. The warm southern climate made use of the dogtrot form more agreeable than it would have been in the Ohio Valley states. The utility of the form is indicated by its continued popularity in Southern frame houses long after the original impetus to its creation ceased.

The dogtrot house in the beginning had only one chimney, and each of the rooms had a door in the long wall. A shed porch added to the front enabled inhabitants to keep out of the weather while going from one room to the other. In time, many houses were built with the entrances to each room opening in the dogtrot and only windows were left to interrupt the long wall. Even "advanced" forms

Double-pen log house, one-half of which has been framed in *(Nacogdoches Co.)*

31

Dog Trot *(Hardin Co.)*

32

Big Thicket log house built in 1940's (*Hardin Co.*)

33

Board-and-batten balloon-frame house (Tyler Co.)

34

with two front windows per room were developed. Windows on the front wall also facilitated upgrading the house into more fashionable forms by covering the logs with weatherboarding and closing the dogtrot with a double door or a single door surrounded by glass panels. Many frame dogtrot houses have been modernized in the same way in recent years.

Studies of eastern U.S. folk housing generally have limited their consideration to the period before 1850 and to the frame and log techniques then dominant. But about the same time as Anglo settlers were arriving in Texas in large numbers (after 1836 and especially after 1845), a new system of construction became available and led to another transformation of folk housing construction techniques. This was the balloon frame.[12]

The principle of balloon framing is replacement of the widely spaced, thick timbers held in place by pegged mortise-and-tenon joints with closely spaced (generally on sixteen-inch centers), thin, two-by-four-inch studs held in place with many nails. Maximum strength on a balloon-framed wall is obtained by nailing sheathing material (commonly boards one-by-four inches) diagonally across the two-by-four studs on the outside and covering the sheathing in more attractive weatherboarding. This extra effort and expense is avoided, at the cost of some strength, by leaving off the sheathing and nailing the weatherboarding directly to the studs. Weatherboard on the outside and shiplapped boards, or just one-by-twelve inch boards butted together, on the inside wall surface provide a great deal of lateral stability.

Much less stability is offered by the application of vertical one-by-twelves to the outside in board-and-batten style, a style that was old in the 1840's. The main contributor to stability in a board-and-batten house was the

sealing boards used on the inside walls, especially when they were installed horizontally as most were. Houses usually were sealed on the inside, but barns and outbuildings usually were not. This is one reason why in old farmsteads outbuildings are often found in worse states of survival than the house.[13] The balloon frame has been compared to the Windsor chair, the lightest and most portable chair made in the colonies, in that each is made of thin structural parts to provide a light but sturdy unit.[14]

Balloon framing marks the beginning of the impact of industrialization on housing. The improvement of sawmill machinery led to widespread availability of stock boards of standard dimensions which were also thin and light enough to be handled by one man. Yet where extra strength was required, as in corner posts, the thin boards could be combined as required. The development of nail-making machinery led to a great reduction of the price of nails and their liberal use in subsequent construction.[15]

The balloon frame was invented in Chicago in the 1830's, became popular by the 1850's, and until the 1870's was known as "Chicago construction." The association with the prairies south and west of Chicago is responsible for the peculiar name of "balloon framing." Detractors predicted that the strong prairie winds would blow the new light buildings up and away like balloons.[16] This author, who grew up in a balloon-framed house on a rural hilltop in the Texas Blackland Prairie, remembers several occasions when he could agree with the scoffers' predictions.

The balloon frame is credited with responsibility for the rapidity of settlement of both urban and rural areas between Chicago and the Pacific coast. In 1865 it was claimed that a man and a boy could do as much as twenty men using the earlier heavy frame style and at a saving of forty percent or more. There may have been a saving of both time and money, but it was at the cost of using more wood and extinction of the craftsman skilled in joinery. Building now came within the reach of anyone who could handle simple joints and a saw and hammer.[17]

Contemporaries called balloon framing the most important U.S. contribution to architecture, but as its use became widespread its significance was forgotten. The European art historian Sigfried Giedion, in the Charles Eliot Norton Lectures for 1938-1939 at Harvard University, was the first to remind Americans of their contribution and its importance.[18] During the U.S. Bicentennial the invention was included among 356 key events in U.S. history suggested by a panel of distinguished historians to the editors of *Life* magazine and was included by the editors as one of "The 100 Events That Shaped America."[19]

Houses which had been built of logs now shifted to the new balloon-frame construction, but kept the single chimney or flue. The central enclosed passageway, and many open dogtrots, disappeared in favor of separate entrances to the two front rooms. This reinforced the log tradition of log cabins with an extra room built on the end opposite the chimney. But whatever the origin of the form, it is called the Southern Lowland double-pen house. Hallmarks of the form are two equal front units, each with its own entrance; there may be a shed porch on the front and a shed-roofed room on the back. The single chimney or flue is found either on one gable wall or is centrally placed. In the later forms shed additions may be replaced by gabled ells, with the chimney or flue moved to the junction of the front structure and the ell.[20]

Shed-roofed additions seem to be a particular characteristic of houses of the Lowland South because they are to be found on both one- and two-story houses regardless of whether the house is built of heavy timbers,

log, or balloon framing. For instance, shed porches and shed-roofed rear additions (sometimes front additions as well) distinguish the Carolina or Southern I house from the Midwestern form.[21]

The Tidewater and Middle Atlantic traditions have provided, via the Lowland South, the single-room log cabin (often later expanded with frame additions), the rectangular log house with or without the dogtrot, the lowland double-pen frame house, and a version of the I house.

The Spanish, the second largest group of immigrants after the Anglos, settled in that part of the state where, as in their homeland, wooden building materials were scarce. In the drier areas of the state, generally west of the thirty-inch average rainfall line, adobe construction was feasible and commonly used, as it had been for so many centuries in Europe.[22] Stone and bricks were used where available. Whatever the final building material used, the largest pieces of wood were used to provide the major framing timbers and to support roofs that were either flat or with very low pitch. Roofing materials ranged from thatch to shingles to tiles, depending on availability and finance. Some walls, in more humid areas, consisted of vertical poles of anything from saplings to sotol stalks either set on a large beam or directly in the ground and plastered with mud inside and out.[23] Weatherboards were sometimes put on the outside.

Examples of these various Spanish building styles are preserved mainly in the southern part of Central Texas, in the upper Rio Grande Valley near El Paso, and in the Lower Rio Grande Valley. Not only are the individual buildings preserved, they still often display the characteristic layout of farm-centered compounds and of towns.

The third largest group of settlers was the Germans and

(*Left*) Board-and-batten frame house with stick-and-mud chimney (*Hardin Co.*)

(*Below*) Log house built in 1930's with stick-and-mud chimney and cooling bench (*Hardin Co.*)

37

Adobe House *(Alpine)*

they are particularly important in Texas folk building heritage because of the large proportion who were direct immigrants from Europe. In general they came from central Germany rather than the Silesian-Czechoslovakia area as the settlers in the Middle Atlantic source region noted above. The most important group of immigrants to Texas came from within the Frankfurt-Brunswick-Erfurt triangle.[24] The earliest Germans to come to Texas, and ultimately the greatest number, settled among the Anglo-Americans already here and within easy access to timber. At least some of their earliest homes featured vertical log walls with mud and wood plastered between the posts and the chinking protected by a covering of shingles.[25] Some settlers built in stone. But it was not long before they were building homes of wood similar to the Anglo styles. The same may be said of the Czechs who settled among the eastern Germans.

Along and west of a line from Austin to San Antonio, however, the Germans settled on a sparsely populated frontier and were able to preserve their traditions far longer and more completely than elsewhere. In the west, wood was scarce and stone was abundant; therefore *fachwerk* or half timbering was widely used with nogging of stone or brick. Often plaster was used to cover the walls both inside and out. Stone was used extensively to build homes, barns, outbuildings, and even fences, in the period prior to about 1885.[26]

Even in the west, Anglo influences had an impact on German forms. Casemented windows disappeared and porches were added. The combination of Anglo and Germanic touches are found on houses of many sizes and different places but are perhaps no more charmingly displayed than on the "Sunday houses" in Fredericksburg and nearby towns. The idea behind the Sunday house is the same as a modern weekend cottage: a place of retreat from the main residence. The difference is that for modern urban dwellers the weekend cottage is usually in a rural setting and designed for recreation, while for the early rural-dwelling Germans the Sunday house was in town and served as the base for weekend visiting, shopping, and church-going.

The Sunday house in many ways is merely a smaller version of the rural German house. There is the same gabled roof with ridge line paralleling the street and space enough under the gable over the front room(s) for sleeping. The upstairs sleeping space was used by the boys in the family and was reached by an outside staircase so that their late arrivals would not disturb the rest of the family. A long shed-like rear roofline helped give the overall house form much the same impression as a saltbox house. A small Anglo-inspired porch across the front completed the form.[27]

Stone buildings in the Alsatian settlements in and around Castroville show many similarities to the German buildings to the north and northwest. Individual buildings, particularly homes, may appear quite Germanic (except for a lower roof angle), but the large central plaza in Castroville and at least one cantilevered balcony reminds the viewer that Mediterranean influence did extend as far north as Alsace in France before it came to Texas.

The Poles who settled in Texas also built in stone in the beginning and in traditional forms and styles. Some examples survive. Rather early, however, they shifted to other materials and styles which were more in harmony with their neighbors. Old World field patterns remain as a distinctive legacy.

Other immigrant groups in Texas either did not come in large enough numbers to establish any regions with

Remains of a rock bordello near the mining town of Shafter (*Presidio Co.*)

40

distinctive styles (with the exception of stone homes and a few surviving palisade-like fences among the Norwegians in Bosque County), or their styles were overwhelmed to the point that nothing remains.

From all directions except west and directly north (unless the Indians are included), settlers have come to Texas—some after long sojourns in the eastern United States or in Mexico, and some directly from European homelands. Building forms and techniques preserved in the state today have long-forgotten roots in customs and practices in seventeenth-century Europe (and occasionally earlier), as well as in innovations developed in North

America barely a century ago. Thanks to the work of the Institute of Texan Cultures and the Texas Folklore Society we now know that the culture groups found in Texas are many. To the resultant variety of building traditions add the diversity of physical environments and building materials available in this sprawling state, and one encounters once more the rich complexity of Texas which is ever a source of wonder and delight to the long-time Texan and a source of despair to the outsider—or new arrival— who wishes to reduce the state and its contrasting traditions to an easy cliche or two.

NOTES:

[1] In the seventeenth century a nog was a peg, pin, or small block of wood used for various purposes. By the early nineteenth century it was used as a verb, "to nog," and it had come to mean to secure by pegs or to build with timber framing and brick, specifically with the brickwork built up between wooden framing timbers. In north England the term was used for a wooden block the size of a brick which was stacked to support coal mine roofs. Thus a piece of any material of approximately brick size, or large pieces of stone whose thickness is about the same as the length of a brick, is called a nog and the total filler is nogging. The term "nogging pieces" is applied to horizontal wooden pieces between vertical timbers to strengthen the frame and is still being used by some carpenters today. See *The Oxford Universal Dictionary on Historical Principles*, third edition (Oxford: Clarendon Press, 1955). John Harris and Jill Lever, *Illustrated Glossary of Architecture, 850-1830* (New York: C. N. Potter, 1966); and Cyril M. Harris, *Dictionary of Architecture and Construction* (New York: McGraw-Hill, 1975).

[2] Fred Kniffen and Henry Glassie, "Building in Wood in the Eastern United States: A Time-Place Perspective," *Geographical Review*, LVI (1966), 42. The cats could be set either vertically or horizontally. The use of mixtures of mud and grass either as cats or as chinking between logs is known in northwestern

41

NOTES (Continued)

Europe, especially Normandy, and also among the Indians of the southern U.S. See C. Johnson, "Missouri-French Houses: some Relict Features of Early Settlement," *Pioneer America*, Vol. VI, No. 2 (July, 1974), 3.

[3]Harris and Lever, *Illustrated Glossary*, Plate 168 especially.

[4]See Seymour V. Connor, "Log Cabins in Texas," *Southwestern Historical Quarterly*, LIII (1949), 115, and Drury B. Alexander and Todd Webb, *Texas Homes of the Nineteenth Century* (Austin: University of Texas Press, 1966), p. 27.

[5]The 1 house was first identified and named in Fred B. Kniffen, "Louisiana House Types," *Annals of the Association of American Geographers*, XXVI (1939), 179-193.

[6]Fred Kniffen, "Folk Housing: Key to Diffusion," *Annals of the Association of American Geographers*, LV (1965), 565. Apparently because of the frequency of occurrence of raised houses in nearby, poorly drained southern Louisiana, observers have been led to attribute similar houses in Texas to influence from Louisiana. The same is true of dormer windows. Both of these house characteristics, however, are to be found in the Tidewater source region and in other places that have no Louisiana influence. One should therefore grant Louisiana influence on Texas houses only cautiously and when there is a good record definitely tying the particular house and its builder to Louisiana.

[7]See Kniffen, "Folk Housing: Key to Diffusion," p. 565; Henry Glassie, "The Types of the Southern Mountain Cabin," *The Study of American Folklore: An Introduction*, Jan Brunvand, ed. (New York: W. W. Norton, 1968), p. 335; and Henry Glassie, *Pattern in the Material Folk Culture of the United States* (Philadelphia: University of Pennsylvania Monographs in Folklore and Folklife, No. 1, 1968), p. 78.

[8]This source region for horizontal log construction of the type used in the U.S. was first identified by Glassie ("The Types of the Southern Mountain Cabin," p. 345) and his conclusion has been accepted by others.

[9]Kniffen, "Folk Housing: Key to Diffusion," p. 553; Glassie, *Patterns in the Material Folk Culture of the United States*, p. 75.

[10]Kniffen, "Folk Housing: Key to Diffusion," pp. 562-563.

[11]The derivation of the Southern barn from the German barn of Pennsylvania is presented by Kniffen, "Folk Housing: Key to Diffusion," pp. 563-564, and by Glassie, *Patterns in the Material Folk Culture of the United States*, pp. 90-93.

[12]Most sources on folk building ignore the balloon frame entirely or mention it only in passing. Glassie is the only worker so far who has devoted even minimal attention to the method. Although the accompanying textual elaboration is scant, there are excellent illustrations of houses typically built with balloon frames in his *Patterns in the Material Folk Culture of the United States*, pp. 103-106. The balloon-framed pioneer house is, I believe, the most neglected aspect of pioneer and folk building in Texas.

[13]Talbot F. Hamlin, *Forms and Functions of Twentieth Century Architecture*, II (New York: Columbia University Press, 1952), 409. The origin of board-and-batten siding on houses in the U.S. remains something of an enigma. The only source this writer has found which treats the style more than in passing concludes that it has probably been a carpenter's way of attaching siding to small buildings since early times, as indeed it is in Japan; see Vincent Joseph Scully, Jr., *The Shingle Style and the Stick Style: Architectural Theory and Design from Richardson to the Origins of Wright* (New Haven: Yale University Press, 1971), p. xlv. This is probably true, yet there seem to be some clues as to the beginning of its popularity which should not be ignored. Scully notes that the use of board-and-batten siding first came to widespread notice in conjunction with the house pattern books which began appearing in the 1830's. This is the same time that balloon framing was making its appearance. The easy availability of stock sizes of lumber, already mentioned as a factor in balloon framing, had an impact on the use of siding as well. With high-speed sawmills turning out stock sizes, the production of one-by-twelves and one-by-twos would have been fast and inexpensive and would have enabled their widespread use in folk housing. The balloon frame and board-and-batten siding derive from the same technological developments, and they spread together over the cultural landscape. Aesthetically, the board-and-batten siding emphasizes the vertical proportions of the building. This was an important consideration for both professional and folk builders when dealing with one-story structures (See Scully, pp. xxxix, xli, xlii.).

[14]Sigfried Giedion, *Space, Time and Architecture: The Growth of a New Tradition* (Cambridge: Harvard University Press, 1954), pp. 352-353.

[15]*Ibid.*, pp. 347-348; Hamlin, *Forms and Functions*, p. 409; Henry-Russell Hitchcock, *Architecture: Nineteenth and Twentieth Centuries* (Baltimore: Penguin Books, 1963), p. 240; James Marston Fitch, *American Building: 1: The Historical Forces That Shaped It* (New York: Schocken Books, 1973), p. 13.

[16]Giedion, *Space, Time and Architecture*, pp. 351-352; Fitch, *American Building*, p. 121; "The 100 Events That Shaped America," *Life Special Report*, Bicentennial Edition, 1975, p. 12.

[17]Giedion, *Space, Time and Architecture*, pp. 348-349; Hamlin, *Forms and Functions*, II, 409.

[18]Giedion, *Space, Time and Architecture*. The lectures were first published in

NOTES (Continued)

1941 and have gone through at least ten printings, with revisions. Even now this is perhaps the most profitable single source to turn to for information on balloon framing because of the length of the discussion and the generous citations to original sources.

[19] *Life Special Report*, p. 12.

[20] See note 12 above.

[21] Kniffen, "Folk Housing: Key to Diffusion," p. 553.

[22] Harrington estimated that perhaps ninety-five percent of the farm construction in the Rio Grande Valley of El Paso County was adobe and that adobe was important also in adjoining Hudspeth County. Adobe structures were present further east in Howard County (Big Spring) and as far as Nueces County (Corpus Christi). See Edwin Lincoln Harrington, "Adobe As A Construction Material In Texas," *Bulletin 90*, College Station: Texas A&M University, Texas Engineering Experiment Station, 1945, p. 10. Biles reports that adobe was used extensively in Cochran County (on the New Mexico border west of Lubbock) after 1925 and was used to some extent also in the northern Panhandle counties of Hansford and Wheeler. See Roberta Frances Biles, "The Frame House Era in Northwest Texas," *West Texas Historical Association Yearbook*, XLVI (1970), 174. Both Harrington and Biles report the use of asphalt and caliche mixed with the adobe to give it more resistance to weathering, and Biles indicates the use of stucco on outer wall surfaces for the same purpose.

[23] A great deal of confusion has developed concerning the techniques of vertical paling or post construction and use of the term *palisado* in particular. One of three basic building methods introduced into the U.S. from seventeenth-century Europe is the construction of walls formed of closely set vertical logs, palings, or planks (Kniffen and Glassie, "Building in Wood in the Eastern United States," pp. 40-41, 43-48). The first usage of the term *palisado* known to this writer is in Alexander and Webb's *Texas Homes of the Nineteenth Century*. The authors made it clear that what they refer to is closely related to wattle and

daub because the vertical palings are hidden under a layer of mud or adobe (See especially pp. 17, 79, 240.). Large vertical poles or roughly hewn planks with the spaces between chinked with mud, clay, or stucco is called picket construction and has the notation that it it is found only in Shackelford County and vicinity, especially around old Ft. Griffin (pp. 31, 236). Kniffen and Glassie use the term in reference to early construction in Saint Augustine, Florida, but do not indicate precisely what is meant by the term. They further complicate things by using the French terminology for vertical construction in the Mississippi Valley ("Building in Wood in the Eastern United States," pp. 47-48). *Palisado* is used by Johnson to mean the same as palisade and is clearly the same as Alexander and Webb's picket (C. Johnson, "Missouri-French Houses," p. 3). Jordan equates the terms *palisado*, palisade, and picket; see Terry G. Jordan, *Texas Log Buildings* (Austin: University of Texas Press, 1978). pp. 4, 27. A half-dozen or more Spanish dictionaries consulted indicate that that cognate of palisade is *palizada*, not *palisado*. This writer believes that in the resolution of the confusion more attention should be devoted to whether or not a sill is present and the vertical members are exposed or covered.

[24] Terry G. Jordan, *German Seed in Texas Soil: Immigrant Farmers in Nineteenth-Century Texas* (Austin: University of Texas Press, 1966), pp. 32-33.

[25] Institute of Texan Cultures, "The Cat Spring Germans," San Antonio: Institute of Texan Cultures, 1971, pp. 3-4 (multilithed booklet accompanying an audio-visual presentation of the same title).

[26] Good sources for German stone construction examples are: Alexander and Webb, *Texas Homes*; Clovis Heimsath, *Pioneer Texas Building: A Geometry Lesson* (Austin: University of Texas Press, 1968); and Terry G. Jordan, "German Houses in Texas," *Landscape*, XIV (Autumn, 1964), 24-26.

[27] Samuel Edward Gideon, "Sunday Houses in Texas," *Pencil Points*, XII (1931), 276-278; Alexander and Webb, *Texas Homes*, pp. 16, 46-57; Jordan, "German Houses in Texas," pp. 24-26.

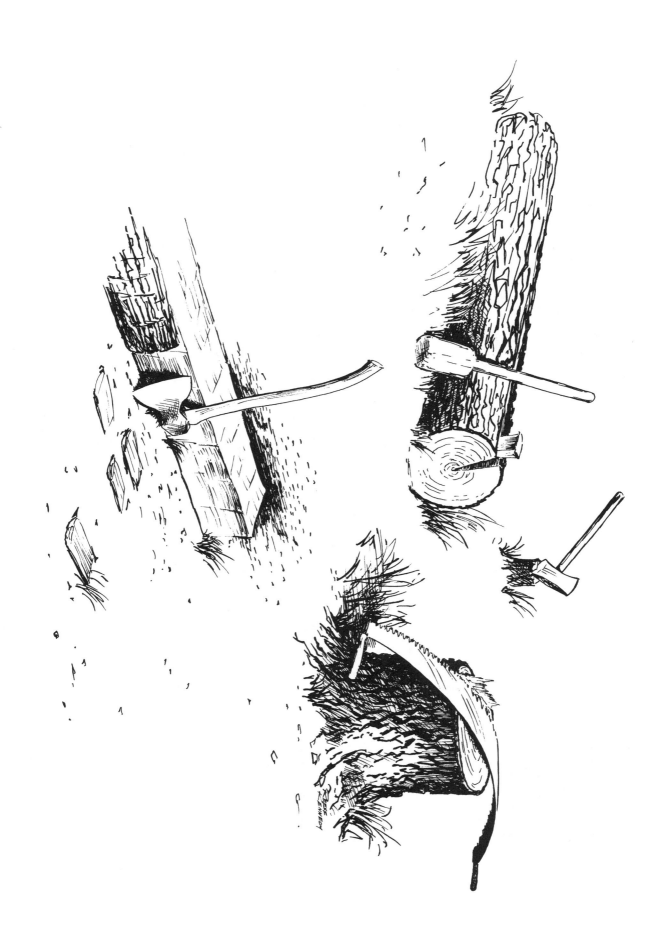

Methods & Materials

The settlers that began drifting from the neighboring states into Texas in the early nineteenth century brought with them their own traditions of building that reached back to their colonial beginnings and beyond. When they got here they had to adapt their own building methods to the materials at hand—pine logs in East Texas, post oak in the Cross Timbers, not much of anything in the Panhandle, limestone on the Edwards Plateau, and adobe out beyond the Pecos. Germans, Poles, Norse, and Alsatians came straight from the Old World with their countries' ways of building in mind and had to adapt to the new land's materials and learn from the older Anglo settlers the methods of putting the materials together.

The method of building depended on the tools at hand.

A good axe, either double-bit or with a driving head, was the first necessity for the Texan building in the timber regions. Beyond that, a broad-axe sped the labor of scoring and squaring the logs. An adze was useful in dressing the matching sides of the logs and smoothing off puncheon floors, and a draw knife was good for the fine work. A froe and a mallet were used to change a pin-oak block into a stack of shingles. And the well-equipped builder had chisels and planes, augers, awls, and saws, and when commerce caught up with him he had nails.

The resultant Texas buildings found in Panna Maria and Castroville, along red dirt roads in Deep East Texas, or near weed-covered fences on the Cap Rock are as distinctive as the state itself and as various as its geography.

Building in Texas, 1844-1845

Prince Karl von Solms-Braunfels

Their fundamental principle, which undoubtedly is correct, is that the first necessity of man is an abode, a roof over his head.

First they select the location for the house. This being done, they proceed to cut down the necessary trees, about fourteen feet in length and about ten or twelve inches in diameter. Of course the amount is generally determined by the number of rooms a family needs, and most of all by the size of the family.

A robust woodsman equipped with a good sharp American ax can cut fifteen or twenty such trees in one day. But one untrained in this trade probably cuts only half of that amount, as it is strenuous and hard labor for him. For such work there is a great difference between an American and a German ax. The former is made of harder steel and remains sharp for a longer period, and naturally makes the work easier. The ax and hatchet are the only tools that the immigrant should buy in America, for they are better in quality and have a longer life than those made in Germany. All the logs cut down are hewed and notched on the two opposite sides in such a way that they fit closely one on top of the other. The work of hewing them can be performed right in the forest after they are felled or at the location where the log house is to be built. Finally the transportation of the logs takes place. A large chain is slung around one or two logs, according to their size, and to that chain are hitched one or two yoke of oxen, and they are dragged thus into the future village.

The first thing necessary for building a house is a foundation. For this one can use posts of a foot to a foot and a half in diameter and seven feet in length. Three feet should be put into the ground and four feet left above the surface. These posts should remain in their natural shape. On them rest the sills and joists on which the floor is laid. The raising of a house four feet above the ground is necessary for protection against insects, especially the ants. After having laid the foundation and made the joists ready for the floor, one should begin to build up the side walls by placing the logs with their flat sides one on top of another. Care should be taken that the spaces necessary for the windows and doors are left open.

Now we come to speak of the roof itself, which is built by putting up two gables on either side and placing across the top of these a ridgeboard. On this are nailed the rafters, which are not planed, but round rough strips. Upon them are nailed the shingles. The best thing to make shingles from is the thick cedar or elms growing in the river bottoms. These round trunks are sawed into blocks three and six feet in length, and are split into small planks of an inch and a half to two inches thick. The shingles of three feet in length are used to cover the roof; those of six feet in length are used to lay the floor, in case there is a shortage of boards or planks. After one has a little practice, the work of making shingles is very easy, and can be done fast. Frames are built into the openings left for doors and windows and in here are nailed hinges (which must be brought along by the immigrants). On those hinges are hung windows, doors and shutters made from the longer shingles. One should lay blocks of any size in front of the door to serve as steps, and the house is finished, except the walls between the rooms and the holes between the logs in the walls. The latter are stuffed close with moss and clay. The length of this square house is thirteen feet; on the inside, of course, one foot is lost. The height is generally ten to twelve feet and the height of the gables is four or five feet more. Hence it is always fairly high in the inside. However, this is necessary on account of the heat radiated by the sun through the shingle. If one has the choice of placing his house wherever he pleases, he should always have the front facing either the north or south, and the windows on the opposite side, so that there are no openings on the east or west. In this manner the entrance of the rays of the sun is prevented, and yet one can keep the doors and windows open so that in the hot season there is a continuous draft.

In the streets of a town where the location and position of the house are always designated, one cannot, of course, follow this rule.

In a hot climate the kitchen is always built outside of the house. It is built in the same manner as the house itself. The chimney is built out of strips of wood in the shape of a pyramid. If one wants a fire in the winter, he will have to build a fireplace in the same manner.

A house built in such a fashion can have a roof extending at both ends. The space under such a projecting roof, which is attached to the house itself and forms a continuation thereof, is called a "gallery." The American uses such a room to hang up his saddles and harness. This is his favorite hang-out in hours of leisure (of which he usually has many every day). It also serves as a sleeping room for the traveler who is looking for a shelter. If the family is large, one

should build two rooms of equal dimensions, standing on a common foundation and under the same roof. Between these two rooms is a passageway of five or six feet in width. Here is really the best place for the dining table, because this room is as a rule very cool and pleasant. A house of such construction can, depending on the ability of the worker, be built in eight days. It takes two Americans six days to construct a one-room house. Our German settlers need a much longer time. The greatest difficulty is really the felling of the trees, as well as hauling them. The actual construction is quite easy.

I have advised all settlers to start their daily work early, i.e., at sunrise, and continue until eleven o'clock in winter and ten o'clock in summer. The hours from ten or eleven until three in the afternoon should be spent at meals and rest. One can work from three until sunset. Likewise one should not go without a hat out of his house or tent, even when it is not hot. One may think that, when a little breeze cools the air, the sun is not so hot, but this is a great mistake. The rays of the sun have on this account certainly no less power over the nerves of the head. Those who have followed these two rules never suffered for observing them. But those who were careless and did not abide by them suffered the consequences. I beg the immigrants to take these two rules to heart. By following them, they themselves and their families can always be in good health.

The house above described is brought only so far as it protects themselves and their property against the weather, without any regard to furnishings which contribute to comfort, since there are more important things to be done. Since such a house is very primitive, and at any rate is to serve only as a temporary abode, one would not build it adjoining the laid-out street, because, when he has the time and means in the following years to build a

new one, he does not want to have this place obstructed. The old one can afterwards be used as a kitchen, or out of its material a stable can be built. Next to this building a space is to be reserved for a pen for a cow or calf. The American manner of building fences is most simple. It is made from logs twelve feet long and eight to ten inches thick. To obtain such a dimension, one cuts a tree not too thick into pieces of twelve feet in length and splits them lengthwise into four parts, and lays the strips one on top of another, to the height desired. One finds in America fields of one or two hundred acres fenced in thus. This sort of fencing is, however, a waste of wood and space, and can be done only on a farm where land and wood are in abundance. But since a fence for a small space like a cow pen does not cause much waste, the settler can always use this type of fencing.

Enclosing a field with this kind of fence has the advantage of keeping out cattle or other animals, especially those that are destructive, as hogs. However, the same result can be had by leaving a space between the rails, but care should be taken lest the spaces are not too large at the bottom. In regions poor in wood, some have already begun to fence in fields by piling the dirt up two or three feet and planting thorny hedges on top. Those in a short time grow to a considerable height and form an impenetrable barrier. This protects the field much better than the other kind of fencing, and is not at all expensive, and it also requires less work. Having the future in mind, the settler can, after planting his first field take a piece of land of five or ten acres, according to the size of his family, and surround it by planting a hedge.

NOTES:

From Karl von Solms-Braunfels, *Texas, 1844-1845* (Houston: The Anson Jones Press, 1936), pp. 108-112.

Reconstructed dugout in Palo Duro Canyon

52

Texas Dugouts

Ann Carpenter

Pioneers who settled Texas prairies and plains usually lived at first temporarily in dugouts, which they also called dirt igloos, molehills, cellars, plains pimples, and log cabins of the plains. These temporary shelters were not regarded with much affection by their residents, and not even Hollywood has been able to romanticize the life in such accommodations. Despite their lack of luxury, dugouts allowed settlers to meet the challenge of finding shelter in a land without wood. Clearly the pioneer Texas dugout was an adaptation of culture to a new environment.

By the 1870's the advancing frontiers of buffalo hunters, ranchers, and farmers had reached westward to enter the great plains area of Texas, that level western section marked by few trees and scant rainfall. At the same time that the Plains settlers' search for shelter was made difficult by lack of wood, their need for shelter was intensified by other climatic features of western Texas, including hot winds, cold northers, blizzards, and hailstorms. Since the sod would not hold together for sod house construction in most of West Texas, the settlers were forced to burrow into the plains like prairie dogs. In short, they built dugouts.

The heyday of Texas dugout construction was roughly 1875-1900, that is, from the disappearance of buffalo and Plains Indians until the arrival of the railroad. By the early 1870's professional buffalo hunters were entering the Texas plains to slaughter bison for the skins; their dugouts appeared at many major waterholes. Among the best known were the hunters associated with J. Wright Mooar,

who killed the only fully white buffalo ever seen. In 1876 the Mooar hunters dug into the banks of Deep Creek in Scurry County. They covered their dugout living quarters with buffalo hides, and their community was called "Hide Town."

Early ranchers often relied on dugouts for their first shelters. The earliest example was Charles Goodnight, who established his JA Ranch in Palo Duro Canyon in 1876 and built a dugout on the canyon floor. Shortly before his arrival, Indians had abandoned their villages there when attacked by the U.S. Cavalry. Goodnight used their tepee poles as rafters to support the dugout roof. The first headquarters for C. C. Slaughter's Long S Ranch was a dugout in the bank of Bull Creek near the Colorado River. Covered with brush and dirt, the dugout had an unusual door: it was a dried bull hide hung by the tail. Other ranchers used dugouts left behind by buffalo hunters, as Mooar's Deep Creek dugout became headquarters for the Nunn Brothers, and in 1878 J. M. Hall purchased a buffalo hunter's dugout to provide headquarters for the Spur Ranch.

Most homesteaders of the 1880's and 1890's had to rely on dugouts for their first homes. To prevent land speculation, homestead laws required each land purchaser to reside on the land at least six months each year for a period of three years before the state would pass title to him. Most homesteaders used dugouts to fulfill the residence requirement. Some were especially creative. Mrs.

53

Josephine Camp owned a T-shaped dugout on Gavitte Creek in Borden County, with each room being in the corner of a different section of land. The occupants thus controlled their claims on all three sections.

Dugouts not only served as private homes. There were dugout stores, schools, post offices, stage stands, commissaries, and line camps. William Henry "Pete" Snyder established a trading post on Deep Creek in a half dugout in 1878; though he had but a small stock of merchandise to trade in his cramped quarters, his store site was later to become Snyder, county seat of Scurry County. Similarly, the town of Sweetwater started as a dugout store operated in 1877 for buffalo hunters by Amos Bouchee and Thomas Knight. The first school house on the Staked Plains was a dugout with dirt roof and floor in Crosby County. The first school in Ira was taught in a dugout about 1893. The late Judge Horace Holley related that a brush arbor that stood in front of the school dugout caught fire, and that both arbor and dugout burned. In the 1890's lumber was hauled from Colorado City to build a half-dugout in the '49 pasture near Gail. Pictures exist of an unusual half-dugout with sod walls that served as post office at Gilaloo in the Panhandle in the 1880's, and another picture shows a dugout used as a post office called Litwalton (near present day Post).

Sometimes a single dugout over the years served in different capacities. For instance, a dugout on Bonita Creek north of Amarillo was first an outlaw's camp; in 1877 it became a line camp for the LX Ranch. Around 1880 the Armstrong and Willingham families lived there, and the dugout was the scene of at least one Indian attack. Later, the dugout was a stop for the "Lightning Express-Daily Mail." Then, in 1884, when a British syndicate bought the LX, the dugout became a commissary.

Dugout living continued to be a common experience for West Texas settlers until the railroad arrived in each area, bringing lumber, brick, and other materials. Before the railroad came, any non-native building supplies had to be delivered from Ft. Worth, Texas, or Dodge City, Kansas, by mule- or ox-drawn wagons, a practice made impractical by the distance, expense, time, and dangers involved. Settlers were forced to construct dugouts from indigenous materials: the prairie itself, rocks, cedar posts, brush, towsacks, rawhide. Once the railroad arrived, the settlers did without everything not absolutely necessary in order to use railroad shipping space for lumber. By the 1890's, eighty West Texas counties had railroads built across them, and no county was more than a hundred miles from the railroad. Not many dugouts were serving as homes after 1910, although existing dugouts were sometimes converted to other uses.

Three main types of dugouts can be distinguished, although dozens of individual variations may be found. The types differed due to the sites chosen and the amount of time and materials available. First, the broken country or lateral type of dugout was constructed by digging a home in the side of a slope, such as a hillside or creek bank. The hill formed the back side of the dwelling, and the front portion was completed with logs, cedar posts, sod, and rock. The dugout was topped with a few poles or posts that held up the roof of grass, twigs, and dirt. A typical roof was made by placing two logs across each end of the dugout. Another log was laid on top of the other two to make a ridge pole. Smaller poles or posts were laid as close as possible to form rafters. Over these, boughs and twigs would form a thatch. Sometimes the sod on top was as much as two feet thick, and the grass and weeds on top kept growing and blooming when it rained. In the end of the room was a hole that led to

the surface to form a chimney.

If the site chosen for the shelter were flat, the plains type of dugout was built. A large pit was prepared, with a stairway leading to the bottom. Posts or poles held up the dirt roof. A typical roof might have several layers of thatching or even towsacks and hay before the final layer of sod was applied. At least in the earliest examples, the entrance was many times at the bottom of the stairs, with any door swinging toward the inside. Later, the roof was lifted a foot or so to allow room for narrow windows, usually one on each side. The roof had a very slight pitch, but it could not have more without causing the sod to wash off during rains.

When some logs or planks were available (as in the Cross Timbers area), a third type of shelter developed: the half-dugout, a combination of burrowing in the ground and building above ground. A hole 4 or 5 feet deep was prepared, so that dirt formed the bottom half of the walls. Above this, walls of wood (or sometimes rock or sod) extended about 4 feet higher, set with an occasional slide window without screens. There would be a door and a fireplace. Later, half-dugouts were sometimes framed with lumber and roofed with cedar shingles. Wood floors might even be added.

Dugouts were nearly always small, one-room shelters, usually rectangular or square in shape, with sleeping arrangements at one end of the room and cooking at the other. Typical sizes were 12' x 16', 14' x 18', 14' x 14', and 16' x 16'. Although sleeping space might be extended by use of wagons or brush arbors outside, still the small dugout had to serve an amazing number of family members. For example, Rich and Alice Miller spent several years (c. 1898-1901) in a dugout nine miles north of Gail. Not only did they have seven children, but they took their turn boarding the school teacher, and they always had a hired hand who stayed with them. Some idea of the cramped interior can be gained from the memories of the Simpson family dugout on Sweetwater Creek; it was considered really spacious because the father did not have to duck his head to walk in as most of the dugout men did.

Interiors of dugouts were naturally crude, but occupants attempted to make them as neat and clean as possible. Dirt floors, walls, and ceilings were covered with a layer of mud and clay that was packed and smoothed to a very hard, even finish. Sometimes stones were packed into the walls. Some settlers plastered the inside walls with a mixture of lime and sand. Others plastered walls with newspapers and pages of magazines. Still others whitewashed walls by baking 'gyprock,' crushing it, and mixing it with water to make plaster; this process helped to lighten interiors where the only artificial light came from candles and kerosene lamps. In some cases, ceilings were formed by tacking cheesecloth, towsacking, or canvas to the rafters—materials that would catch falling debris, yet could be washed when dirty. Dirt floors were at times covered with buffalo hides, or towsacking could be nailed to the ground at each edge and changed when needed.

Dugouts did not always have an actual door; a blanket, buffalo hide, or wolf skin might cover the entrance. The entrance usually faced south, both to benefit from summer breezes and to avoid north winter winds. If the dugout had a single shelf, it was just inside the door to hold water bucket and washpan; this was a handy arrangement for throwing water out the door. If there happened to be a door on the dugout, it had no lock. All visitors were welcome, and it was common practice to keep food on the stove for strangers or neighbors—even when the owner was away. A popular story concerns two men who, while riding through the Panhandle, discovered a padlock on a dugout door. Although they did not wish to enter, they considered the lock an indication of mistrust. Before riding on, they tore off both lock and door and scattered parts of both over a long distance.

Some dugout occupants chose to cook outdoors, but apparently most did cooking in a dirt fireplace at one end of the dugout. Still standing is one unusual "two-story" dugout that the Dorwards built near Gail in 1892; it had a fireplace upstairs and down. In later years a bootlegger used the lower fireplace to cook his mash while beans boiled in the upper chimney. Some settlers were fortunate enough to have a stove, usually a round-bellied "bachelor" stove with a drum inserted in the stovepipe for baking. Fuel included buffalo chips, cow chips, and mesquite roots. Water was hauled in barrels—usually for miles—although many attempted to build their dugout near springs or streams.

Furnishings for the dugouts were meager and mostly homemade. For example, the Bley family living in a dugout in Section 467 near Fluvanna around 1901 had just a few store-bought items to serve them and their six children: the stove, sewing machine, and some cane-bottomed chairs. The beds and plank table were homemade; goods boxes (that is, wooden boxes once used to ship merchandise to stores) served as kitchen cabinets and clothing trunks. Although a few dugouts may have had fine furnishings (such as a dugout on the Wheeler Ranch said to have been outfitted with a fine organ and Oriental carpet), most had little furniture at all. When the Herman Garrett family brought their sheep to Midland in 1884, they dug a room-sized hole, put a tent over it for a roof, and heated it with a stove burning mesquite roots; inside they had two narrow beds and some crates for chairs. Other settlers merely had

hay for a bed, or they spread buffalo hides on the dugout floor and slept on them. One pioneer recalled an unusual way of making a bed; Andrew J. Long said cedar poles were driven into the sides of the walls, and cords were stretched from one pole to the other for springs. Another description of bedding was given by Dr. P. C. Coleman, who described a dugout he visited around 1900 some forty miles south of Colorado City; twelve people spent the night in the 15' x 15' dugout, and he was given the choice bed—under the bed of the sick baby he had been called on to doctor.

The plains settlers seemed always to have been determined to give some touch of home to the dugout. Some kept rag rugs on the floor and a white counterpane on the bed. Others planted flowers at the window or swept a path in front of the door. It was said of many pioneer women, as it was of Martha Killough near Amarillo, "She keeps the dugout like a parlor."

Rough as they were, dugouts had advantages. Making use of locally available materials, settlers found dugouts easy and fast to build as well as economical to build and maintain. Since the plains were sparsely settled, it was necessary that two or three be able to construct the shelter. The dugouts were fire resistant (though not fire proof), termite proof, and weather and storm proof. Tales exist of families surviving not only hailstorms, blizzards, and tornadoes in their dugouts, but also devastating prairie fires. Furthermore, dugouts were well insulated, relatively cool in summer and warm in winter. Newspaper accounts of the great blizzards in 1886 praised the dugouts, for people survived in them while residents of frame houses were freezing to death. Aesthetically, the dugout fit the plains environment; the indigenous materials made the dugout seem nearly to grow from a hill or canyon.

Dugout living had its problems, too. Constant dirt was

difficult to escape. Even in dry weather dirt and other material sifted down from the ceiling. One woman recalled her terror at spending her first night in a dugout and feeling something like fine hail falling on her face; she was not much comforted when told that it was just the building materials being moved around by the wind. Although residents might joke about such things as having to make up their beds with a hoe or rake, dirt was a constant and dreary fact of life.

No matter how many layers of posts, brush, grass, clay, and sod were packed on the roof, the dugouts always leaked. During downpours, the roofs leaked like sponges, and then they dripped three days before drying. The dirt floors became swamps, and mud dripped from the ceiling. Tight lids had to be kept over the pots and pans to keep the mud out of the food. When the roof quit dripping, all clothes and bedding had to be hung out to dry. Nothing could eradicate the dank, unpleasant smell, especially as it mixed with the buffalo-chip smoke from cooking.

There was the danger of things falling into dugouts—usually cows. The George Cowdens lived in a dugout near Midland around 1883 when one of their "Palo Pinto" cows fell through the roof and onto their bed. They had to dig the bank off the dugout to get the cow out. Philanthropist John G. Hardin told a similar story of a cow stumbling into his dugout in Wichita County during the night. Sometimes a herd of cattle would run over a dugout, and many times baby calves fell into the chimney. Also, there are stories of Indians attacking dugout residents by riding horses onto the roof. If these problems weren't enough, sometimes dugouts fell in all by themselves, and they were known to wash away during rains.

Dugouts had other small but terrifying hazards. Tarantulas fell from the ceiling, sometimes even into the

food, and rattlesnakes slithered down the walls, under the beds, and even into the clothing. Field mice, garter snakes, and lizards were commonplace, and so were centipedes, scorpions, and vinegarroons. Some settlers also complained of bedbugs and fleas. As one pioneer said, "You don't have to keep a dog to have fleas. Just have a dirt floor, and you'll have fleas for sure." Mosquitoes were a nuisance in some areas.

Because of these obvious limitations, dugouts were never regarded as more than temporary solutions to the problem of shelter. As soon as lumber was available, settlers moved to more conventional accommodations. Perhaps their attitude toward the dugout is best preserved today in the present description of some poor shelter as being merely "a hole in the wall" or "a hole in the ground." Just about every county history in the area has the frequent statement that a certain family "lived in a dugout until a house could be built." In Borden County there was actually one half-dugout in Section 461 that served many newcomers as a home until they could provide some type of shelter of their own, which most often was at first just a dugout. Apparently all settlers longed to have a lumber house.

Many interesting but confusing variations have resulted from the pioneers' habit of adding onto their dugouts. One example still stands west of Crowell, in Foard County. The original dugout (possibly a stage stand) was said to have existed already when New Yorker Louie Weber bought the place in the 1890's. First, he built a half-dugout and connected it to the dugout. Still later, during the 1920's, he built a lean-to of vertical rock. A fascinating house is the result.

One of the common ways of adding onto the dugout was to add one or two frame rooms above ground, attached to the dugout, but not above it. The new rooms were most often used as living room or bedrooms. When the Bleys near Fluvanna added two above-ground rooms in 1904, they invited friends for a dance in the new addition and settled the children to bed in the dugout. One daughter remembers a woman losing her petticoat during one dance and fleeing to the dugout in embarrassment. This method of adding rooms above ground was naturally followed by conversion of the original dugout to something like the present-day cellar: a place to store food and a haven from storms. The insulation and protection aspects of the dugout were too good to be discarded, and as "the cellar," the dugout has continued to be a significant part of plains country life for one hundred years after its heyday.

Attempts are being made to preserve Texas dugouts and information about life within them. Some county historical groups are involved in projects to record locations of dugouts and to preserve them. A few dugouts can still be seen in conditions close to their original states, ranging from Goodnight's dugout in Palo Duro Canyon to the two-story Dorward dugout in Borden County. Two such structures have been moved to the Ranching Heritage Center at Texas Tech University in Lubbock: one is a half-dugout from the Matador Ranch, and the other a full dugout with a second story above ground from C. C. Slaughter's "Long S" Whiteface Camp in Garza County. Others have worked in creative ways to preserve dugout history. Mondel Rogers has included dugouts among his original paintings, now published as *Old Ranches of the Texas Plains.* Jane Gilmore Rushing has given a novelist's view of life in a Texas dugout in several of her books, including her prize-winning *Mary Dove.*

Along with preservation of the dugout structures themselves, it is well to preserve the spirit of those early builders and occupants. One such occupant recalled when, as a young bride, she moved into a dugout. She remembered standing in front of the cookstove, holding an umbrella in one hand and stuffing buffalo chips in the stove with the other. With her skirt pinned up and with rubbers on her feet, she was wet, muddy, tired, and afraid. Considering her story and the many like it, one can understand why the rate of settlement slowed down when it reached the plains. The dugout was one clear way that culture adapted to the new environment. It was one means by which people of great stamina conquered the obstacles they faced.

BIBLIOGRAPHY

Although any study of Texas dugouts must rely mainly on first-hand interviews and site observations, the following published sources provide helpful overall views.

Borden County, Texas: The First Hundred Years. Gail: Borden County Historical Commission, 1976.

Coleman, P. C. "Experiences of a Pioneer Doctor," *West Texas Historical Association Yearbook.* VII (June, 1931), p. 38.

Griffin, John Howard. *Land of the High Sky.* Midland: First National Bank of Midland, 1959.

Hamner, Laura V. *Light 'n Hitch.* Dallas: American Guild Press, 1958.

Hamner, Laura V. *Short Grass and Longhorns.* Norman: University of Oklahoma Press, 1948.

Kraenzel, Carl F. *The Great Plains in Transition.* Norman: University of Oklahoma Press, 1955.

McMillan, Edward. "The Cowboy, Product of His Environment," *West Texas Historical Association Yearbook.* XXXI (October, 1955), pp. 85-89.

Rogers, Mondel. *Old Ranches of the Texas Plains.* College Station: Texas A & M University Press, 1976.

Smith, Ruby. "Early Development of Wilbarger County," *West Texas Historical Association Yearbook.* XIV (October, 1938), p. 54.

Adobe house *(Presidio County)*

60

Adobe: Earth, Straw, and Water

John O. West and Roberto Gonzalez

Many of the ancient arts of earlier civilizations have been lost or greatly modified by succeeding civilizations, but the use of earth to make bricks for construction still remains relatively unchanged in the American Southwest. From Africa to China, from Peru to the American Southwest, adobe's history is a living thing. In Chapter 5 of Exodus the making of sun-dried bricks was a job given to the children of Israel. As a special punishment, Pharaoh ordered the Israelites to make the bricks without providing them the straw needed, so that it was often impossible for them to make their daily quota.[1]

Through the years various civilizations have used the word "adobe" as well as the building-block. The word *tobe* appears in the Coptic language, which is said to have come from the Egyptian. The word came into Arabic as *tuba*, or *at tuba*; the term and the technique were taken by the Moors from North Africa into Spain during their conquest of the Iberian Peninsula. The Spanish use of the word *at tuba* eventually came out *adobe*, the term in widespread use today for both the sun-dried brick and the clay-like soil from which it is made.[2]

While the Spanish did bring the Egyptian-Moorish techniques of brick-making with adobe mud to the American Southwest, the use of earth—or adobe—as a building material was already well established here. When the Conquistadores first came to New Mexico in the 16th century, they discovered that the Indians were living in great boxlike apartments, which the Spaniards called

"Pueblos." And where adobe was not the main material used, it was included in the construction as mortar to help bind the stones together to make sheltering walls.

The use of adobe in the Indian pueblos was wide and varied. The majority of the early structures was built by laying the "mud" walls in solid courses or layers about two feet thick, and in most cases shaped by hand. Each layer of the wall was allowed to dry before the other layers were laid, much like the "pise de terre" technique used by the French. Examples of this type of construction can be seen in the ruins of the Picuris and Pot Creek Pueblos which are said to date back to the year 1150.[3]

The period from 1250 to 1598 AD saw the appearance of the numerous tribes of Indians in the Rio Grande Valley and the introduction of the multi-storied housing complexes that were built by these Indians, typified by the pueblos found in Taos, New Mexico.[4] At the Acoma and the Hopi Pueblos, Castañeda in 1540 noticed that a different technique was used in building the pueblos. The Indians set the grass and brush on fire and, while the ashes were still smouldering, water and earth were mixed with the ashes. This mixture was later rolled into balls which were allowed to harden in the sun. These balls were then used instead of stones to form the walls of many of the pueblos. These crude adobe bricks or balls were cemented together with adobe and mortar. The ash apparently produced a kind of lye binder.

After the arrival of the Spaniards, several changes took

Adobe roof (Terlingua)

62

Shafter *(Presidio Co.)*

63

place in the construction of the adobe buildings of the area, particularly the introduction of the rectangular adobe brick which provided the basis for variety.[5] For example, the Isleta pueblo buildings standing today were made with a variation of the brick-making technique: marshy sod was cut into brick-like pieces, set aside to dry, and used to build with, as any other bricks would be. This technique (called *corte de terrón*) is still being used in the Isleta area—and they don't need to add straw for binder, since grass roots in the sod do the job.[6] Southwest Indians also built huts of intertwined branches and plastered them with mud, giving an adobe-like color and appearance; the result was much like the wattle-and-daub huts of early Anglo-Saxons.[7]

Today many of the techniques used by the Southwestern Indians to construct their homes can be studied only in ruins, but the basic materials used by them still tell the story of the significance of adobe in the Southwestern United States. And living examples of the art can be found being built today in the area once occupied by the Conquistadores.

The Spanish Southwest is particularly good for the use of adobe: the sparseness of rain makes it possible for adobe structures, unprotected by plaster, to stand literally for centuries with little wear from the elements. And with reasonable repairs, there is hardly any limit to the life expectancy of adobe. Add to this permanence the simplicity of the process of making adobe bricks and the economy and ready availability of the materials, and a near perfect combination is at hand.

Commercial adobe makers vary the proportions of clay and sand according to the climate: a more humid area requires more clay, and a dry area needs less. On the average, 70% clay and 30% sand is the optimum,[8] but the folk fabricator is a pragmatist, using the soil that's at hand.

Often a family in need of a room—or a house—will simply use the earth from the back of the lot to make bricks for the front of the lot! And oat straw, the best "binder" for good adobe-making, is easily replaced with hay, dry grass clippings—even leaves, if that is all that is available.

Making adobe requires few tools—*pico, azadón, y forma* (pick, hoe, and form)—and the process is easily learned. Earth is chopped thoroughly with a hoe, with rocks, twigs, and foreign matter picked out. A miniature volcano-shaped pile is formed of the earth, and water, in small amounts, is added and chopped into the earth. Too much water slows the drying process and makes concave bricks—something like a cake that has fallen; too little water and there simply is not enough mud consistency to hold together. A couple of handfuls of straw binder will serve to make a dozen adobes; it too is mixed in so that it is spread throughout the mixture.[9]

The form, usually two or three adobes in size, is a simple box without top or bottom. The "standard" adobe measures 10 by 16 inches, or 9 by 18 inches, four inches thick—a weight of about 35 pounds—but in practice the adobes can vary considerably, up to 12 by 24 inches and six inches thick, weighing over a hundred pounds.[10] The dampened form—visualize a short, three or four step ladder—is laid flat on the ground and the mud-straw mix—called *mezcla*—is slopped into it with some force, so that each corner is full (some workers tramp the mud in with their feet); the top is smoothed with a very simple tool—the hand. Excess mud is scraped off and flung back into the mixture pile for future use. The form, which is often left soaking in a barrel of water overnight, is slick so that the worker can lift it straight up, leaving two or three adobes lying flat on the ground. A dripping wet rag is wiped around the inside of each rectangle of the form, to remove residual mud and

Making adobe bricks pp. 65-70

65

67

prepare for the next filling. Laid flat near the last group of adobes, the form is ready to be used again and again. A good worker alone can easily make a hundred bricks a day, working at a relatively easy pace. And with a *mozo* carrying water and helping prepare the *mezcla*, two or three hundred a day is not unusual.

Under typical sunny Southwestern skies the adobes lie as they were formed—*tendidos* or stretched out—three or four days until they can be turned up on the long side—*candiados*—so the air can get to them. They stay thus for two or three weeks, depending on the weather, and then they are stacked—*trinchados*—loosely so air can still circulate around each one. The top of the stack is covered with tarpaper, cardboard, or whatever is handy, to reduce the danger of rain showers melting the bricks before the sun has baked them hard. After a couple of weeks the adobes are ready for use.[11]

Adobes are used much as the more familiar fired bricks are used, except that users of adobe are often more relaxed about procedures. A foundation may be of concrete, or mud-mortared rock, or even the bare ground (preferably a bit higher than the surrounding area.) A layer of adobe brick is laid, with mud or lime-and-sand mortar, and another course is laid, with joints overlapping, and another and another. Openings are left for windows and doors as the walls go up; the openings are capped by dressed 2 by 6's or peeled logs (city codes often specify quarter inch steel plates, as if cottonwood logs had not held up for two or three centuries!) and then adobes go on, marching across the tops of the openings, making the wall a continuous line again.

The roof problem is handled in any of several fairly standard ways, depending on the availability of materials. The "old" way, perhaps the closest to the folk process, is probably the most interesting. Traditionally, peeled logs five to six inches in diameter—*vigas*—were laid atop the walls, about two feet apart. A slope was managed by having one more course of bricks laid on the front wall than the rear one. Then the walls went on up, a foot to 18 inches above these beams. Across these *vigas* smaller peeled branches (*latias*) about an inch in diameter are laid, as closely together as possible. Then a layer of *carrizo*—reeds—goes atop the *latias*, to a depth of an inch or so. Four or more inches of earth piled atop the reeds completes the job, waiting only for the first shower to dampen and seal the roof.[12]

Finishing the adobe part of the building is a fairly simple thing. The tops of the walls are protected from erosion by a layer of tile or stones or lime-and-sand plaster. The outsides of the walls today may be covered with small mesh chicken wire and heavily plastered with lime or cement plaster. Older methods used more of the *mezcla* (generally without straw), simply flung onto the wall and slicked over to produce a smooth surface. Paul Horgan says Indian workmen building Spanish missions along the Rio Grande used wet sheepskins—wool to the wall—to smooth the mud plaster.[13] These days a tow sack does the same job, if the plaster is used. Often a wall will stand naked to the sun for several months, curing to a flint-like hardness that makes plastering only a decoration.[14]

Windows and doors are framed as in brick buildings. Centuries ago, when mesquite grew large, hand-hewn planks of twelve to fourteen inches made doors and shutters to swing on hand-forged hinges and pins. Today steel casement windows and fancy millwork doors often are used—but many a simple home still uses the skills of the local *carpintero* who builds each door or window to fit the hole the adobe mason left. Standardization and six-foot-eight-inch doors are not always necessary.

Water is the chief enemy of adobe buildings, yet usually rain falls with impunity on Southwestern walls. But let a determined drip send a steady flow of water etching its way down a wall and a centuries-old structure can acquire a deep scar in a hurry. And of course a flooded yard melts the walls from the bottom in a matter of days if not drained and sun-dried. Water in another way, via capillary action, erodes adobe from the foundation upwards, several inches to a foot, making the surface appear acid-etched two or three inches deep. The remedy is simply to fill the eaten-away part, with *mezcla* or with lime or cement plaster (if the owner has the money to spend). Unchecked, this capillary action can simply eat the bottom of the wall away, causing the whole thing to tumble down.[15] Thus exposed to wind and water, the fallen wall in a few years has returned to the earth from which it came, indistinguishable from any other hillock. In time, given the need, the pile of earth that once was adobe brick may be chopped up, watered, and made again into useful adobes to shelter man or beast—and there is no need to search for straw this time.

One-room huts, spacious haciendas, even modern mansions use the lowly adobe for building material. Adobe walls nearly a foot thick (which once served beautifully to stop Indian arrows or Comanchero rifle slugs) provide natural insulation, making homes warm in winter and cool in summer. And with exposed *vigas* and colorful tile roofs to top them off, adobe homes still preserve much of the charm and utility of ages past, when Moorish Spain met American Indian to produce the perfect building material out of earth, straw, and water.

NOTES:

[1] G. E. Middleton, *Build Your House of Earth: A Manual of Pise and Adobe Construction* (Sidney: Angus Robertson, 1953), pp. 8-9.

[2] Arthur Oden, "Mud, Sticks, and Stones" (Unpublished Master's Thesis, Texas Western College, 1959), pp. 1-13

[3] Bainbridge Bunting, *Taos Adobes: Spanish Colonial and Territorial Architecture of the Taos Valley* (Santa Fe: New Mexico Press, 1964), p. 6.

[4] *Ibid.*, p. 3.

[5] Roland Dickey, *New Mexico Village Arts* (Albuquerque: University of New Mexico Press, 1970), pp. 32-38.

[6] Interview with Carlos Chávez, El Paso, Texas, September, 1974. Mr. Chávez was raised in the area where *corte de terrón* was common.

[7] Dickey, p. 40; see also Paul Horgan, *Great River* (New York: Rinehart, 1954), I, 48-51.

[8] United States Department of Agriculture Farmers' Bulletin, *Adobe or Sundried Brick for Farm Buildings* (Washington, 1970), pp. 1-13.

[9] Interview with Señor Del Rio, Juarez, Chihuahua, Mexico, March 1973; Señor Del Rio has made and built with adobes since early childhood.

[10] United States Department of Agriculture, p. 4.

[11] Interview with Señor Del Rio.

[12] Interview with Richard Copenbarger, Socorro, Texas, September, 1974; Mr. Copenbarger is an authority on adobe architecture, reconstructing an early 19th century Comanchero house now named a historical site by the State of Texas.

[13] Horgan, I, 224.

[14] Interview with Señor Del Rio.

[15] Interview with Richard Copenbarger.

Riggs Hotel (*Fort Stockton*)

73

Riggs Hotel *(Fort Stockton)*

Adobe church in Shafter *(Presidio Co.)*

75

Details of adobe construction

Adobe house *(Presidio)*

76

Adobe Church *(Terlingua)*

77

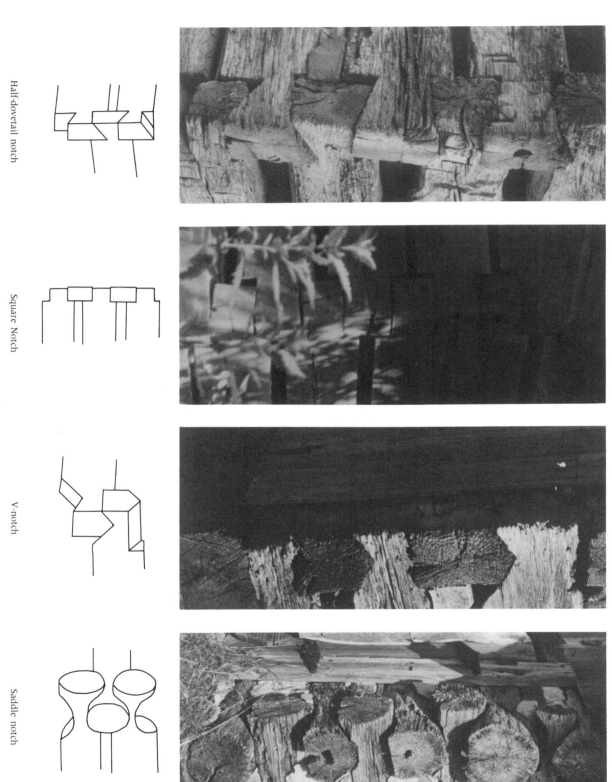

Figure 1: The most common types of log corner-notching in Texas. *(Drawing, Terry G. Jordan)*

Half-dovetail notch

Square Notch

V-notch

Saddle notch

78

Log Corner Notching in Texas

Terry G. Jordan

In the eastern half of Texas, the pioneer folk architecture was based mainly in log construction. For at least a century and a quarter, roughly 1815 to 1940, log buildings were erected by folk artisans and rank amateurs alike.[1] If any single element can properly be called the key to log construction, it is the corner notch, the joint where logs from adjacent walls are attached to one another. The entire weight of the building, exclusive of the sills, rests on the four corners and therefore on the notches. Not only is the notching weight-bearing, but it also holds the walls laterally in place by preventing horizontal slippage. If the notching is faulty, the entire structure is faulty.

Four major notch types are found in Texas, all of which were derived from the eastern United States and German Central Europe, the major source region of American log construction techniques.[2] These four types are the *half-dovetail*, *saddle*, *V*, and *square* notches (Fig. 1). The half-dovetail accounts for about thirty-five percent of all log dwellings in Texas, based on a field survey of over 500 houses, and is found most frequently in Central and North Texas. The V notch, confined even more exclusively to interior parts of the state, especially the Hill Country and Cross Timbers, is seen on about one-fifth of all Texas log houses. A quarter of the log dwellings are square notched, a type most common in East Texas but occurring through parts of Central Texas as well. Saddle notching occurs on only about fifteen percent of the log houses, but on over half of all outbuildings, particularly barns and cribs. On houses,

the saddle notch is most common in East Texas, particulary on dwellings erected since 1900. To generalize, then, the half-dovetail and V notches prevail in most of Central and North Texas, while the square and saddle types are found mainly in East Texas.

The half-dovetail seemingly evolved in Central Europe from a more complicated type of cornering. It was first used extensively in the border region of Virginia and West Virginia and became dominant through most of the Upper South and Ohio Valley, in areas as far-flung as the hills of Arkansas, the North Carolina Piedmont, and the southern half of Ohio. The half-dovetail is so-named because it has a dovetailed splay or slant only on the top side of the tongue of the log (Fig. 2). The result is a superior notch, difficult to fashion but producing a firmly locked joint which has the added advantage of draining rainwater to the exterior of the notch. Half-dovetailing is generally a sure indicator of fine craftsmanship and occurs usually on logs that are neatly hewn on two sides. It is particularly prevalent when hardwoods, mainly various species of oak, are used in construction.

The saddle notch is probably the most ancient of all types. It is used almost exclusively on logs that are left round rather than hewn, and is fashioned by hollowing out a saddle-shaped depression near the end of the log, shaped to fit the rounded contour of the adjacent log or another saddle. Two subtypes of the saddle notch can be distinguished, the "single" and "double." The double saddle is formed by cutting depressions into both the top and bottom of the log, while the single saddle notch, the simpler of the subtypes, has a depression cut only on one side of the log (Fig. 3). Both subtypes of the saddle notch form a locked joint, and the ends of the logs are left projecting beyond the corner, rather than being cut off flush as in the half-dovetail type. The single saddle notch with the depression cut on the bottom of the log drains rainwater better than do the other saddle subtypes, since it lacks a depression on the top side of the log which could catch and hold moisture. Pennsylvania Germans seem to have been responsible for the introduction from Central Europe of the subtype notched only on the bottom. Saddle notching is most common in softwoods, mainly pine and cedar, and its use on dwellings is closely identified with poor whites and blacks in the Deep South.

V notching, so-named because of its inverted V-shaped joint, was developed in Europe, apparently as a variant of the saddle notch (Fig. 4). The Schwenkfelders, a German religious sect from the province of Silesia, seem to have introduced the V notch into Pennsylvania in the 1730's, and it became the most common type on Pennsylvania German log houses. Its spread west was mainly by way of the Central Appalachians and Ohio Valley. It is the dominant type in the mountains of western Maryland and Virginia, and occurs widely through Kentucky, Ohio, Indiana, Illinois, and Missouri.

In Texas, V notching is very closely associated with settlers of upper southern and German heritage. It occurs almost exclusively in the interior central and northern parts of the state and is extremely rare in East Texas. Clearly V notching reached Texas by way of the Ohio Valley and Missouri. The Hill Country Germans of Central Texas presumably learned how to fashion the V notch from upper

southerners in their vicinity, since the large majority of Texas German immigrants was not derived from provinces where this type of corner notch was known.

The V notch forms a solid, locked corner, and is used both on hewn logs and on those left in the round. If the logs are hewn, the corner is boxed, but round logs are left projecting beyond the corner, as with the saddle notch. Rainwater is drained out of the joint fairly well, though the V notch is inferior to the dovetail and single-saddle types in this respect. V notching occurs frequently on both oak and cedar logs. It is not uncommon to find saddle and V notching intermixed on walls, an additional suggestion that the V is derived from the saddle type.

The square notch, often called a "quarter" notch in Texas, is apparently derived from the half-dovetail type and possibly also from V notching. It was developed in Europe and is common in northern Bohemia, a principal source area of American log construction.

We might best regard square notching as a degenerate type because it requires much less skill to fashion than most other styles and does not produce a locked joint. It probably evolved as less-skilled craftsmen decreased the angle of dovetailing, or both angles of the V notch, until the angle reached 90°, forming a notch consisting only of right angles (Fig. 5). Because this notch is not locking and cannot hold together simply by gravity, each joint must be pegged or nailed to assure the survival of the structure. Pegging the logs provides sufficient shear strength, at least until the pegs rot out from the rainwater that tends to collect on the flat surface of the notch. Square notching is normally found on hewn logs.

Degenerate forms of material culture, such as the square-notch, often prevail when uninitiated culture groups accept a technology from another group, usually on a periphery or

Figure 3: Single saddle notching on a crib in the East Cross Timbers. (Texas Log Cabin Register, Denton Co. No. 7). *(Photograph by Terry G. Jordan)*

Figure 2: Half-dovetail notching on a hewn log house near Gainesville. (Texas Log Cabin Register, Cooke Co. No. 38). *(Photograph by Terry G. Jordan)*

81

Figure 4: V notching on hewn oaken logs, North Texas. (Texas Log Cabin Register, Cooke Co. No. 16).
(Photograph by Terry G. Jordan)

82

Figure 5: Square notching on sawn logs, Northeast Texas (Texas Log Cabin Register, Red River Co. No. 3.)
(Photograph courtesy Dallas County Heritage Society)

outer zone of usage. In the case of the square notch, the first widespread acceptance occurred among settlers of English ancestry in the interior coastal plain and Piedmont of Virginia. Most likely, the Virginia English were attracted to this least complex notch style because log construction was to them an alien technology. Their descendants carried square notching across the inner coastal plain of the South, eventually reaching East Texas. It is normally an indicator in Texas of lower southern origin of the builder. Most often, detailed research reveals that square-notched structures were built by immigrants from Alabama or Mississippi.

To generalize, we can say that in Texas half-dovetailing suggests hill southern origin, particularly Tennessee, and occurs most often in oak; V-notching reveals Appalachian or Ohio Valley background; square notching usually indicates lowland southern origin in Alabama and adjacent Coastal Plains states; and saddle notching, on dwellings, is representative of the poorer socio-economic groups of the deep southern pine forests.

Notching is only one trait of log construction, but a very important one. From it we can learn much about the diversity of Texas log buildings and about the different backgrounds of the folk who built these structures.

NOTES:

¹The only general reference on log construction in Texas is: Terry G. Jordan, *Texas Log Buildings: A Folk Architecture*. Austin: University of Texas Press, 1978. Chapter 4 deals with corner notching in much greater detail than does the present paper. Data and illustrations in this book and in the present article were derived from the Texas Log Cabin Register, a manuscript collection housed in the Archives of the North Texas State University Historical Collection and Museum, Denton. The collection is open to interested persons.

²A good general source on corner notching is Fred B. Kniffen, "On Corner Timbering," *Pioneer America*, Vol. 1 (Jan. 1969), pp. 1-8. See also: Terry G. Jordan, "Log Corner-Timbering in Texas," *Pioneer America*, Vol. 8 (Jan. 1976), pp. 8-18.

Tie barn (*Comanche Co.*)

84

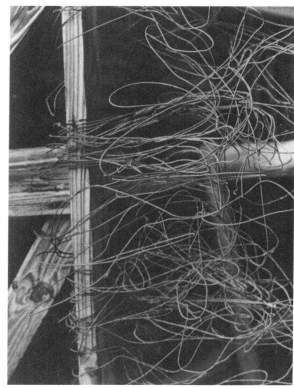

Baling wire

Texas Tie Houses

Pat Ellis Taylor

In the plains and desert areas of Texas where wood is at a premium Texans have had to use their ingenuity in finding lumber suitable for building homes, utility buildings, and fences. One unique source of lumber has been from discarded railroad ties. Tie structures are usually found close to railroad lines; there is a typical cluster around the Southern Pacific lines coming into and out of El Paso. But isolated tie houses are also found dozens of miles away from the nearest track.

The durability called for in railroad construction is a plus when the ties are later used for home building. When ties were first made for the railroads, high quality hardwood was used to prolong their rail life. Several tie camps were erected in East Texas north of Dallas where the ties were hewn out of the abundant oak timber found there. Now, even though ties are made of softer, less durable woods, the creosoting process strengthens them so that they are at least as sturdy as hardwood ties. Southern Pacific now gets its ties from a creosoting plant in Houston; the Santa Fe has a plant in Albuquerque; and the largest tie manufacturer in the United States is located in Tennessee. In some of the better built tie houses in which the exteriors have been carefully plastered, it is only the smell of creosote which identifies the original building material.

Texas at present has approximately 21,000 miles of railroad track. The ties which support these rails have a lifespan of about thirty years. So there is quite a bit of lumber which eventually becomes available simply from

this inevitable wearing out process. Up until a few years ago, the spikes which were used to anchor ties were dated so that at a certain time a whole section would be pulled up and replaced. Now, however, ties are pulled individually when they show signs of wear. In addition to ties on existing lines being pulled, there are times when a whole section of line is abandoned and the tracks pulled. This happened to a Denver Northern branch one hundred eleven miles long between Wellington and Pampa in 1970 as the section was no longer economically viable. When this occurs, a great many ties are suddenly available for construction purposes. An interesting early example of this occurred at the turn of the century when a company was selling stock in a coal mine supposedly located a few miles west of Valentine, which in fact was totally worthless. In their advertising, they also claimed there was a railroad spur line leading to the site which branched from the Southern Pacific line at Chispi. When the entrepreneurs came to court, the judge ruled that they could either go to jail or build the railroad. The railroad was built, then promptly abandoned. When the Sixth Cavalry set up an outpost at Evett's ranch in 1916, they used the ties on the abandoned line to build barracks and stables. Unfortunately, they made the mistake of building their camp in the bed of Diez y Ocho Creek which became a raging torrent with the first big rain, washing their tie camp into the Rio Grande about nines miles away. Luckily, W. D. Smithers, the well-known Texas pioneer photographer, recorded the camp for history before it disappeared.

There are several methods used for tie construction. Roger L. Welsch, who has studied tie houses in Nebraska, enumerates three basic methods: (1) laying the ties vertically using horizontal sills; (2) laying the ties horizontally butted against a vertical corner post, and (3) laying the ties horizontally so that they alternately overlap, as in log construction, this last being the most popular type which he found.[1] The roof can be either hipped or gabled. If hipped, one or two ties are laid horizontally across the front for slant. If gabled, ties are usually cut on a diagonal and placed at the ends, although other materials are also used to form the gable, including adobe brick and plywood.

By far the most popular method I observed in Texas tie houses was that of vertical ties set into a concrete base. A good example of this construction is a building outside of Anthony, Texas, which was built twenty-seven years ago. It consists of two rooms which form a "T". The front room was built by Carlos Nevarez who worked for the railroad at the time. He seated the ties vertically on concrete, then chinked the building with additional concrete, covering it with chicken wire and plaster. About twelve years afterward an uncle by marriage, Jose Navarrete, added the second room; the ties are exposed on the addition so that the method of construction is easily observed. Although the Nevarez building was originally constructed for storage, it has been used by various members of the family to live in from time to time.

The most unusual laying of ties I found in the construction of an abandoned outbuilding outside of El Paso across a dirt road from the Southern Pacific line. It was part of a large cluster of buildings, including a plastered farmhouse, haysheds, fences and chicken pens, all built from ties. It alternated vertical and horizontal

placements. The horizontal ties were staggered for strength and the corners were wrapped around with four to five strands of barbed wire which were stapled into place to give added stability.

An example of a house built partially of ties belongs to Mrs. Kay Niewald in El Paso. The house was originally a barn and stable and was converted by George Kuper who used railroad ties which he picked up between Deming and Columbus in New Mexico. Ties are used for support beams for the ceiling, window sills, door frames, and the entranceway. The longer, thicker beams across the living room's ceiling and door arches were pieces from a railroad trestle bridge which was disassembled and cut to size. Foot-long L/braces join the beams at the corners, bolted into the wood. Kuper also built a fence around the house from ties by setting the verticals into place, then holding the horizontal ties steady with baling wire. He would then drill a hole through the two pieces and insert a length of re-bar, bending down the end with a hammer. Kuper died several years ago, and Mrs. Niewald now rents the house to two families.

Although the ties allow for thicker walls than those of a typical clapboard house, they apparently do not have the temperature regulating properties of adobe brick. Jewel Babb, a 76-year-old goat-herder who lived for many years in a tie house, reminisced about its cooling and heating properties (or lack of them) when I interviewed her. Her house is located approximately thirty miles south of Sierra Blanca on a desert ridge and was built by Dixie, her oldest son, in 1946. In addition to the house, he also built various sheds and fences on the property from railroad ties. The house is large but the facilities primitive, having no electricity and no running water. Dixie had originally built it for himself and his wife, but it had been abandoned for

Feed trough

Shed roof

Tie barn interior

Details of tie barn (*Comanche Co.*)

Details of tie barn *(Comanche Co.)*

The tie house built by Dixie Babb in 1946
(Photograph by Pat Ellis Taylor)

Close-up of Babb house, showing ties set vertically in the ground
(Photograph by Pat Ellis Taylor)

90

several years before Jewel Babb moved into it. Cattle had chewed off the tarpaper covering it, so there were gaps between the ties as much as half an inch wide which Mrs. Babb tried to stuff with paper and pieces of plastic.

"The first winter it got so cold," she said, "we had to heat rocks and put our feet on 'em to keep warm. Our wood-burning stove didn't have a flue. So we'd pile up dead sotol in it and all the heat would go straight out the chimney. We'd haul water in in glass jars and they'd be broken in the morning from the freeze." On the other hand, in the summer, she said the house would get so hot that she would wet a towel and put it on top of her head, covering it with a head scarf, in order to cool down a little. Regardless of its discomforts, Mrs. Babb lived at the house for over ten years up until the fall of 1976, and the house is still standing and in good condition.

When these structures were built, railroad ties could be obtained for free if a person knew when and where ties were going to be pulled up. Les Standiford, who now lives in the Niewald house, tells of how railroad families would follow the construction crews in pick-up trucks so that the ties could be thrown directly into the truck beds. Other times the ties would simply be thrown at the side of the track for anyone to pick up, and sometimes for only a few cents apiece the railroad would sell ties from stockpiles. However, in recent years railroad ties have been increasingly popular with building contractors. The Southern Pacific now sells its ties for $2.00 apiece to construction firms, which price does not include picking up the ties from the right of way. The contractors in turn sell the ties for as much as $4.50 each. Ties are now found as part of fashionable decor in chic restaurants and expensive homes and are popular for use in flowerbeds and garden walkways. As a result, railroad ties are no longer available to the person interested in cheap construction materials, and the tie house will increasingly become a structure of a by-gone era.

NOTES:

'Roger L. Welsch, "Railroad-Tie Construction on the Pioneer Plains," *Western Folklore*, XXXV (April 1976), 151-152.

Style & Form

Snow is rare in central Texas, but some of the old Alsatian and German houses still show the steep roofline that was necessary during the white Christmases of the Old World. In East Texas many of the finest of the old homes have beautifully decorated double doors or a single door framed by etched-glass windows to fill the gap left by the old-time open central hall, or dog trot. And there are lower east side blocks in Texas' big cities that are populated, row on row, with shotgun shacks that are so uniformly built and spaced that identification would be almost impossible without house numbers. Style is in the eye of the beholder and builder.

The story of building in Texas is the story of the evolution and blending of styles. The Anglos, who had several

generations of building experiences in their pioneering across the southern states, set the styles and forms which the European newcomers incorporated into their own forms. Thereafter style evolved, usually becoming more sophisticated as the level of culture improved. Simple adobe houses added gabled roofs. Log houses were boarded over with milled siding. Rock houses were plastered over and whitewashed, at least on the front and the sides that could be seen from the road. The time eventually came when it was un-stylish to live in one of these old homes, no matter how they were veneered, so the dwellers built frame houses in town and turned the old houses into barns.

Comanche Tepees

Ferdinand Roemer: 1847

In the afternoon several friends and I visited the camp or tent village of the Comanches which lay near our own camp, however, on the opposite side of the river. After crossing the San Saba which was about forty feet wide and two feet deep at this point, and similar to the Pedernales and Llano, flowing rapidly and clear, we saw the tents and huts standing about in irregular order. Probably several hundred horses were grazing round about us. The wigwams were serviceably and comfortably made. They are round, twelve to fourteen feet high, and made of tanned buffalo hides sewed together and spread over a framework made of poles sixteen to eighteen feet long, crossing each other on the top. Near the ground is an opening which serves as a door, but which is usually closed by a bear skin. On the top is a small slit, which can be protected against pressure from the wind by two flaps, ingeniously arranged, and which serves as a vent for the smoke. The door and the vent of the tents always faced east, opposite the prevailing winds during this time of the year.

Soon we had an opportunity to enter one of these tents to see the interior, as several of the occupants invited us to do so with friendly nods. Upon entering one we were urged to sit down on buffalo and bear skins, which had been spread in a circle on the ground. Thus we had an opportunity to examine the arrangement of the house leisurely. The master of the hut sat in the rear, opposite the door. At his side were his wives, either engaged in caring for the children whom they fondled lovingly, or doing beadwork. The latter, done on strips of leather, was intended exclusively for the men, for unlike civilized people, the men and not the women among the Indians lay particular stress upon outward finery. The poor squaws are the slaves of the men, and forgetful of themselves, they are concerned only to adorn their lord and master and to gain his approbation. In the middle of the tent was maintained a little fire in a hollow which was adequate to warm the tent and at the same time served to roast the meat. A leather rope fastened to a stake driven into the ground and reaching up to a point where the poles cross each other, was evidently placed there to give the tent more stability and to keep it from being blown down during a strong wind.

Other huts which we visited later resembled the first one and differed only as to size, according to the rank and wealth of their occupants. The wigwams of the Comanches deserve particular mention since they are so serviceable and comfortable. I am sure they afford more protection in inclement weather than many of the ordinary log houses found in Texas. This shows that the Indians possess an inventive mind when one considers that these tents are so arranged that they can be easily dissembled, loaded upon pack horses and transported.

From Ferdinand Roemer, *Roemer's Texas*, Oswald Mueller, trans. (San Antonio: Standard Printing Co., 1935), pp. 244-245.

Pueblo Indian Housing in Texas: Ysleta del Sur

Thomas A. Green, Jr.

Among the first immigrant builders in Texas were the Tigua Indians of the community of Ysleta del Sur (Ysleta of the South) east of El Paso. Although the Tiguas are native Americans, they are not native Texans. Their housing traditions appeared in our state only at the close of the seventeenth century, although their legends claim an earlier arrival.

While I prefer the romance of the Tigua assertion that they settled in the area after avenging the atrocities committed against the Pueblos by the Spanish explorer Coronado, most commentators state that they came in the aftermath of the Pueblo Revolt of 1680.[1] Driven beyond endurance by Spanish domination, several of the Pueblo villages rose in unison under the leadership of the warrior-priest Popé in the holy war to rid the Southwest of foreign influence. Those Europeans who managed to escape death fled. In the company of the expelled Spanish were many Tigua natives from Isleta Del Norte, south of modern Albuquerque, as well as a scattering of other Indian peoples from the New Mexico tribes.

Rather than returning to their homes in the west, a

sizeable band of Tigua established a settlement in Texas in the community that came to be known as Ysleta del Sur. In spite of the resettlement, throughout their residence in Texas the Tigua have adhered to traditional Pueblo social structure, culture, architecture, and building traditions.

Despite this remarkable tenacity, they came frighteningly close to being ignored into oblivion. During the Spanish Period the Tigua were awarded a large grant of land by Spain. The rights to this territory were protected by the Treaty of Guadalupe Hidalgo when this region was eventually taken over from Mexico by the United States. Unfortunately, during the War Between the States when the land rights of the other Pueblos were formalized by President Abraham Lincoln, the tribe's residency in the Confederate state of Texas prevented the granting of legitimate status of the Tigua. This historical accident nearly doomed the group to extinction.

In the 1950's the city of El Paso annexed the town of Ysleta, subjecting most of its Tigua residents (at least those who had been able to retain their land) to property taxes amounting to a major portion of their average annual income. In the face of this threat, the Tigua retained the services of El Paso attorney Tom Diamond who, after an extended legal battle, was able to help the tribe obtain the protected status to which it was entitled. Thus, after almost two centuries, we came to recognize what the Tigua had known all along—that the Tigua are a Pueblo enclave in Texas and, as such, are entitled to the protected status and land rights awarded to the rest of Indian America.

The Pueblos of the Southwest were given their name by the Spanish explorers because when they were first encountered by the *conquistadores* they resided in permanent towns—*pueblos*. This sedentary lifestyle was made possible by the development of agriculture prior to the period of initial European contact. Many of these early settlements contained multi-storied buildings constructed from stone and sun-dried adobe bricks. These native Southwestern dwellings were rivaled in size by contemporary Euro-American apartment houses only in the twentieth century. Among the surviving Pueblo groups of New Mexico and Arizona similar buildings still stand and are in regular use.

Various commentators have noted that the native American's adobe dwellings presented no novelty to the Spaniards, since the use of sun-dried brick is common in arid regions of the Old World. Adobe construction was known in Spain well before their excursions into the Western Hemisphere in the fifteen hundreds. The conquerors, however, brought with them important architectural modifications for the adobe dwelling, among them being brick-making techniques, the substitution of first-story doors for roof hatches, and chimneys.[2] The Spanish also introduced the *horno*, a beehive-shaped adobe oven still used by the Pueblos, as well as other less welcome changes to the Pueblo way of life.

The Tigua of Ysleta del Sur never constructed multi-

storied dwellings. Their housing was consistent, however, with the prevailing Pueblo architectural style and bore a striking resemblance to the houses one may still see in their ancestral home of Isleta del Norte.

For the most part, the houses of Ysleta del Sur have been small, often a single room and rarely exceeding three or four rooms, and suitable for a single family. These dwellings were constructed of rectangular adobe bricks composed of mud with a straw or grass binder, dried in the sun. By the time of the Tiguas' arrival in Ysleta the Indians of the Southwest had adopted from the Spanish the technique of forming adobe bricks in wooden molds. As the bricks were laid they were bonded together with mud, and the walls were plastered inside and out with additional layers of mud. The walls of the traditional Pueblo buildings are significantly thinner than those built by the Spanish, for they rarely exceed one foot in thickness. Coupled with the smaller windows of the Indian dwellings, this was sufficient to keep them relatively cool in the summer and warm in the winter.

When the walls were erected to the desired height, about seven feet in the examples with which I am familiar, *vigas* (beams) were installed across the top. Across the beams were placed *tules* (reeds) and an earth covering. Earth floors are common in the traditional Pueblo style house, although a floor of flat stone could be added.

In spite of the fact that the traditional Tigua houses were composed only of dried earth, in the desert climate these buildings are extremely durable if the outer walls are maintained by replastering when they become weathered. In fact, many of the adobe structures that still stand along Juno, Palla, and other streets in the old Indian neighborhood of Ysleta del Sur were built longer ago than most members of the tribe can remember. Successive residents have modernized these dwellings by the addition of new doors, windows, or concrete floors, but the essential quality of the traditional dwelling remains.

Nowadays most of the Tiguas live in modern housing of their own or in a recently completed tribal housing project. The construction of the Pueblo-style dwelling, therefore, has ceased to be a living tradition in their community. This house type, however, does represent an important mode of Texas folk building. Such housing incorporates both the basic native American adobe architectural style encountered by the Spanish explorers in the sixteenth century and subsequent modifications adopted by the Tiguas and other Pueblo peoples after exposure to European construction techniques.

NOTES:

[1]See, for example, C. W. Hackett, *Revolt of the Pueblo Indians of New Mexico and Otermin's Attempted Reconquest, 1680-1682,* (Albuquerque: University of New Mexico Press, 1942), II, 159, and Texas Commission for Indian Affairs, *Brief History of the Tigua Indians,* (El Paso: Texas Commission for Indian Affairs, 1970), p. 2.

[2]For a brief discussion of some of these contributions see William W. Newcomb, Jr., *North American Indians: An Anthropological Perspective,* (Pacific Palisades, California: Goodyear, 1974), p. 157.

Storage cabin for medicine pots, drums, rattles, flutes, and other ceremonial equipment and supplies

(Photograph courtesy of Smithsonian Institution National Anthropological Archives)

Alabama-Coushatta Buildings

Howard N. Martin

Construction practices of the Alabama-Coushatta Indians developed in common with those of other tribes in the Southeastern Woodlands cultural province, which extended across the southern part of the United States from the Atlantic Ocean to the western edge of the Big Thicket region in Texas.[1]

Alabamas and Coushattas were members of the Upper Creek Confederacy and were living near the present city of Montgomery, Alabama, when the French contacted these two tribes in 1702. After 1763 members of both tribal groups left their homes and migrated to Louisiana. Less than two decades later, they began moving across the Sabine River into Spanish Texas. This vanguard, followed within a few years by substantial numbers of Alabamas and Coushattas, settled in the Big Thicket primarily because this awesome region offered numerous advantages for subsistence and as a refuge from encroachment by white settlers. Since the decade of the 1850's, descendants of these two tribes have occupied a reservation in Polk County, Texas.[2]

Construction Tools

One of the principal tools used by the early Alabamas and Coushattas was an axe made by cutting a hardwood stick about two feet long, splitting one end approximately three or four inches, inserting a stone axe head into the split stick, and securing the stone with strips of deer hide. Some of the knives were made of bone, shell, and stone,

but most often a short piece of cane hardened by fire was used as a cutting instrument.

Split logs were used extensively in a variety of construction activities, and two additional tools—hardwood mauls and wedges—were essential in splitting logs. The first step in the log-splitting process was to fell a tree by girdling. This procedure involved the use of axes to cut a groove through the bark of the tree and extending the groove around the entire circumference of the tree. Pine gum or resin was poured into the groove and set afire. The burned material was removed by axes and knives. Then more burning resin was applied to the groove. This process was repeated until the tree fell. After cutting off the limbs, a workman used an axe to cut a notch at one end of the log. The final step was to drive hardwood wedges into the lengthening notch with wooden mauls until the log had been split.[3]

Public Buildings

Prominent in Alabama-Coushatta construction were public structures around a community's square ground. Each Alabama or Coushatta town consisted of a central square ground and a series of neighborhoods, scattered for miles through the surrounding woods or along streams, and connected by a network of trails.[4]

The public square was located near the center of each town or community and was used for assemblies of various types—governmental, diplomatic, religious, ceremonial, and entertainment. Each square was formed by four buildings of equal size, facing inward, and enclosing an area approximately forty feet on each side. The square was laid out so that the sides faced the four cardinal points—north, east, south, and west.[5]

Pitch-pine posts sunk in the ground and forked at the top supported a brush roof for each building, which resembled a shed or brush arbor. The seats in these buildings were usually cane platforms or split logs laid with the flat sides uppermost.

The number of buildings around the square was gradually reduced.[6] A picture of an Alabama square ground in 1912 shows only two brush arbors—one on the east side and the other on the west.[7] The eastern arbor was reserved for the chief; other principal men of the tribe sat in the arbor on the west side. Split logs on the northern and southern sides of the square usually were occupied by women, children, and visitors.

A small cabin made of rough boards split from logs provided storage for medicine pots, drums, rattles, flutes, and other ceremonial equipment and supplies. This building was located behind the shed or arbor occupied by the tribal chief.

Residential Buildings

Early Alabama-Coushatta residences were rectangular houses, fifteen to eighteen feet long and ten to twelve feet wide.[8] The floors were earthen, and the wooden walls were six to eight feet high. Pitch-pine uprights were sunk into the ground at each corner of the new house. Also, one post was set at each side of the door, and another was placed in the middle of the opposite side.

The tops of the uprights were connected by horizontal poles tied with baksha, a coarse, tough fiber known also as

bass cord. Other horizontal poles were fastened half-way up except across the door.[9]

The wall framework was covered by crude planks or split logs standing on end. The wall covering was held in place with baksha cord.

The frame for the gabled roof consisted of eight to ten rafters on a side. Over these were laid a number of horizontal strips. The top layer of the roof usually included thin boards, pine bark or, preferably, cypress bark. Poles laid over the roof and tied on the rafters held the roof in place.

Fires were built on the bare floor, usually in a depression clayed up on all sides. A smoke-hole was provided at the top of each gable-end of the house, one to let fresh air in and the other to let the smoke out.

Alabama-Coushatta houses had only one ground-level entrance and no windows. Many of the cabin entrances did not have any type of door; others were covered with the skins of animals. Later, doors were made of one or more rough planks swung on side hinges of leather. Cross pieces for bracing were added if the door was constructed of more than one plank.

A series of benches or beds extended around the interior of the house next to the walls, except at the doorway. The framework for each bench consisted of four or six forked posts, about three feet high, supporting long canes over which cane crosspieces were laid. Cane mats were placed on top of the framework. The skins of bears, panthers, or deer were added to these benches when they were to be used for sleeping purposes.

Near each dwelling was a granary or provision house constructed of rough boards or split logs. This building provided storage for corn, potatoes, berries, roots, and other food items.

Usually each family had only one house, but prominent families occasionally added a second house for use in the summer. In October, 1839, a German traveler, Gustav Dresel, visited the Fenced-in Village of the Alabamas in present Tyler County. He observed that the tribal chief (Antone) had a principal cabin made of logs and a second house with cane-covered walls that was used as a dwelling during the summer.[10]

Sweat-houses

Alabamas and Coushattas used sweat baths to enhance supernatural powers and to cure the sick. A sweat-house was usually a small lodge constructed of skins or blankets thrown over a framework or poles. Other types included small houses built with closely fitted, plastered logs, and structures consisting of cane mats placed over a pole framework and plastered with a mixture of mud and grass or moss. Red-hot stones were placed in the center of the sweat-house, and from time to time water was thrown over the stones to generate heat and steam. Persons using the sweat-house usually stayed in the heated enclosure long enough to perspire freely and then would depart to dive into the nearest water, preferably a cold stream.

Before going on hunting trips, members of both tribes used this combination of sweat bath and cold swim to improve their luck while hunting.[11]

Construction Changes

Alabama-Coushatta construction tools, materials, and methods changed gradually over the years. Stone axes and non-metallic knives were among the tools replaced by iron and steel implements soon after contact with the white traders and settlers. While tribal construction tools were improved rapidly, alterations in structural features of buildings were effected at a slower pace. Except for a reduction in the number of brush arbors, the square ground and its related brush arbors on the Alabama-Coushatta reservation existed otherwise unchanged until the early years of the twentieth century, when the square ground was gradually replaced by the Presbyterian Mission building as the tribal meeting place.

By the 1830's the exteriors of Alabama-Coushatta residential buildings usually consisted of notched pine logs arranged horizontally, similar to the exteriors of the white settlers' log cabins. In August, 1838, another German traveler, F. W. von Frede, visited Colita's Village and observed that the people of this Coushatta community lived in cabins made of young unhewn trunks.[12] Gustav Dresel, after visiting the Alabamas' Fenced-in Village, commented favorably on the quality of the buildings in comparison with those of neighboring white settlers.[13]

In 1854, the Alabamas and many of the Coushattas settled on land deeded to the Alabamas as a reservation, marking the end of their homeless wandering in the Big Thicket and the beginning of stabilized community development which included substantial alteration in the construction of their dwellings. Texas had been admitted to the Union in 1845, and the number of white settlers arriving to build homes in the Big Thicket increased rapidly after that year.

Alabamas and Coushattas observed the building of the white settlers' houses and duplicated many of their neighbors' construction features. They built mud-plastered fireplaces and chimneys, and they no longer included in their building plans either smoke-holes in the gabled roofs or fires built in the center of the cabins.

During the latter part of the nineteenth century, cabins built of saddle-notched pine logs continued to be used, but

(Right) Log house used by Alabama-Coushattas at the turn of the century. *(Photograph from Mrs. Fain Williams' Collection)*

(Below left) Frame cottage built by the State of Texas in 1929 *(Photograph by Howard N. Martin)*

(Below right) One of the latest Alabama-Coushatta brick houses *(Photograph by Roland Poncho)*

other features were added. Houses were constructed on hardwood blocks above ground, floors were built of planks, and front porches became customary.

Many of these log cabins were replaced in 1929 when the State of Texas appropriated funds to build two- and four-room wooden cottages for the Alabama-Coushattas. Today 148 brick homes have been completed on the reservation through a Mutual Help Housing Project administered by the Department of Housing and Urban Development. The owner of each new brick home participated in the construction of his house by contributing part of the labor. The newest eighteen of these homes have fireplaces and chimneys.

The completion of these new homes, which do not differ significantly from those in most other parts of the country, marks the end of a distinctive Alabama-Coushatta tradition in construction techniques. These new homes also symbolize substantial progress in Alabama-Coushatta dwellings—from cabins with smoke-holes to expel smoke from fires built on earthern floors, to modern brick houses including fireplaces and provided with exterior brick chimneys extending above composition roofs near television antennas.

NOTES:

[1]John R. Swanton, "Notes on the Cultural Province of the Southeast," *American Anthropologist*, 37 (1935), 373-385.

[2]Howard N. Martin, *Myths & Folklores of the Alabama-Coushatta Indians of Texas*, (Austin: The Encino Press, 1977), xvii-xxii.

[3]Nineteen of the oldest residents of the Alabama-Coushatta Indian reservation in Polk County, Texas, were interviewed by the author of this article during the decade, 1930-1940. These informants supplied most of the information about Alabama-Coushatta construction activities after 1800.

[4]John R. Swanton, "Social Organization and Social Usages of the Indians of the Creek Confederacy." *Forty-second Annual Report of the Bureau of American Ethnology*, (Washington, D.C.: U.S. Government Printing Office, 1928), 181-182, 263-265.

[5]*Ibid.*, 183-186.

[6]*Ibid.*, 187-188.

[7]*Ibid.*, Plate 5 (b), opposite p. 225.

[8]T. T. Waterman, "The Architecture of the American Indians," *American Anthropologist*, 29, New Series (1927), 212-213.

[9]John R. Swanton, *The Indians of the Southeastern United States*, Bureau of American Ethnology, Bulletin 137, (Washington, D.C.: U.S. Government Printing Office, 1946), 394-395.

[10]Gustav Dresel, (Max Freund, trans. and ed.), *Gustav Dresel's Houston Journal: Adventures in North America and Texas, 1837-1841*, (Austin: University of Texas Press, 1954), 65.

[11]Swanton, "Social Organization and Social Usages of the Indians of the Creek Confederacy," 444-445.

[12]F. W. von Frede, *Biographical Sketches of the United States of North America and Texas*, (Cassel, 1844). This book, printed in German, was translated by Oswald Mueller, Houston, and the English version is in possession of the translator. Material cited for this article appears on page 110 of the translator's typescript.

[13]Gustav Dresel, *Gustav Dresel's Houston Journal: Adventures in North America and Texas, 1837-1841*, 65.

All photographs in this essay are The Old Koch House.

The Old Koch House

Connie Hall

The limestone-and-log house, shaded by live oaks older even than it is, sits slightly below the caliche road against a backdrop of rock-wall fences. Abandoned since the 1920's the old Koch house now harbors only an occasional hunter who camps there for a few days during the winter months of deer season. Yet this old house, battered by the years but beautiful still, remains as a testimonial to the people who built it. Like the other German houses of the Hill Country, it reveals and reflects the ingenuity, industry, determination, and integrity of the German-Texan settlers.

The house is situated in Blanco County, in Central Texas, an area settled largely by German immigrants. These people first arrived in the Hill Country in the 1840's under the auspices of the *Mainzer Adelsverein,* the Society for the Protection of German Immigrants in Texas, an organization formed in Germany by a group of noblemen to promote German settlements in Texas. These pioneers were led initially by the well-meaning but inept Prince Karl von Solms-Braunfels, founder of New Braunfels, and later by the more capable Baron Hans von Meusebach, who established Fredericksburg. The immigrants left Germany primarily to escape economic privation and political persecution yet encountered on their arrival in Texas many of the same old problems cloaked in new forms. They were confronted with starvation and disease, a devastating epidemic of a sickness they called cholera, the ever-present threat of Comanche Indian raids, the hostility of their slave-holding neighbors, and, not the least, the loneliness of

the isolated, rock-hard region they had settled. Yet these immigrants found the freedom they had come for. The German settlers persisted, and their staying power is reflected in the durability of the houses they left behind them.

According to Koch family descendants, Arnor Koch and his sister Linda, the old Koch house was built in 1856, fairly early in the forty-year period from the 1840's to the 1880's which witnessed the construction of the majority of the German-Texas houses. Its builders were Gottlieb Koch and his two sons, Carl and Herman, men of a strong, tough family whose story is echoed in countless other sagas of the Hill Country Germans. The family—father, mother, and two sons—arrived in Texas in 1854, debarking at Indianola and settling first at New Braunfels, where they remained for two years and where Carl met and married a young German immigrant, Karoline. The Kochs then set out for their permanent home in the Twin Sisters community of Blanco County, arriving after a hard journey saddened by the death of the mother, who was buried on the way. The life which awaited them there was, in many ways, as difficult as its beginnings. Not only were they forced to do battle with the soil and the elements, but they had also to contend with their Anglo-Texas neighbors. Having left Germany in part to escape military conscription, Carl and Herman nevertheless found themselves in the 'sixties unwillingly embroiled in the American Civil War, Carl impressed into service with the Rebel forces and Herman

107

fighting with Union troops. The years took their toll. In the small, fenced graveyard in the field behind the house lie three Kochs—two of Carl's and Karoline's five children, and a daughter-in-law—who met untimely deaths: Rudolph a victim of appendicitis, Adolphine dead of childbirth, and Emil killed by his own hand because of unrequited love, according to family tradition. Carl and Karoline, buried also in the family plot, survived into their seventies, and their descendants, some of them, still live in the caliche hills and the German communities of Blanco County.

An emblem of the family's staying power, the old Koch house, too, endures. As yet unrestored, but patched up and shored up by my father, Luther Hill, who bought it in 1951, it remains to tell its own story of the early German houses in Texas. Like the other German colonial houses, it represents, first of all, a merging of the old world with the new; here construction methods which were essentially German met and were modified by the exigencies of the new world, particularly those dictated by the warm climate and primitive frontier conditions in Texas. Secondly, the old Koch house marks a progression over the years in construction practices; for this house, like many others, was built in stages, rooms being added as time permitted or the growth of the family demanded.

The house appears to have been built in a number of separate increments. There is no way to be certain, however, as to what comprised the original house, what additions followed, and in what order. We can only guess as to how the old house stretched and grew.

The original house, a story and a half high, probably consisted of a front porch, two attic rooms, and two ground-level rooms joined by a dog-run, or open hall. Such a floor plan was not uncommon for the German houses of

this period. Both Ferdinand Roemer, who travelled through Texas from 1845 to 1847, and Federick Law Olmsted, who visited the state in 1856, described in their books German houses of identical or similar design. The dog-run design was borrowed from the Anglos, who had brought that house type with them from their journey through the Southern states.

Originally, the front porch of the Koch house extended across the width of the entire house, shading the dog-run and the two lower rooms. As was customary in Texas, where the summers were hot, the porch faced south to obtain full benefit from the prevailing southerly breezes. The inclusion of the porch, as well as the dog-run, marked a departure from the houses the settlers knew in Germany, where the climate was colder, and demonstrated the manner in which the immigrants modified their house plans to fit the needs of the new land. The Germans selected these features from the Anglo-American houses which they observed on their journey through Texas from Indianola, their main point of debarkation.

The exterior walls of the original house were built of cedar logs cut on the builder's own land. This use of cedar in the construction of house and barn, as the use of rock for fencing, served a double purpose, in that the rancher cleared his land at the same time that he took from it the materials he needed. And this early builder had to make do, first of all, with what was available; he had to raise his house almost literally out of the land on which it stood. These cedar logs were hand hewn to form square pieces of timber and were then anchored to one another at the corners of the house with dove-tail joints. Each log was notched at both top and bottom, and the logs did not extend beyond the corners of the house. The logs were then placed so closely together that little or no interstices

Deer-horn hanger

Lap joint on plate

Joint of plate, joist, rafter of cedar logs

109

Cellar entrance with protecting gate

Cellar steps

Unplastered log siding with rock lean-to

111

Sleeping loft with grain storage bins

remained, this close fitting of the logs in accordance with German building practices. Such interstices as were left, however, were chinked with a limestone mortar which remains hard and solid to this day. Perhaps, and this can only be conjecture, the German builder had picked up some pointers from his Mexican neighbors and mixed cactus juice as a binder into his mortar, as the Mexican builders did when they built the missions in San Antonio.

These hewn log exterior walls were later covered with a variety of materials. The west wall was covered with cypress shingles and the east wall with milled pine board and batten, which might have been added at a later date. The south, or porch, wall was coated with a limestone plaster, but only to a certain level. The upper two or three feet of the log wall were left exposed, perhaps because that part was not visible from the road. In the last decades of the century the terms "log cabin" and "log house" had come to be used pejoratively, in the sense that they were equated with both poverty and backwardness, and our builder might have concealed his walls with the idea in mind of adding some sophistication to his house. However, in Germany it was customary to cover walls with both plaster and shingles, and the builder might simply have been following traditional building practices. Certainly, the coverings made his walls more airtight.

From the porch we enter the dog-run, or dog-trot, a hall ten feet wide, originally open at either end. In the warmer weather, particularly during the hot, dry days of summer, these dog runs became additional rooms — cool, breezy places — where the ranchers took their ease from the mid-day heat, where the wives shelled peas and tended to other household chores, and where the animals liked to languish, hence the name, dog-run or dog-trot.

At either side of the dog-run, doors open into the two original ground-level rooms. These rooms are very similar in appearance; however, the west room, which contains a fireplace, proves to be the more interesting of the two. This fireplace stands in the center of the west wall, its exterior chimney extending up to and beyond the peak of the gabled roof. Both the fireplace and the chimney were built of cut limestone and covered with a lime plaster. Originally, this fireplace was used for cooking as well as heating; however, no evidence of this, such as iron poles or swinging cranes in the small "firebox," remains today.

The attic, or loft, is reached from the front porch by way of a steep enclosed ship's ladder. This ladder, made of milled lumber, probably was added at a later date, replacing a rough log ladder. Usually, access to the attic in these old German houses was gained by an outside staircase, a New World innovation which would have been highly impractical in the colder climate of Germany but which served here in Texas as a welcome space saver. This attic, which occupies the space provided by the gable roof, contains two rooms and a storage area. The two rooms were used as bedrooms, as it was customary for the older children to sleep in the loft. The area between the two rooms consists of a narrow passageway flanked by wooden bins, which were used to store seed grain. The sides of the bin, which were removable, were made of milled lumber. The lettering upon one of the planks still clearly reads, "Buy your lumber/from Loomis and Christian/Old Courthouse/Austin, Texas."

The first addition which the Kochs made to their home might have been the small front room on the east side of the house. This room, which was formed by walling in one end of the front porch, is particularly interesting in that it furnishes the only example in the entire house of *fachwerk*, or half-timbered construction. This building technique, which dates back to medieval times, was quite popular with the German immigrant builder, and the *fachwerk* wall remains one of the distinctive features of the German colonial house. This type of construction entailed the building of a heavy timber frame with a diagonal bracing member, which was then filled in with stone or brick. In Germany brick was generally used and in Texas, stone. The builder of this little room used hewn logs for the frames and braces and then filled in with adobe bricks, an adaptation reflecting the influence of their Mexican neighbors.

The next addition to the house was, perhaps, the shed-like structure which extends across the rear, or north side of the house. A shed-room addition at the back of the house which balanced the porch at the front is characteristic of the Texas colonial house, and it is difficult indeed to find a home of this period without one. This addition to the Koch house not only provided two new rooms, making the house now two rooms deep, but also lengthened and enclosed the dog-run. The walls of this part of the house, which abut the hewn log walls of the original structure but do not tie into them, are made of yet another building material: cut limestone. This limestone had always been readily available in the Hill Country but was not used earlier by this builder because, perhaps, of the difficulty of cutting the limestone blocks or the problems involved in transporting it. As a rule, the German settlers, in need of shelter in a hurry, constructed their first homes of log and later, in a more leisurely fashion, either built new homes of limestone or attached limestone additions to the original house. The stone walls of this shed addition are quite thick, eleven inches in width; the walls of the log section of the house, by comparison, measure eight inches. However, the walls throughout the house, as it existed up to this point, were finished inside in the same manner, with a layer of mud

and straw which was then coated with a limestone plaster.

Next, perhaps, feeling the need of a cool place to store food and other items, the Kochs dug out the cellar. Occupying the space below the two eastside rooms, this cellar extends from the south log wall of the original structure to the north stone wall at the rear of the house. It is reached by circular stone steps which descend from an opening in the front porch, the steps apparently placed in this circular pattern in an effort to encroach as little as possible on the adjacent *fachwerk* addition. Even so, it appears that in order to accommodate the staircase, this small room was forced to relinquish some of its area. Its west wall, curving along the lines of the staircase opening and made of boards, is unlike the other three walls, and it probably replaces one torn down earlier to make way for the stairs. In the cellar we find two vertical logs supporting one large log beam which spans the ceilings. Originally, this beam was supported by limestone pillars which now lie toppled on the earthen floor.

The entire house, or rather what comprises the house thus far, is protected by a high gabled roof, the ridge of which runs parallel to the front of the house. The steep pitch of this roof is yet another feature which reveals the German origins of the builder, for in Germany, where the snowfall was heavy, such a roof-line was mandatory. The roof was covered originally with wooden shingles, probably cypress, but these were later replaced by galvanized iron.

The last addition to the house—and its tacked-on appearance shouts addition and afterthought—is the gabled board-and-batten structure attached at right angles to the center of the rear wall of the house. Even this most recent construction, however, is hardly new. In 1973 Rudolf Liesceman, then in his eighties, told my father that,

Board-and-batten, rock, and log come together

115

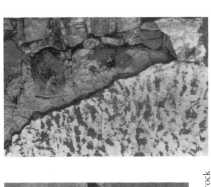

Details of plaster over log and rock

Hat peg

Store bought door lock

Cellar entrance

Dog-trot with gate to keep out cows

Stairs to loft

Fachwerk addition to Koch house

Fachwerk and timber joint

Fachwerk with adobe fill

117

Mud with straw binder used as sealer

Plate and stud joint

Harness hanger

118

as a child, he had played with the Koch children and that the house, even then, contained this last addition. Entered through a door at the enclosed end of the dog-run, the addition consists of two small rooms, one opening directly into the other, in the fashion of the shotgun house. The rear room served as a kitchen. It contains an interior chimney, and a flue hole still gapes in its north wall. The front room is notable chiefly for its gutter, which runs along the upper corner of the entire south wall. Because the builder neglected to tie the roof of the addition into the roof of the main structure and even allowed the house's roof to intrude into the room, he then had to attach a gutter to the roof edge to carry off the water which drained directly into the room. The care with which the rest of the house was built is not much in evidence in this addition, and the house, when restored, would be more attractive without it.

Hopefully, the old Koch house will indeed one day be restored, as so many German houses in the Hill Country have been in recent years. For it is nothing short of tragic to lose these houses—and too many which were left for years to shift for themselves are already gone. These homes speak to us of their times, the life in Texas as the German settlers knew it a hundred year ago. And they tell us about the beauty of houses that are simple and honest and are at one with their surroundings.

When I think of the old Koch house, I see it as it is in the evening, when it seems to settle down and blend into the land upon which it rests and from which it was built. The silver cast of the logs and weathered boards merges with the color of the tree trunks, and the mellow grays and soft yellows of the limestone melt into the hues of the earth.

NOTES:

[1]Ferdinand Roemer, *Texas* (Waco: Texian Press, 1967), p. 163; and Frederick Law Olmsted, *A Journey through Texas* (New York: Burt Franklin, 1969), pp. 177, 189.

[2]Interview with Rufus Walker, Consultant to the San Antonio Conservation Society, August, 1976.

119

Alsatian Architecture in Castroville

Alsatian Architecture in Medina County

Terri Ross

Just west of San Antonio, in Medina County, a unique community reflects the Alsatian heritage of its residents. When Henri Castro brought over five hundred families from the French-German borderlands, he established three towns that today represent a distinctly European element in Texas. The Alsatian immigrants of the 1840's threw together huts of logs and clay until they had cleared the land and planted their crops. None of these early homes remains today, but the following generation had time to build more permanent structures that can still be seen throughout the Castroville, Old D'Hanis, and Quihi area.

Alsatian architecture can be distinguished by an odd, sloping roof line, by the regularity of its rectangular shape, by wooden dormer and casement windows, and by the unusual and sparce placement of chimneys and exterior openings.

Typically, older homes in Medina County look like the owners chopped off the symmetrical extension of the steep gable, creating a short-side roof line forward and a long side aft. Although this imbalance is not unique to this small community (Shaker homes in the northeast were built the same way, from middle European design), it is an unusual feature in a flat land that experiences more sunshine than snow. The peaked gables were designed for snow-shed, but the immigrants built them in Texas because that was what they knew best, and perhaps because the style reminded them of home. Gradually, the pitch of the roof flattened on newer homes as the need to shed snow became less important than the need to balance materials on those sharp angles. Many of the early roofs were made of thatch, but later cyprus shingles weighed more and were more difficult to maneuver. After the Civil War, builders used galvanized tin for roofing, and sloped the roof less, but in the same manner as the early roofs. Lean-to's extended the floor space and lengthened the rear roof line and added to the long rear slope. Roof lines frequently came within five feet of the ground and resembled their European counterparts.

Another striking aspect of Alsatian architecture is its rectangular shape. Early homes were similar in their rectangular design. Henry Castro, founder of the community, helped build several 16' by 32' homes. Within these compact homes, every inch of space was utilized. Sleeping quarters were generally located in lofts above the main room, which could also function at night as sleeping space. When a shed room was added to the basic structure, it was attached to the rear wall, creating another rectangle with an additional eight to nine feet in width. Because the original wall first served as an exterior wall, older homes in Medina Valley have fourteen-inch walls between some of the rooms.

Some of the homes incorporated their kitchens into the rear, lean-to addition. Other homes, such as the old Vance House, had separate buildings for the kitchen. If the kitchen were separate, it was built along the same proportions as the house.

A variation of the 16' by 32' dimension can be seen around Quihi, where several buildings combined living space and barn under one continuous roof. Human quarters were separated from the barn by an open passage, usually large enough for a wagon to pass through. Although the interior design was somewhat different, the sloping roof remained the same. Ray Boehle's house, built in the 1850's, served a unique triple purpose as a home, a court house, and a school in the upper loft. Today the building is used as a barn for grain and machinery, but still has its red tin roof, wooden window boxes, and large wooden doors and windows.

Several buildings combined living space with business space. Two examples of this duality of purpose are the Carle

House and the House on September Square, both in Castroville. The Carle House, built by Castro and Leopold Menetrier before 1850, is two-story limestone. The lower front section of the building was used for a store, 25' by 40', and faced the main square near the first church. Kitchen, dining room, and a warehouse were downstairs also, supporting the upstairs residence. Because of the commercial nature of the building, apparently, the house has three doors facing the street.

The House on September Square (1869) was apparently also built for business, because of the large double doors that face a main street. Residents theorize that the building was originally a store or saloon. Today, the house is again part of the commercial establishment, doubling as both house and shop for local artists.

Part of the uniqueness of this section of Texas' architecture is the deep, wooden, casement windows. Casement windows, which opened either in or out, still exist in upper windows or windows built on the lean-to sections of the houses. Set deep in wooden frames, the casement windows were popular with early settlers and were another direct reflection of their homeland. Slowly, the traditional windows were replaced by double-hung forms because they became available commercially and were popular among the Alsatian's Anglo neighbors. Also, the double-hung windows had larger panes of glass and let in more light. These deep casement windows frequently had solid wood shutters over them, a vivid reflection of the old country. Mrs. Peg Gillette's house in Castroville still has these solid early shutters. Double-hung windows, held in place by pegs and later with cords with counter-balancing weights, allowed for a lighter shutter, with modern slats which can be seen on most windows in the area today.

A curious characteristic of the earliest Alsatian homes is

Ray Boehle barn at Quihi (*Medina Co.*) Rock building served as court house, school house, and home before becoming barn.

123

an asymmetrical arrangement of the windows. Because Alsatians constructed their homes piece-meal, adding bit by bit as the need arose, window placement was not an integral part of the original design. Rather, windows were impromptu affairs built for function more than aesthetics. If an added wall blocked the air and light flow, residents cut another window, creating occasional side-by-side windows on some walls and leaving other exterior walls window/less. The asymmetrical openings are a reminder of the growing structure rather than a particular community need for design.

Few examples of Medina Valley's original construction systems can still be seen, but the houses were built along three basic construction methods: vertical logs set in the ground with spaces filled by mud and straw; vertical logs set into a timber, with the spaces normally filled with stone; and a combination of both stone and logs or stone and frame. Obviously, earlier homes used mud and straw, while later homes added timber and stone. Examples of the horizontal and vertical logs supported by stone can still be found throughout Medina County, where both rubble and cut stone support the structure. In these homes, additional protection was created through the use of lime plaster, which also created a smooth surface. Lime plaster over rough stone is prevalent throughout the area, whether it was part of the original structure or was added later.

Two-story houses had stone walls for the first floor and the vertical log arrangement on the second floor, typically European. Both one- and two-story houses had masonry north walls to protect them from northern winds.

Another European feature in this Alsatian community is the battered, or sloped chimney top. The angular tops resemble older French homes and can be seen in French settlements throughout the United States.

The Alsatian sense of chimney placement is sometimes startling. Rather than adhering to more typical concepts of architecture and locating the chimney tops directly above the fireplace—concomitantly with flues running perpendicular from ceiling to roof—they occasionally placed their chimney tops above windows or doors, leaving the observer uncertain as to the connection between the fireplace and a distant chimney top. This unconventional appearance is created by the flue, which is not always perpendicular to the ground. Rather, it may angle from the fireplace within the walls of the house toward the owner's choice of exterior position for the smoke's exit.

Exterior openings on Alsatian homes are both asymmetrical and infrequent. The relatively few openings may be an indication of an attempt to protect themselves from the weather, or a carryover of their village's need for solid walls. However, descendants of the early settlers increased the number of exterior openings and began to reflect a more symmetrical design, where openings indicate floor plan.

The addition of a porch is definitely non-European, and the settlers probably adapted the covering for practical reasons. When the immigrants travelled a year through Texas from the Galveston port, they had the opportunity to observe native customs of protection against the sun. The porch, a West Indies device, was used extensively by both Mexicans and Indians in Texas. So although the lines of the early homes are basically French, they also reflect the mixture of cultures in their addition of protection against the sun. Many of the two-story homes have balconies, creating a silhouette reminiscent of the Spanish style.

An additional borrowing from natives is the catercorner fireplace used by Mexicans and Indians in Texas. Although most of the older homes have fireplaces against one wall,

Carle house (*Castroville*)

Signature of builder (*Castroville*)

125

Alsatian house with Anglo porch and a veneer of lime plaster over stone

Unveneered rock house with inside chimneys

Bath house behind Vance Hotel

127

Typical Alsatian house with added Anglo porch

128

some, like the Vance House, have catercorner fireplaces. Caesar Monad, who built the house (now the Landmark Inn) in 1853 as a home and a store, used Mexican laborers and built the catercorner fireplace as a major heat supply. The Vance House has another architectural device unusual in Alsatian homes, the arch. Between the main section of the house and a projecting wing, a large arch supports part of the ceiling. Typically, Alsatians made no use of the arch.

Some of the older Alsatian buildings are rotting away. Others have been turned into barns and storage sheds. Nevertheless, some are still used for homes. In fact, several modern homes have been built using the old architectural lines of the early settlers. Gabled roofs, sloping roof lines, and small wooden windows are suddenly reappearing on new homes, suggesting that a new generation is concerned with retaining its architectural heritage.[1]

NOTE

[1]This paper is indebted to suggestions by Anthony Crosby in his "European Building Techniques in the Alsatian Communities of Medina County," presented before the 1975 meeting of the Texas State Historical Association.

The Gawlik House, erected in 1858, Panna Maria. The rear roof of this house, which comes quite near to the ground, is typical of Silesian Polish folk architecture. (*Photograph by T. Lindsay Baker*)

130

Silesian Polish Folk Architecture in Texas

T. Lindsay Baker

"You want to know what kind of house I live in. Here one can get his house very easily and everybody builds his house for himself."[1]

In these words, John Moczygemba, one of the pioneer settlers at Panna Maria, Texas, in May, 1855, informed his family and friends in Poland that the immigrants in Texas built their homes for themselves. The settlers did so by using the building techniques they carried from the Old World when they began erecting their new homes on the frontier.

Panna Maria was the mother colony for a number of Polish communities founded in central Texas during the mid 1850's. After the initial settlement, established in 1854, within two weeks other Poles moved to Bandera to establish a colony there. These two communities were followed by the founding of several Silesian Polish settlements at such places as Czestochowa in Karnes County, Yorktown in DeWitt County, St. Hedwig in Bexar County, and even an identifiable Polish Quarter within the city of San Antonio. In all these places, except in urban San Antonio where housing was available, the immigrants built homes as they would have done in Europe. Many of these interesting structures remain intact today.

The Poles who immigrated to Texas in the 1850's were almost exclusively peasants from the region of Upper Silesia, at that time the southeasternmost tip of the Kingdom of Prussia. They actually came from a small subregion within Upper Silesia located east and northeast

of Opole, the principal adminstrative center for the area in the mid-nineteenth century. Originating from such a small territory, probably no more than forty miles long and thirty miles wide, they brought with them a homogeneous folk culture which in Texas provides, in addition to other cultural elements, a distinctive and identifiable form of architecture.[2]

Upon their arrival on the Texas frontier, the immigrants immediately needed shelter. They followed traditional practices in building this first cover by constructing dugouts and crude log houses, almost invariably covered with thatch roofs made from prairie grass. As one writer early in this century recorded, after interviewing a large number of original settlers, "the newcomers camped in the shade of the wide-spreading oaks, and proceeded to build shelters for themselves of stakes and brush, using strands of grass to make the roofs."[3] An American who visited Panna Maria in November, 1855, later wrote that the immigrants there were living in "sod houses" and "dug outs," while in another place he noted that he found them "huddled together on little patches of land living in their pole cabins & sod houses."[4] Yet another contemporary writer described them as living "in burrows covered with dry twigs and stalks."[5]

The first primitive shelters gave way to more substantial houses made from logs, lumber, and stone. The techniques used by the Silesian peasants sometimes surprised their neighboring Americans. Stanisław Kiołbassa, a native of

131

the village of Swibie in Upper Silesia,[6] moved from Panna Maria to Bandera, where in the mid-1850's she built a house described by an American writer as "the first and only one of the kind in the country." It consisted of "grooved mesquite blocks," "mesquite being the most readily available wood to the builder.[7] More common were ordinary log cabins, which were built in all the settlements where wood was plentiful. All of these original log structures have disappeared, although they were once quite common. For example, Father Adolf Bakanowski, just after his arrival at Panna Maria, where he served as pastor from 1866 to 1870, described the houses in that settlement as "made of wood, similarly to Lithuanian houses."[8]

Within three years after the initial arrival of the Polish settlers, stone houses began appearing in the Silesian communities. Probably the first of these was the cottage built by John Gawlik at Panna Maria in 1858. He was a stonemason by trade and soon his handiwork could be seen throughout the Karnes County area.[9] As early as 1855 the need for stonemasons and builders had been felt at Panna Maria, for in May of that year one immigrant wrote home to Poland that "there are no cottages," adding further, "and masons are needed."[10] Perhaps it was Gawlik who came in response to that need. At any rate, stone houses became more and more common in all the settlements. Owners of some of the early stone cottages at Panna Maria, for example, included Albert Kasprzyk, John Rzeppa, Philip Przybysz, and others, and many of these century-old houses remain standing today.[11] Several of these structures were recorded in 1936-1937 and 1977 by field teams from the Historic American Buildings Survey and thus photographs and detailed measured drawings of several Silesian homes are available in the Library of Congress.[12]

All the immigrants were impressed with their isolation

in the vast country where they had settled. Instead of living in villages, as they had in Europe, they settled on their own land, sometimes far from their neighbors. One peasant wrote home in 1855: "There are no villages. One cottage lies from the other 10 miles or even more. . . . We live quite a distance from the church. It is farther than you live from the manor."[13] Father Bakanowski, writing in 1866, noted that "When one comes to Panna Maria, the church welcomes him from a long distance—and here it seems that the church is standing by itself—the houses of the inhabitants are hidden in the woods."[14] From St. Hedwig in Bexar County, Father Teofil Bralewski wrote in 1869: "I am all by myself in the forest like a hermit, because the houses of the Poles are situated far away from the church in the brush, and I can see only clouds and trees."[15]

The houses built by the immigrants were almost identical to those in their homeland, whether made of wood or stone. They almost invariably had steeply pitched roofs, designed for snow to slip off easily, but in Texas the immigrants only rarely saw snow. These roofs originally had straw thatch covering, a roofing material which remained visible in the Silesian Texan communities into the twentieth century. First wooden shingles and then more modern roofing materials replaced thatch. Often rear roofs reached quite low, sometimes as low as five feet from the ground. In the early years many of the Silesian houses were in reality both homes and barns combined. Farm animals and farm families often shared opposite ends of the same structures, usually with the residence made of stone and the stable made of wood. At least one such house is still preserved at Panna Maria. The upper floor rooms or lofts of Silesian Texan houses had access by inside staircases or outside stairs or ladders. These upper rooms usually were ventilated by pairs of windows at one or both ends. One

(Right) The August Moczygemba house in Panna Maria, erected during the Civil War.
(Photograph by T. Lindsay Baker)

(Below) Silesian Polish cottage at Panna Maria, showing the traditional combination of home and stable under one roof. The family lived in the stone end of the structure while the animals were kept in the wooden stable at the opposite end.
(Photograph by T. Lindsay Baker)

133

interesting element of Upper Silesian folk architecture which was transferred to Texas was the use of the interior smoke rooms connected with the fireplaces for smoking meats.[16]

A striking alteration which the Silesian immigrants made to their traditional form of house building was the addition of porches to the south-facing windward sides of their homes. This was a modification which the German immigrants in Texas in the 1840's had made to their folk architecture[17] and it is a quite understandable change. Coming from northern Europe, the immigrants fully felt the heat of semi-tropical Texas summers. As Father Bakanowski wrote for a newspaper in Upper Silesia, "The climate [in Texas] is very hot in the summer, there are cool, refreshing winds."[18] In a letter to his superiors in Rome about the same time, he noted that "We are living on a hill, so we have the wind constantly, something that the people here want very much. Nearly all the people sleep outside or inside the house with the windows and doors open."[19] The cool shade of the veranda soon became the most popular place in the Silesian Texan home. There the residents engaged in almost all their daily activities from preparing meals to dressing animal hides, and the porches became the natural places for such items as saddles, washtubs, comfortable chairs, and flowering plants.[20]

Although the architectural legacy of the Silesian immigrants in Texas remains for the most part intact, it is slowly slipping away due to the action of the elements and to lack of interest by owners. Many of the cottages in the settlements are unoccupied and have fallen into disrepair, leaving a great challenge to the present generation to preserve this important part of their European and Texan heritage.

NOTES:

[1]Johann Moczigemba, Panna Maria, [Texas], to [Friends and Relatives, Pluznica, Regency of Opole Prussia]], 13 May 1855, in Kingdom of Prussia, Regency of Opole, Department of the Interior, Die Auswanderung nach den Amerikanischen Staaten—Concesirung von Vereinen u. Agenturen zur Beforderung der Auswanderer [Emigration to the American States—Concessions of Societies and Agents for Transporting Emigrants] (15 May 1847 to 13 September 1855), p. 56, Regency of Opole Collection, sec. 1 vol. 12132, Archives of the City and Voivodeship of Wrocław, Wrocław, Poland. This letter is available in the original Polish in Andrzej Brozek and Henryk Borek, Jeszcze jeden list z Teksasu do Pluznicy z 1855 roku [One More Letter from Texas to Pluznica in the Year 1855] (Opole, Poland: Instytut Slaski w Opolu, 1972), pp. 14-19, and in English translation in T. Lindsay Baker, ed. and trans., "Four Letters from Texas to Poland in 1855," Southwestern Historical Quarterly, LXXVII, No. 3 (January 1974), 383-386.

[2]Among the general histories of the Silesian Poles in Texas are the following works: T. Lindsay Baker, The Early History of Panna Maria, Texas, Texas Tech University Graduate Studies No. 9 (Lubbock: Texas Tech Press, 1975); Andrzej Brozek, Slazacy w Teksasie: Relacje o najstarszych osadach polskich w Ameryce [Silesians in Texas: Accounts of the Oldest Polish Colonies in America] (Warsaw: Panstwowe Wydawnictwo Naukowe, 1972); Edward J. Dworaczyk, The First Polish Colonies of America in Texas (San Antonio: The Naylor Company, 1936); Jacek Przygoda, Texas Pioneers from Poland (Waco: privately printed, 1971).

[3]S. Nesterowicz, Notatki z podróży po północnej i środkowej Ameryce [Travel Notes on Northern and Middle America] (Toledo: A. A. Paryski, 1909), p. 201.

[4]Thomas Ruckman, "The Census Taker—A Complete Description of the County of Karnes—In South West Texas—by Thos. Ruckman June, 1890," pp. 39, 45, in Thomas Ruckman Papers, University of Texas Archives, Austin, Texas.

NOTES (Continued)

¹Wacław Kruszka, *Historja polska w Ameryce* [Polish History in America], 2nd rev. ed. (Milwaukee: Drukiem Kuryera Polskiego), 1937.

⁶T. Lindsay Baker, "The Kiolbassa Family of Illinois and Texas," *Chicago Genealogist*, V, No. 3 (Spring 1973), 78-82.

⁷*A Twentieth Century History of Southwest Texas*, 2 vols. (Chicago: The Lewis Publishing Company, 1907), I, 189.

⁸Rev. Adolf Bakanowski, Panna Maria, [Texas], to Our Dearest Father Superior [Rev. Hieronim Kajsiewicz, Rome, Italy], 13 November 1866, Adolf Bakanowski Letters Sent, Archives, Congregation of the Resurrection, Rome, Italy, item no. 9330, collection hereafter cited as Bakanowski Letters.

⁹Dworaczyk, p. 21.

¹⁰Moczigemba to [Friends and Relatives], 13 May 1855, p. 54.

¹¹T. Lindsay Baker, "Panna Maria and Płuznica: A Study in Comparative Folk Culture," in *The Folklore of Texan Cultures*, ed. by Francis Edward Abernethy, Publications of the Texas Folklore Society, Vol. 38 (Austin: Encino Press, 1974), 201-202, 219-220; Dworaczyk, 21-22, 44, 66-67, 73.

¹²Robert A. Steinbomer, *Three Early Polish Houses in Panna Maria [,] Texas* (n. p.: privately printed 1977), pp. i-iii, 1-33; U. S., Department of the Interior, National Park Service, Historic American Buildings Survey, Structures Nos. Tex-311, Tex-312, Tex-314, Library of Congress, Washington, D.C.

¹³Moczigemba to [Friends and Relatives], 13 May 1855, p. 54.

¹⁴Bakanowski to [Kajsiewicz], 13 November 1866, Bakanowski Letters no. 9330.

¹⁵Rev. Teofil Bralewski, Martinez [St. Hedwig, Texas], to Reverend Father [Peter Semenenko, Rome, Italy], 14 March 1869, Teofil Bralewski Letters Sent, Archives, Congregation of the Resurrection, Rome, Italy, item no. 41202.

¹⁶*Budownictwo ludowe opolszczyzny* [Folk Architecture of the Opole Region] (Opole, Poland: Prezydium WRN Wydzial Kultury w Opolu, Towarzystwo Przyjaciol Opole, and Muzeum Wsi Opolskiej w Opolu, [ca. 1970]); Jozef Matuszczak, *Z dzie jow architektury drewnianej na Slasku* [From the History of Wooden Architecture in Silesia], Rocznik Muzeum Gornoslaskiego w Bytomiu, Art Series no. 5 (Bytom, Poland: Muzeum Gornoslaskie w Bytomiu, 1971); *Spichlerze opolszczyzny* [Granaries of the Opole Region] (Opole, Poland: Muzeum Wsi Opolskiej w Opolu-Bierkowicach, 1967). For comments on thatch roofs in Texas, Elias J. Moczygema, Panna Maria, Texas, to T. Lindsay Baker and Krystyna Baker, interview at Panna Maria, Texas, 10 August 1973. Many of the observations in this paragraph are based on the author's field research in Texas in 1970-1975 and in Upper Silesia in 1972 and 1975-1977.

¹⁷Viktor Bracht, *Texas in 1848*, trans. Charles Frank Schmidt (San Antonio: Naylor Printing Company, 1939), p. 135; Arthur L. Finck, Jr., "The Regulated Emigration of the German Proletariat with Special Reference to Texas" (unpublished M. A. thesis, University of Texas, Austin, Texas, 1949), p. 64; Ferdinand Roemer, *Texas, with Particular Reference to German Immigration and the Physical Appearance of the Country*, trans. Oswald Mueller (San Antonio: Standard Printing Company, 1935), p. 93.

¹⁸[Rev. Adolf Bakanowski], Panna Maria, Texas, to [*Zwiastun Gornoszlazki*, Piekary, Regency of Opole, Prussia, Spring 1870], *Zwiastun Gornoszlaski* (Piekary, Prussia), 14 April 1870, p. 120.

¹⁹Rev. Adolf Bakanowski, Panna Maria, [Texas], to Our Dearest Father Peter [Semenenko, Rome, Italy], 28 June 1867, Bakanowski Letters no. 9344.

²⁰Mrs. Mary Mika, Panna Maria, Texas, to T. Lindsay Baker and Krystyna Baker, interview at Panna Maria, Texas, 11 August 1973; Moczygemba to Baker and Baker, interview, 10 August 1973.

Figure 3

Figure 2

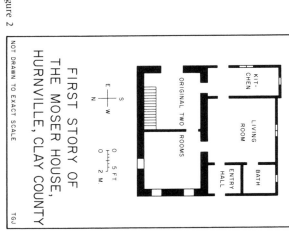

FIRST STORY OF
THE MOSER HOUSE,
HURNVILLE, CLAY COUNTY

NOT DRAWN TO EXACT SCALE

KIT-
CHEN

ORIGINAL TWO ROOMS

LIVING
ROOM

BATH

ENTRY
HALL

N
S W─E

0   5 FT
0   2 M.

TGJ

136

Figure 1

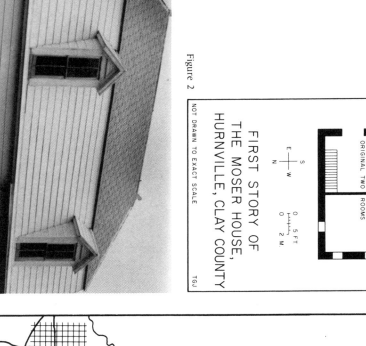

HURNVILLE, A RUSSIAN-GERMAN
SETTLEMENT IN CLAY COUNTY,
NORTH TEXAS

■ HURNVILLE STORE
● MOSER HOUSE
▲ BAPTIST CHURCH
△ LUTHERAN CHURCH
☐ SEVENTH-DAY ADVENTIST
⊞ GERMAN CEMETERY
── ── BORDER OF GERMAN-
        SETTLED AREA

HENRIETTA

HWY. 1197

LITTLE WICHITA RIVER

HWY. 287

HWY. 2332

HWY. 171

HWY. 2332

OKLA.
TEXAS

RED RIVER

0   1   2   3   4 MI.
0 1 2 3 4 5 6 KM.

TGJ

A Russian-German Folk House in North Texas

Terry G. Jordan

Out on the rolling black prairies of Clay County, north of Henrietta and east of Wichita Falls, is a most unusual ethnic settlement. Its name, Hurnville, does not suggest anything out of the ordinary in this dominantly Anglo county, but a close inspection reveals the settlement to be one of the few Russian-German colonies in Texas (Fig. 1). Those familiar with the northern Great Plains know that Russian-Germans are very common from Kansas up through the Dakotas and into the Canadian Prairie Provinces, but in Texas they are quite unusual. The presence of a few scattered colonies of Russian-Germans in the Texas Panhandle, particularly Lipscomb County, has attracted the attention of various scholars, but the Clay County settlement has gone largely unnoticed.[2]

The ancestors of the Russian-Germans migrated from Germany to Russia in the 1700's, settling in many different provinces and districts.[3] The forefathers of the Hurnville people settled in the Ukraine in the late 1700's, coming mainly from southwestern Germany, especially Swabia. Their principal home villages in the Ukraine were Rorbach and Grossliebenthal, both located about fifty miles northeast of Odessa in the open steppes of the Nikolayev area, near the Black Sea.[4]

After about a century in the Ukraine, many Russian-Germans grew discontent, particularly when land reforms threatened their landownership. These discontented ones emigrated, generally to the American Great Plains, a movement which began in the 1870's. Those who came to

Hurnville were later participants in this migration, arriving in America in the early 1890's. Typically, they went to stay initially for several months with relatives who had come earlier to Nebraska and South Dakota. Somehow they heard of cheap land available in the Clay County area, and several families came south to establish the Hurnville colony beginning in 1893. In all, some fifteen families from Rorbach and Grossliebenthal were represented.

Of the cultural relics observable in this Russian-German settlement, none is more visually striking than the traditional folk-architecture. The best surviving example is the house of Mr. and Mrs. Leon Moser, which displays many architectural traits found in the Russian-German settlements of the northern Great Plains and echoes the folk houses of the German communities in Russia and even Swabia.[5]

The original part of the Moser house consists of two rooms side-by-side above a cellar, forming an elongated floorplan (Fig. 2). These rooms have rock exterior walls two feet thick, built of native stone gathered locally and cemented with a dirt-and-straw mortar. The stone walls were later covered by milled wooden siding on the exterior, so that the stone is now completely concealed from view. An enlargement in 1910 added a second half-story, and another in 1930 almost doubled the size of the house.

Covering the original two-room portion is a striking hipped gambrel roof, into which several dormer windows are cut (Fig. 3). No chimney or fireplace is present, and a front door and porch are lacking.

A number of these architectural features are also seen on Russian-German folk houses in Kansas. This similarity, perhaps partly explained by the brief sojourn of the Hurnville colonists in the settlements of the northern Great Plains, as well as by a common Russian house prototype, is seen in the milled siding over stone construction, elongated original floorplan, hipped roof, mud cement, dormer windows, absence of a front door and porch, and story-and-a-half enlargement. The hipped roof and dormer windows, moreover, can also be seen in Russia and Swabia.

One of the most interesting features of the enlarged house is the small entrance hall on the west side beneath a shed roof (Fig. 2). A similar entrance chamber, called a *kriliz*, is a common feature of German houses in Russia. There, on the steppes of Eastern Europe, the *kriliz* is a useful cold-climate feature, but it makes less sense in Texas. Of all the features observed in the Moser house and those of Kansas, apparently only the stone construction and milled siding are absent in Russia. The great thickness of the walls is typically Russian, though the dominant old-world building material was sod. The antecedent of the gambrel roof profile is less certain, but likely lies in southwest Germany.

In almost every respect, the Moser dwelling differs from Anglo-American folk houses of the Clay County area. The Anglo homes are of frame construction and typically have multiple front doors, porches, one story, and gabled roofs. If built before about 1875 or 1880, the Anglo houses have a fireplace and prominent exterior chimney. They lack hipped or gambrel roofs and dormer windows. Clearly, the Moser folk house was shaped by an alien architectural tradition. The presence of this structure in the North Texas landscape is made even more striking by the many differences between it and the Anglo houses.

Hurnville, like most rural Texas communities, is dying. Its distinctive Russian-German subculture will soon vanish from the countryside. One can only hope that Leon Moser's fine house, so splendid a visual record of the Russian and South German heritage of these people, will somehow survive. We Texans who value the past, the rural, the folk culture, should not allow such structures to disappear.

NOTES:

[1]See: Richard Ballet, *Russian-German Settlements in the United States*, trans. by L. J. Rippley and A. Bauer, Fargo: North Dakota Institute for Regional Studies, 1974, and Albert J. Petersen, "German-Russian Colonization in Western Kansas: A Settlement Geography," unpublished Ph.D. dissertation, Louisiana State University, 1970.

[2]See: F. S. Reisdorph, "A History of the German People in the Panhandle of Texas and Ellis County, Oklahoma," unpublished M.A. thesis, West Texas State University, 1942, and Elsie M. Wilbanks and Austin H. Montgomery, "The Other Germans," *Texana*, Vol. 9 (1971), pp. 230-248. An exception to the neglect of the Clay County Russian-Germans is: William C. Taylor, *A History of Clay County*, Austin: Jenkins and Pemberton, 1972, pp. 78-79, 94-96, 109, 117, 125, 144.

[3]Karl Stumpp, *The German-Russians: Two Centuries of Pioneering*, Bonn, W. Germany: Atlantic-Forum, 1964, and Robert Low, *Deutsche Bauernstaaten auf russischer Steppe*, Berlin-Charlottenburg, Germany: Ostlandverlag, 1916.

[4]The information on the Hurnville Germans, unless otherwise noted, was derived from an interview with Mr. Leon Moser at his home in Hurnville, May 24, 1975. Mrs. Moser, nee Linstaedt, also provided information at this interview. She is not of Russian-German extraction, but instead the daughter of *Reichsdeutsche* immigrants from the village of Zartin, Pomerania.

[5]All information on Russian-German folk houses in the northern plains is derived from: Albert J. Petersen, "The German-Russian House in Kansas: A Study in Persistence of Form," *Pioneer America*, Vol. 8 (1976), pp. 19-27.

Church of the Immaculate Conception at Panna Maria

139

Panhandle shotgun shack (*Photograph by Sylvia Grider*)

140

Shotgun Houses and Shacks

Sylvia Grider

The "boom" has been a characteristic feature of the economic development of the United States. In many instances, these booms were over almost as suddenly as they came, leaving in their wakes a whole spate of ghost towns. Others were more lasting, and the "boomtowns" they created are lasting monuments to their success. There have been gold booms, silver booms, lumber booms, coal booms, and, most recently, oil booms. A common feature of these economic outbursts is that they involved the discovery of a valuable natural resource that was usually located in an isolated and uninhabited part of the country. In order for the exploitation of the natural resource to be a financial success, great numbers of workers were required to extract or process the material at the site of the discovery. One problem that this vast working force created was the need for cheap and immediate housing. A common solution for this problem was for the company to provide housing for the employees. In the oil and lumber boomtowns of Texas and Louisiana, the shotgun house took precedence over all other types of company housing.[1]

The shotgun house is generally one room wide with the alignment of the rooms end to end and the front and back doors in the narrow gable ends. The term "shotgun" is of disputed origin but it has acquired a folk etymology which explains, "If you fire a shotgun through the front door it'll go straight through and out the back."[2] Fieldwork has proven, however, that the front and back doors are nearly always offset, although one or the other can be found

aligned with one of the inner partition doors. Until recently the origins of this distinctive folk house type have been as obscure as its etymology. However, Professor John Vlach of the University of Texas demonstrated through meticulous and extensive fieldwork that the shotgun is basically a West African house type which was brought to the islands of the Caribbean, especially Haiti, by slaves.[3] From Haiti the house type spread to the Southern United States where it was used extensively as slave housing. Eventually free blacks and slaves established the house type in New Orleans, where it remains to this day as a characteristic example of the architecture of the older parts of the city.

As was previously pointed out, because so many of these little houses could be crowded together in a limited area and could be built so quickly and inexpensively, they were readily appropriated as company housing when the great economic booms of the first quarter of the century were in their heyday. The need for housing was most acute in the lumbering areas of East Texas and Louisiana as well as in the oil fields of West Texas and the Panhandle. As a result, the shotgun was quickly adapted to all of these areas. However, because of the high prevailing winds of the Panhandle (as well as simplicity of construction), a distinctive curved roof was developed there and this sets the Panhandle shotguns apart typologically from those further south and east. Because of this low curved roof, shotguns in the Panhandle are generally referred to by the local people as "shacks" rather than as houses.

The best way to understand shotgun houses or shacks in general is to examine one in some detail. In one corner of the pasture on the northeast edge of Pampa, Texas, is a vacant shotgun which exhibits all of the major characteristics of this unusual house type.

This tiny two-room shack is approximately 12' wide, 24' long, and 8' high (measuring on the corner and thus not taking into account the added arc of the covered roof). It is constructed of sawmilled boards of standard dimensions. The siding is wide vertical boards with the cracks covered by a narrow splice board, a technique generally known as "board and batten" but locally called "clapboard." The front room has no separate interior wall so there is no trapped air space or insulation—just one layer of boards serving the exterior and interior. These thin walls would have made such houses uncomfortable in both winter and summer.

The front door of the house is "store bought" or factory made, ca. 7' x 3'. It is set on the far side of the front gable end, not in the center as the folk etymology of "shotgun" implies. The screen door appears to be homemade. There is a short overhang of shiplap nailed over the door and covered with tin to deflect the rain. A small window, 3' square, is centered between the door and the opposite edge of the house. This window is set quite high and the top sill is flush with the top of the siding.

The front room of the house is approximately 11' square. There is one window on the right wall and a narrow, triple-hinged board-and-batten door on the opposite wall. The back room is the same size. There is a sheetrock partition between the two rooms with a doorway cut on the left and aligned with the back door but not the front. The rear door is also of factory make and has a pane of glass in the top panel. There was apparently no screen door in back. There

are two windows in this room, one on each side. The walls of this back room are the backs of the raw, wide boards of the clapboards, whitewashed instead of covered with sheetrock as is the front room.

As has already been mentioned, the roof is the most distinctive feature of the shotgun shacks of the Panhandle oil fields. In addition to being wind-resistant, the curved roof was apparently the simplest possible method of construction and one that required the least amount of time and skill. A carpenter built the roof of one of these buildings by first laying a 2 x 12 edgewise, like a ridgepole, with one 2 x 6 half way to the edge, parallel, on each side. Then 1 x 12's were bent crossways over the tops of these boards, nailed down, and covered with tarpaper or ninety-pound felt paper. The shallow, curved gable opening was covered with a single 2 x 12, usually chopped to fit with a rig axe instead of being sawed. An experienced carpenter or rig builder did this by first drawing a long-radius arc in the dirt with a stick attached to a string. Then he laid the 2 x 12 over the arc and chopped the curve accordingly.

There was no attic or ceiling below the underside of the roof of this particular shack, although in others sheetrock or plywood was nailed to the bottoms of the 2 x 12 ceiling joists. However, this lowered the headroom so much that it was not a general practice.

The floors of this and all other shotguns were made of 4" wide, milled tongue-in-groove floorboards, laid longitudinally. Sometimes the floor was covered with cheap linoleum, but rugs were rarely used because of the dirty conditions resulting from a combination of the blowing dirt of the Dust Bowl and the oil and mud tracked in by the oil field workers. There were never any dirt-floored shacks because the standard method of construction was to use heavy rig timbers as a foundation,

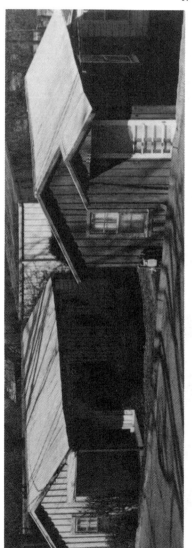

Shotgun houses *(Nacogdoches Co.)*

Shotgun house *(Nacogdoches Co.)*

143

Country shotgun (*Harrison Co.*)

144

which raised the building up off the ground so far that board flooring was required.

Today shotguns are scattered throughout Texas and other parts of the South, and are easily recognizable because of the long, narrow floorplan with the door in the gable end. However not many new shotguns are being built today because the ubiquitous trailer house or mobile home has practically replaced the shotguns whenever cheap, quick housing is needed. Nevertheless, the little shotguns which do remain are outstanding examples of folk architecture in an increasingly homogeneous and mass-produced society.

NOTES:

This article is an abridgement of a longer version, "The Shotgun House in Oil Boomtowns of the Texas Panhandle," in *Pioneer America* 7:2 (July, 1975): 47-55. The original research was done for a presentation at the 1971 meeting of the Texas Folklore Society in San Antonio.

[1] Previous studies of the shotgun in Louisiana include: Fred Kniffen, "Physiognomy of Rural Louisiana," *Louisiana History* 4 (1963): 291-300; Yvonne Phillips, "The Shotgun House," *Louisiana Studies* 2 (1963): 176-79; and George Stokes, "Lumbering and Western Louisiana Cultural Landscapes," *Annals of the American Geographers* 47 (1957): 250-66.

[2] This folk term has already appeared several times in print. See, for example: Dorothy Bracken, *Early Texas Homes* (Dallas: Southern Methodist University Press, 1956), overleaf; Mitford M. Matthews, *Dictionary of Americanisms on Historic Principles* (Chicago: University of Chicago Press, 1951); and Yvonne Phillips, "The Shotgun House," p. 178.

[3] John M. Vlach, "The Shotgun House: An African Architectural Legacy," *Pioneer America* 8:1-2 (January and July, 1976): 47-70.

145

Barns & Outbuildings

The farm complex included the house, the barns, and all the outbuildings necessary for the family to maintain its self sufficiency. After the house was built and the family was out of the weather, the settler built his crib or barn to protect his corn and his tools and ploughs. The barns continued to grow by necessity, being doubled-penned in the same way as the houses, with extended roof lines to add sheds and lean-tos. Chicken houses, pig pens, cow lots, and gardens were added and fenced in to keep animals and crops separated for the owner's good.

As the farmer prospered he built water tanks and milk houses and stock troughs. He fashioned a long furnace with a chimney to hold the long pan for making syrup. He dug a cellar to store his root crops in, a place where he could keep the summer's canning at a fairly constant temperature. He built a smoke house where he could cure and keep his meat.

The placing of the buildings was for the greatest efficiency, with the milk house and smoke house near enough for the wife to use easily, and the outhouse and the hog pens and chicken house far enough away to dilute their characteristic aromas. The barns and cow lots and stables were situated so that the least movement got the most work done. All of it made one architectural whole, a working unit that served its maker with its greatest efficiency.

Barns and Outbuildings

Thomas J. Stanly

The early Texan built the buildings on his farmstead in the order of his greatest priorities; hence the corn crib came before the blacksmith shop. Since most were initially subsistence type farms before they became specialized in production of a single crop or could qualify as a ranch, the farmer's greatest need for structures beyond the house followed a common pattern. The function of each building and the availability of material dominated the order and type of construction more than did the urge to duplicate the lifestyle and physical appearance of the place of origin of the many different migrant groups of farmers.

Determining Factor of Economics

Economics was the primary factor in determining both the building and the sequence. The majority of early settlers came to Texas by choice. Cheap land was the golden fleece that was advertised so widely and successfully by early land impresarios. The carryover influence of primogeniture among Anglo-American groups—whether from the Tidewater, Blue Ridge, Appalachian, Middle Atlantic or Lowland South regions—was not a small factor. Cheap land was equally enticing to European emigrants. It has been said that Texas was a land of second or further removed sons who spent all their cash for land and were content to live in humble dwellings wearing simple garb so long as they were living on their own land. Hence farming and ranching were near the total of industry in early Texas. This resulted in the farm production unit dominating the

beginning of building in the area. This influence still prevails up to our city limits and to a degree within.

Land settlement policies beginning with the Spanish and Mexican grants, through United States efforts including preemption and homesteading, have resulted in the continued wide distribution of individual land holdings in the state. This pattern of land ownership is basic to a stable agricultural industry and has been a major factor in Texas' being one of the dominant agricultural states in the union. Farm buildings, therefore, take on added significance as a part of this primary economic production unit in the state.

A second economic consideration in regard to supporting farm structures was limited cash for building anything beyond a room large enough for a "cookstove and sleeping scaffold." Building resources, consequently, were those of the land as well as the hand of the settler. This shortage of money prescribed what, how, and when farm outbuildings were built.

Materials and Styles

The typical settler used what money he had for land and the trip to Texas, whether he came by overland wagon or by boat from the coast. Transportation costs and limited capital dictated use of material on hand. To the East Texan it meant pine logs; to the Central and Cross Timbers Texan it meant oak logs or rock construction. The High Plains resident combined logs with his dugout, and the Mexican-influenced South and Southwest Texas farmer adopted adobe construction.

Log construction where trees were available receives the most attention of researchers. Stones or rocks were used most frequently as structural material in areas settled by emigrants from Europe. Most of these ethnic groups by design or chance settled where there was a geological outcropping of rock formations. Their heritage was strong in masonry construction.

One must consider that labor and talents of the builder were the primary inputs into all construction since the material was necessarily of the land. Noticeable style of the building, then, whether dwelling or outbuilding, was that of the builder—the settler.

The abundant supply of pine logs in East Texas, often available for the cutting on unclaimed land, generally restricted barn design to the single, double, or in fewer instances, the triple pen square or rectangular basic construction form. This pattern was true to a lesser extent westward and southward where cottonwood, hardwood and cedar logs were substituted for the easily worked pine. Total use of rocks or rocks mixed with logs permitted or mandated deviation from the typical pen construction.

As the small or what came to be known as the "pecker wood" sawmill began to appear, sawed boards were integrated into the construction of farm buildings. In the absence of planking during the earlier years, shingles or rived boards, as they were commonly called by early Texans, were nailed on pole laths to substitute for planking or siding where needed when support was not needed. An example of this would be the enclosing of the gables of a crib or barn.

Split slabs were frequently used, usually in a vertical position, as siding and support on a pole frame for buildings no more than twelve feet square. If used for flooring

(puncheons), doors, or shutters, the artisan settler would dress the boards to varying degrees of smoothness to accomplish a closer fit.

Rived boards or shingles were the most common roofing material. The hearts of pine, cypress, and cedar trees were the source of the best boards. For lesser farm buildings with a roof run of six feet or less, or when the settler was just making out, he sometimes used the slab in lengths of the entire run, double layered in thickness with staggered joints. A man who had the ability to pick a straight splitting board tree from a stand of timber was considered to possess a special talent. Unique enough to mention but limited strictly to the marshlands of south Texas and the river bottoms where the palmetto grew, the fan from this plant was occasionally layered in the manner of shingles for temporary roofing and siding on such farm buildings as chicken houses and temporary sheds.

The substitution of sheets of corrugated tin for covering old and new buildings, began in the early 1900's as a practical choice. Tin was more efficient, easier to lay and relatively cheap. The rural landscape is now scarred with rusty tin roofs hiding the original shingled roofs that had mellowed with age.

Examples of improvisation by early Texans were quite evident in their door latches and hinges for barns and outbuildings. Though products of function and available material, their design had to meet specifications beyond just keeping the door shut. The best example of why one would go from an ordinary latch string, turnbutton, or drop latch was that sooner or later, every farmer would come up with a latchwise mule or horse. Rending appeals to the Almighty or classic bursts of profanity, depending on the spiritual leanings of the settler—though both served the same purpose—have resulted from the early morning view

Barn Latches

Plank and Hewn-log Barn (*Hamilton Co.*)

of the posterior of an old mule protruding from the crib door. To compound matters, the animal would usually founder or colic from gorging.

The hinging of doors was totally a matter of function though different methods were used with varying degrees of efficiency. A damning comment regarding a farmer's enterprise was that every door on his place would drag. The rawhide and pivot rod hinged doors at best would put a man in this category. The wagon hub rings that were often used as pivot rod retainers were about the only evidence of technology in hanging these doors. Wrought-iron strap hinges and other designs of metal hinges were seldom available to the remote homesteads of early Texans even if they could have afforded them. Later years showed some residents who still chose not to compromise their ingenuity by using manufactured hinges. The rawhide was replaced with short sections of heavy fabric machinery belting discarded from cotton gins and sawmills or with a square cut from the sole of an automobile tire. These modern substitutes hinged the door but it still dragged.

Outbuildings and the Priority of Construction

The settler, if moving from a distance, would usually spend his first year with relatives. He often worked for a share of the crop and his keep. When he did move into his own house—most commonly a single-pen log structure with no room for tools—he was confronted with the universal question of what must be built next. Most moving to a new homesite was done between crops. The house would have been started the previous year after "laying by" his crops. He would make the house tight enough to move into shortly after harvest. When the move was a great distance, the farmer would sell his corn and trade it for livestock delivered after the winter. If moving within the

vicinity, he would often move his grain to the new location. The crib or corncrib, therefore, was needed immediately as much as a barn to shelter the livestock. A multipurpose structure, consequently, serving both these functions was the obvious choice. This building frequently was used for many other functions until resources and time permitted special purpose buildings. This circumstance accounts for "barn" being a general term used in referring to all outbuildings in Texas as in other farm cultures.

Barns and Cribs: The first log pen or basic unit of the barn was ordinarily built to the rear of the house close enough for animal distress to be heard. Exceptions to this relative location frequently resulted from the course of the roads. Roads usually meandered along the crests of the ridges for the sake of dryness. The best site for a home was along an established wagon road. Often the best drained site remaining was the other half of the hill across from the house. Hence the barn was often placed on the other side of the road, dividing the homestead.

The barn structure was enclosed by the "lot" fence. As one moved westward in the state, this term was supplanted by the ranch oriented term "corral." The first building was most likely to be a crib with an open lean-to being added as soon as possible. How soon depended on the level of animal care to which the settler was committed. Many early farmers were content to hang on the side of the crib a half-log trough fashioned from a hollow tree trunk as his concession to the well-being of his stock. By contrast, in days when Indians and marauders were a threat, secure log stables with inside latches were constructed.

The crib when constructed of logs was built on sills resting on piers of large rocks or hewn wooden blocks. In the east central portion of the state where long leaf pine was common, rich pine or "lightered" blocks were used.

153

"Pore lightered" blocks from loblolly or shortleaf pines were not as permanent. When hardwood blocks were used the sapwood of large trees was split off and only the heart wood was used.

Split or rived slabs sometimes called puncheons were used for crib floors before sawed boards were available. They were pegged or nailed on peeled pole sleepers or floor joists. Nails were often the most expensive material in this type of building. Some slab floors were laid without nails. In rock construction the base of the wall was the foundation. Stones supporting the floor joists were "hipped" inside the wall or else the joists were extended through and rested on the wall. The pole ceiling joists and rafters rested on the plate logs or the last tier of rocks. Frequently the board or slab gables were made with doors through which corn could be thrown.

The story is told of the old farmer in the Sabine River Bottom where saddle notched pine log crib construction was dominant, who used to brag each year to his neighbors of always making a crib full of corn. Dry year or wet, he filled his crib up to the plate log. Once following a particularly dry spring resulting in crop failure and most people making just a few "nubbins" of corn, an observant traveler learned his secret. The farmer just jacked up the plate logs on his crib and removed enough of the wall logs—one at a time—until what remained of his crib was full.

Some farmers with time and resources went beyond the single level concept of barn construction. They would go up about half wall height with the log or rock wall—three to four feet above the ceiling joists—before laying the plate for the rafters. Thus a loft or upper half-story was available for hay or fodder storage. Occasionally the ground level without a floor was used as stables with the upper level

providing feed storage.

The second and subsequently the third pens were added as the farmer prospered. Each pen was placed on a gabled side of the existing barn with enough distance between to allow passage of a wagon. The roofs were joined, covering this hallway. Designation of the front and rear was changed from the gabled to the eave sides at the openings of the hall. As the pens were added they were used for the various needs that were not provided by the first structure. The inevitable lean-to was usually a part of the additions. Some roofs were cantilevered, initially, to the eave sides to provide lean-to or side space extending beyond the basic pen.

The stalls for workstock that were included in the barn complex were commonly furnished with the aforementioned hollow log troughs. Harness was usually hung by sets at various intervals along the hallway. The hanger might be a peg set in a log or one prong of a V crotch cut from a tree limb or sapling and nailed to the wall. The walls and unused space in the cribs or stalls were handy for storage of tools, equipment, and supplies until a wagon or plow shed could be provided.

In the areas of the state where shallow wells of twenty to forty feet were possible, a well could be dug in the main barn complex for watering the stock. Until this was done, they were watered at a flowing stream, spring, or in a trough at the house well. Penned hogs were sometimes watered from a cistern filled from gutters on the barn roof.

Horse Stalls and Wagons Sheds: Barns were often limited to two pens. When additional space was needed, supporting barn buildings more specialized in design relating to function was added. Among the first of these was a building that most frequently provided two purposes—stalls for the workstock and shelter for the

(Right) Double-pen barn of dressed oak
(Freestone Co.)

(Below left) Barn roof of rived boards
(Tyler Co.)

(Below right) Harness hanger
(Nacogdoches Co.)

155

Double-pen barn with split-rail fence (*Tyler Co.*)

157

Double-pen barn built in 2-stages with dressed (*right*) and peeled (*left*) logs (*Panola Co.*)

Grain chute

158

Barn built around former slave quarters. Roofline can be seen in barn wall
(opposite) (Mason Co.)

Interior of barn built around slave quarters (*Mason Co.*)

160

wagons. In order to combine these functions the building ordinarily was located with one slope of the roof space in the lot and the other half outside the line of the lot fence. With this divided access, the animals, when loose in the lot or "stomp," as the enclosed area was sometimes called, were not exposed to injury from running into plows and the equipment was protected from the animals.

These stalls were designed in a rectangular pen partitioned by log walls in combination of two, four, etc., since the farmer normally added workstock in pairs. Most wagons were double team as were the majority of the breaking plows used for land preparation. The stalls, opening to the eave inside the lot, were recessed about eight feet under a roof that was either cantilevered or a lean-to. This provided a linear shed covering the stall entrances. Harness was hung on the walls. The covered space also provided a shelter for harnessing, or as often referred to, "gearing up" the work animals. It prevented the stall entrances from becoming boggy. Tradition has it that these stalls were favorite places to bury money, since the stomping of the animals would erase any sign of fresh digging. The gables were slabbed or boarded in. Frequently ceiling joists were added over the stalls forming a loft which was used for feed storage. Some farmers cut holes about 2' x 2' in the loft above each stall and would drop hay into feed racks on the wall of the stall.

The wagon shed side of this structure was more likely to be enclosed or be made as a separate building as people moved westward in the state, particularly in the German settlements.

Although the wagon shed served as storage space for all tools, it took its name from the largest piece of equipment stored therein. Dry storage for the iron-rimmed wooden-wheeled wagon was vital, since, when exposed to sun and rain, repeated swelling and shrinking of the wooden inner-rim would result in stretching the iron rim, causing it to slip off in dry weather. Soaking in the creek overnight would tighten it temporarily. A work bench, the antecedent of the blacksmith shop, was often set up under this shed.

Blacksmith Shop: As farming operations expanded and forge work was needed, the blacksmithing operation was moved to a small separate building due to the hazard of fire. This shed frequently was slab sided or of board-and-batten construction. Normally the floor plan was a bench running the length of one side wall. The forge with bellows was most commonly located in the rear corner opposite the bench. The anvil, anchored on a vertical wooden block, was positioned toward the center near the forge. The vice, commonly a leg vice, was fixed to the bench. If available in the landscape, a big shade tree furnished a desirable place to locate the blacksmith shop. The tree would provide shade for this hot task and furnish a limb for use as a hoist. The tree would make this spot a social center for idle farm hands and visitors, since blacksmithing was often done when work could not be done in the fields. A water barrel for tempering iron was a fixture outside under the eave of the roof. A smaller container filled from this source was positioned by the anvil.

Smoke Houses: Most early Texans were first subsistence farmers so the food supply was a first priority. As soon as possible a small structure was built for a smoke house in which meat was cured. The more complete smoke house had cantilevered plates extending from the gabled end far enough to provide space for hanging the animal carcasses. The building was, because of function, tightly constructed. When not constructed of rock, as was common in central and west Texas, the cracks in the logs were chinked with chimney mud, rocks, or covered with rived boards to hold the hardwood smoke during the smoking process. In most smoke houses a low bench was used on which rested boxes in which the meat was salted or the meat was stacked between layers of salt. The salt removed the moisture. Small hardwood poles or sticks were placed in a perpendicular direction on the ceiling joists for hanging the meat. "Bear grass," a sandy land version of the palmetto family, was used when available as ties for the meat to be hung on the sticks. Sausages were looped over the sticks. After about a ten-day to two-week smoking period the meat was allowed to hang in place and the sausages were often stored in earthen crocks in lard rendered from the fat of hogs.

Potato Houses: Irish potatoes and sweet potatoes were basic foods for early Texans. Until he could do better, the settler stored his Irish potatoes on a crib floor or in dry sand under a house or crib floor. Sweet potatoes were kept in a "potato bank." This potato bank was most common in East Texas. It was an inverted cone-shaped pile of potatoes covered first with two to three inches of pine straw over which a four to six inch layer of dirt was added. An opening at the top of the cone, normally covered with a waterproof tub, was allowed for ventilation. The bank was opened from the ground level to assure protection from moisture. This improvised structure did a good job of preserving sweet potatoes from the rain and freezing temperatures, but it did present one problem. It was a perfect haven for tarantula spiders. Few frightening experiences compare with reaching one's hand into a dark hole, grasping a potato and, upon withdrawing, seeing a gleaming black tarantula three inches in girth sitting atop the hand.

The potato house was the equivalent of a root cellar in other areas of the United States. It served not only as storage for root crops but also as a cool place for storing

food preserved in jars and later in cans.

One common design of the structure was a dugout. The upper portion of the walls would be built with inner and outer walls of a thickness of about twelve inches so they could be filled with sawdust for insulation. Where rock masonry was common the thickness of the stones provided insulation. The floor was earthen. You had to stoop to enter the door and go down a couple of steps into the room.

Cowsheds: As farmers expanded into livestock enterprises, little additional building was required. Occasionally a stall in the existing barn might be set aside for a milk cow where she could be fed and milked separately from the woods or range cows. Normally there was an outside entrance from an adjacent cow lot since mules or horses were inclined to kick, frequently resulting in injury to the cow. The cow lot adjoining the horse lot seldom included any shelter beyond perhaps a lean-to across one of the gabled sides of an outside pen of the main barn. When milking was done it normally took place in this open lot. The milk cows' calves were kept in a fenced pasture during the day, insuring that the cow would return home at night. One or two tie posts were conveniently located in the cow lot to tie off the calf while the milker, usually the woman of the house, milked half the cow's milk for the family and saved two "tits" for the calf. It took a pen full of these range cows to fill a lard bucket of milk. The calf tying posts doubled as anchor posts for stretching a calf during branding and castration.

Chicken Houses: An old hen and a "settin'" of eggs were a common gift from a neighbor to a new settler or young couple. The flock grew to need a house. Chickens were among the first tenants on a farmstead but had to wait some time before they were accommodated with a special house. Meanwhile they used for roosts the closest trees,

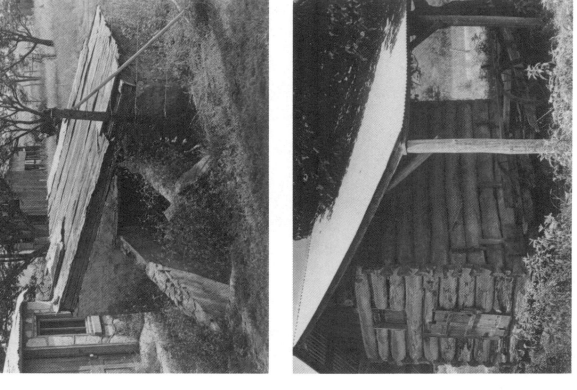

Storm cellar also used for food storage (*Coryell Co.*)

Single-pen corn crib with wagon shed (*Lee Co.*)

163

Smoke house (*Blanco Co.*)

Corn crib with wagon and feed shed and puncheon floor (*Rusk Co.*)

Furnace for syrup
making
(Nacogdoches Co.)

board fences, wagon bed frames, or whatever would keep them away from marauding varmints. Straw-filled boxes nailed to the various shed walls served as nests. The chicken of that day, bred primarily by survival of the fittest selection process, could fly to the top of the tallest tree if necessary. It was quite self-sufficient.

When the chicken house was built, it was another pitched roof, shed type structure normally not over twelve feet square. It was closed in with boards or rived slabs on all sides except the south. The top half of the south wall was often slatted or even latticed with small laths for ventilation. Openings between the laths had to be small enough to turn 'possums, mink, fox, and other predators. Small-mesh chicken wire replaced the slatting when wire became available.

A double or triple row of nests would be fixed to one wall. Placement of the nests at eye level was important because it was common for a chicken snake to coil in the nest while swallowing an egg. Thus it was somewhat hazardous for the person gathering the eggs to stick his hand in a blind nest. The roost supports were two poles inclined from the ground to one of the other full walls. Small roost poles traversed these supports at about fourteen inch intervals. The bottom roost pole did not come closer than two feet from the ground—again as protection from varmints.

The turnbutton latch on the door was sometimes supplemented by a lock in the depression years of the early 1900's. For several reasons, the chicken lent itself to being stolen more often than did any other of the farmer's livestock.

Hog Pens: Hog pens were often just outside the horse lot near the corn crib for convenient feeding. The pens were constructed of saddle-notched logs placed about waist high.

They had no permanent roofs. In the parts of the state where there was a hardwood mast—acorns, beech mast, etc.,—hogs roamed the woods. Most farmers in the wooded sections of Texas owned hog dogs that were trained to drive the wild hogs up in the late fall when the two- and three-year-old mast-fattened barrows or "bar hogs" were penned and finished on corn. Farmers in the treeless areas of the state commonly kept their hogs confined year round.

Goat Sheds: These shelters were common in East Texas and other areas where Spanish goats were raised as a source of fresh meat. The shed was most commonly of pole construction with a rived board roof. The north, east, and west sides would be enclosed with vertical slab or sawed board siding. A run of the same size would be extended on the south side enclosed by a board or slab fence. The entrance was a style which the goats could negotiate but which other animals could not. It was located on the downwind side of the house for obvious reasons.

Slaughter Houses: Initially slaughter houses were uncommon, but around the turn of the twentieth century larger farmers or ranchers would slaughter for the developing local city markets. Slaughter houses were usually not much more than a taller-than-average pole-barn-like structure which in later years might have had a concrete floor, tanning vat, and wire screening. One strong ceiling joist spanned the structure for use in hoisting the animal carcasses. This need made the extra height of the building a necessity.

For lesser farmers, slaughtering of the home meat supply generally took place under a tree near the "wash pot." A hoisting rail was placed in the crotch of a tree and supported on the other end by a braced post. A barrel with the butt end buried in the ground on angle was usually evident for use in scalding hogs in order to remove the hair.

Syrup Mills: Making syrup from ribbon cane or sorghum was common in all parts of the state where there was enough rainfall to grow the crop. Little construction was involved. The layout was the greater interest. The mill was anchored on a platform supported by four solid posts. The space required for stacking the cane and circle for turning the arched log mill lever by the mule made shelter impractical. The furnace upon which first the round syrup kettles and later the rectangular evaporator pans were set required a large mud smoke stack. Only the cooking area was covered with a pole shed with a slightly pitched roof. Commonly seen hanging from roof laths were utensils used by the syrup maker: skimmers, juice pushers, a pot, and a stained rag for blocking the flow of juice in the evaporator channels. Sometimes a wooden barrel covered with a sack strainer would be placed near the furnace of the skimmer for collecting the skimmings. When full, a prescribed amount of shelled corn was added. After two weeks or more of fermentation, a somewhat cloudy timid yellow brew called cane beer was offered to visitors who dared to partake. The syrup mill was a social institution for farm residents. Since many farmers in a community used one mill on shares, several families were involved. The "chews" or pulp from the crushed stalks of cane were usually piled just beyond the circle made by the mule pulling the mill lever. This was a natural place for small children to develop their acrobatic prowess. This also served as a prime hiding place for the beer after it was jugged if made under clandestine circumstances. When operating late in the evenings a fire on a raised platform covered with dirt (called a "Nigger Boy") provided light. A choice diversion for young courting couples was to walk to the glowing syrup mill, ostensibly to drink some of the fresh cane juice.

Ratproofed Corn Cribs: Rats have always been the nemesis of the farmer. After a few years of trying unsuccessfully to store corn in the main barn, many early farmers would attempt to build a ratproof crib. This crib would be of a design similar to the cotton house but on a much larger scale. It was built upon posts of lasting wood, high enough to prevent a rat from jumping up to the crib from ground level. Often this crib would be high enough for stock to loaf underneath and for the farmer to bump his head when running the stock out. The ratproofing consisted of placing an inverted tub or some other slick metal cylinder over the top of each post before the crib sills were laid, placing a retractable ladder at the door, and locating the structure away from a fence or tree or any other object from which rats might jump. For one reason or another this design seldom prevented rat infestation. Rainy day or Sunday afternoon sport of a rat killin' played by young men and boys armed with sticks and hoes, flanked by house cats and yard dogs survived as a rural entertainment until the day of organic poisons.

Cotton Houses: Fifteen hundred pounds of seed cotton were required to yield an average sized (500 lbs.) bale of lint cotton. Temporary storage was needed for the seed cotton until that amount could be accumulated and hauled to the gin. The cotton houses, found primarily in East Texas, were located in the fields or patches convenient to the cotton plantings. They were commonly of one-pen saddle-notched log construction, or board-and-batten, supported by wooden blocks or rocks, and displaying gabled, shingled roofs. The dimensions were approximately 12' x 15' x 6'. Sometimes the board roofs were cantilevered to the front gable to provide cover for weighing and hanging the scales. These structures served for general storage of field tools and supplies at other times of the year. When located near a creek or river, they frequently provided a sleeping place at

Cotton shed and wagon *(Medina Co.)*

167

Cotton shed and cotton wagon (*Medina Co.*)

John's house *(Milam Co.)*

169

One-holer *(Hamilton Co.)*

Double-pen barn (*Panola Co.*)

night for boys running their "set hooks."

Wells: Well houses were not common on Texas farmsteads nor were spring houses, although many early settlers used springs for their water supply. The closest structure to a well house was the open well shed usually constructed as a shingled gabled roof over the well on more developed farmsteads. In the absence of the traditional "dairy," or spring house, it was common for the housewife to cool milk in a jug submerged in a spring or to drop a container of milk on a line into the northeast corner of the well. Casual research has not yielded any meteorological or geological reason for that particular corner being the coldest but it was believed to be so.

Wash Sheds: Manual labor by farmers required a heavy clothes washing load elevating this chore to one of high priority on farmsteads. As a farm developed beyond basic necessities, the wash shed would make its appearance. Close to the well a bench would be placed upon which tubs could be set. If the well was close enough to the house, this bench would be positioned against the wall under the overhang of the roof. In more affluent circumstances, a designated shed would be built near the well expressly for washing. A wash pot was placed near the bench or shed for boiling the clothes before scrubbing them on the scrub board. The necessary clothes line with a prop pole was located nearby.

Outhouses: The outhouse, designed for human comfort, was not a direct component of the farm production complex but was nevertheless a structure of vital function. Though not confined to farmsteads, it was certainly more conspicuous in the open landscape of the rural home than in towns. Placement of the outhouse (or toilet, as it was frequently termed by rural residents) was far enough behind the house to avoid odors but close enough to reach

in case of emergencies. The family desired to locate it behind another building to provide private entry and exit.

The outward dimensions of this board-and-batten structure was usually about four feet square, if designed for single occupancy. The pitched roof was adequate for this small building. Before the days of the pit design introduced by the Works Progress Administration architects during the New Deal 1930's, the back wall did not extend below the level of the seat. This opening provided access for cleaning by man or nature—usually nature. The only other visible change that the finest minds among the WPA architects made was to do away with the standard eye level diamond shaped cutout between two of the center boards in the back wall. The classic half-moon cutout apparently existed only in the minds of cartoonists drawing outhouses. This vertical space in the "government" toilet was covered by a board vent running from the pit back of the seat through the roof. This visible capped vent was a singular monument to the limited progress in redesigning this classic structure.

Large families or public buildings dictated a rectangular shape of this building to provide more seats on the bench. The seats in the traditional design were diamond-shaped cutouts of an appropriate size between two wide boards serving as cover for the bench. The front of the bench was sheeted with boards. Comfort conscious builders would fashion a modified circular cutout with chamfered (rounded) edges. Some builders would vary the sizes of the seats to accommodate people of various ages. Unless the two seat boards were well mortised in some manner, an uneven distribution of the occupant's weight could result in a severe pinch to sensitive parts.

The door had outside and inside turnbutton latches. A favorite prank for a youngster was to slip up and shut the outside latch on the unsuspecting occupant to test his Houdini techniques.

Bunkhouses: The bunk house, heralded in songs and stories of the old west was not typical. As portrayed in movies, the bunkhouse existed on relatively few large ranches in the class of the XIT, Pitchfork, and 6666. A single room added as a lean-to to a barn or some other structure was most frequently used to house a hired hand or more than one in peak seasons. This humble abode, typically furnished with a bunk and chair, was commonly given the first name of the first occupant. It was usually called by this name after his departure. The most common designation was "John's Room," since there was an inordinate number of John Smiths looking for secluded work in the early days of Texas.

Woodsheds: Split stove wood was the chief source of fuel for food preparation. As resources permitted and women became more assertive, their demand for dry wood was heeded in building a woodshed. The shed was normally located just outside the back yard fence with an entrance from within the fence. A three- to four-foot square opening was placed on the side wall to the outside of the fence so that wood could be thrown conveniently from a wagon.

In conclusion, Texas settlers used the skills handed down from their ancestors, the materials of the land, and the will of the dreamer to fashion the often unique structures that cradled what is today a great agricultural industry. The switch from the subsistence farm, where the farmer produced all he needed, to the specialized one crop, mechanized modern farms of today, may have left behind the opportunity to identify visibly each man by his style of building.

(Top row and left) Outhouses
(Above) One-holer with adapter for children

173

Gates & Fences

A stout fence, tight strung, punctuated regularly with straight posts set plumb is a classical work of art. It stands for order and separates territories with such exactness and definition that there is no room for argument. A romantic is able to satisfy the function more casually with fences made of split rails that worm their slow ways around a corn field or with long meanders of stacked flat stones. Pole fences and palisades can be as regular or random as the builder chooses. Whatever its style and structure, a good fence maintains social harmony and improves the chances and quality of neighborliness.

One fence in the Panhandle left a cattleguard at the corner of a small cow pasture and headed west as straight as a line of sight. It was a five-strand fence—hog tight, horse high, and bull strong—that ran through two draws, then up where the prairie flattened out, till finally it went out of sight

and beyond the imagination over the horizon. A water gap made out of an old truck tailgate guarded the ditch at the first draw while a piece of roofing tin, hung crossways, protected the other. A bluebird nested in the hollow of the thirtieth post from the cattleguard, and scissor-tails in pairs rested regularly before looping up into the sky again. Lizards hung grotesquely from barbs, impaled along with a variety of grasshoppers by a butcher bird who believed in laying up his treasures on earth. One of the men killed a coyote with a .32 automatic pistol once and hung it four posts down from the cattleguard. He said it would scare away other coyotes. A snake hung belly up on the fence would make it rain. On the other hand, a crow sitting on the fence was the announcement of a spell of dry weather. The fence went right through the middle of a prairie dog town located on the level between the two draws. They never noticed.

Corral fence built by F. E. A. with railroad ties in 1940 (*Hamilton Co.*)

176

Rails, Rocks, and Pickets: Traditional Farmstead Fencing in Texas

Lonn Taylor

By the time that Bing Crosby recorded "Don't Fence Me In" in the 1940's, two generations of Texans had come to think of a fence as a device for keeping something—usually cattle—within an enclosed area—usually a pasture. The word "fence" itself conjured up distasteful images of a post-hole digger, stacks of fence posts, rolls of barbed wire, and thirty-foot walks from posthole to posthole. However, to Texans who lived before the era of barbed wire, that is, before the 1870's, a fence was a structure that kept something—sometimes cattle, but more often hogs—out of an enclosed area—usually a cornfield.

The wire fence and its western cousin, the barbed wire fence, were creations of the Industrial Revolution, by-products of the technology that created durable wire in great lengths to meet the demand generated by the invention of the telegraph. They were not common in Texas until after the Civil War, although smooth-wire fencing was advertised in Southern agricultural journals as "railroad fencing" in the late 1850's. Instead of wire fencing, Texans used various forms of traditional fencing which reflected both the cultural origins of the builders and the materials provided by the local environment. In eastern and central Texas, the wooden fence in several forms was common; in the Hill country, German settlers built stone fences. On both the coastal plain and the blackland prairie of North Texas, farmers experimented briefly with hedging plants, an idea evidently introduced from England into the treeless midwest. Prince Carl of Solms Braunfels reported

seeing hedge fences in the treeless regions of Texas in the mid-1840's; he wrote that "some have already begun to fence in fields by piling the dirt up two or three feet and planting thorny hedges on top. Those in a short time grow to a considerable height and form an impenetrable barrier. This protects the field much better than the other kind of fencing, and is not at all expensive, and it also requires less work."[1] Some Texans continued to build traditional wood and stone fences well into the twentieth century, and scattered examples of both types, as well as a few builders, are still with us. This article is about some of those survivals and survivors.

Fences served various purposes on a nineteenth-century Texas farmstead, which was in fact a labyrinth of enclosures. Of foremost importance was the field fence, which enclosed the cornfield and the cotton field. The corn field was the breadbasket and food supply of the farm, because corn was necessary for feeding men, horses, mules, and hogs, and the cotton field was the source of cash. A typical East Texas yeoman farmer in 1860 might have ten acres in cotton and two or three in corn, so that the fences enclosing these fields were considerable structures. Next came the cow pen, usually with a shed along one side, where calves were penned during the day so that their evening cries would bring their grazing mothers home at night to be penned, milked, and turned out again the next morning. On more prosperous farms, a separate horse and mule pen might adjoin the cow pen. A vegetable garden,

177

surrounded by a varmint-proof fence, was usually located in a well-drained spot between the animal pens and the house. Finally, the swept-earth yard around the house was surrounded by a yard fence, designed to keep wandering stock away from the porches, decorative shrubs, and flower beds. The yard fence generally enclosed house, kitchen, smokehouse, wash house, and well, and sometimes had a decorative front gate as well as plainer side and rear gates. The overall effect was that of a maze, and the walls of the maze were substantial fences.

Most of these fences, and especially the field fence, were made necessary by the principal of American common law that permitted stock owners to graze their stock unattended on any unfenced land, no matter who the owner was. In sixteenth and seventeenth century England, the common law had required owners of livestock to pen their animals or use herdsmen, and had held the owners responsible for damage done by their livestock to unfenced crops. But in Colonial America, with its surplus of land, the onus was placed on the farmer, and the law required him to fence his fields against free-grazing livestock. This continued to be the law in most Southern states until well into the latter nineteenth century, even though the "fence law question" was hotly debated by farmers and agricultural journals. The *Southern Cultivator*, published in Augusta, Georgia, in the 1850's, described the fence law as "the heavy tax to which American agriculture is subjected by reason of that early colonial system of compelling every cultivator to fence his crops instead of requiring every owner of livestock to keep them out of his neighbors' fields" and went on to argue that "corn and cotton never travel off their owners' land to injure others. As much cannot be said of hogs, sheep, cattle, and horses."[2]

The worst threat to crops was hogs, which in the South were allowed to run loose and forage for themselves through the summer and fall before being rounded up with dogs and slaughtered to provide winter pork. A hog-proof field fence was an expensive necessity and was so much trouble to build that Southern agriculturalists argued that even a law requiring just the penning of hogs would be desirable, since "the expense of fencing against cattle is about one-half that of fencing against hogs."[3] In Texas, however, laws requiring the fencing of any kind of stock were not forthcoming until the advent of barbed wire made cheap range fencing possible, and even then the legislature simply provided for local-option elections on the matter. A state law was passed in 1959 (*Vernon's Annotated Texas Civil Statutes*, Article 6971a) that made it unlawful for stock to graze on state and national right-of-ways and made the owner of the stock liable in case of accidents. This finally put the responsibility of control of animals on the owners, who were then forced to fence *in* their stock.

Until the early stock laws were passed, and in some places for many years afterward, farmers in East and Central Texas protected their corn and cotton with several varieties of a traditional Southern rail fence called in the nineteenth century a "worm fence," a "Virginia worm fence," a "zig-zag fence," or most frequently a "rail fence" or "split-rail fence." The latter term seems to be the common twentieth-century term. This form was introduced into Texas by settlers from the old South, where it was common in the eighteenth and possibly the seventeenth centuries, and it was quickly adopted by other immigrant groups who came into the area, including the Germans who settled in Fayette and Austin Counties. They coined a Texas-German word for it: *Riegelfens*, from the German word for "rail" and the English word "fence" (A

(Left) Stake and rider rail fence (Round Top)

(Below) stacked split-rail fence (Tyler Co.) (Photograph by Robert C. Boykin)

179

180

(Right) Rock fence (Hamilton Co.)

(Below) Rock fence (Bosque Co.)

fence is a *Zaum* in German).

In its simplest form, a split-rail fence is built up of panels of rails, usually ten to twelve feet long, stacked seven rails high. The ends of each panel interlock with the ends of both adjacent panels, somewhat like the corners of a log cabin, although the rails are usually not notched. Each panel leans against its neighbor at an angle of about one hundred twenty degrees, and it is this angle that gives the fence stability as well as its zig-zag configuration. The angle also produces a series of corners, ideal places for weeds, vines, and other destructive vegetation to gain a foothold.

A more complex and more stable elaboration of the rail fence is the "stake-and-rider" variety, in which each corner is held in place by two stakes which cross over the top rail. A final rail, heavier than the others, is then laid in the forks of the stakes. This is the "rider," whose weight helps to hold the stakes and panel in place. While cattle and hogs, or even a high wind, can push over a laid-up split-rail fence, it is almost impossible to break through one that has been staked and ridered.

The first step in building a stake-and-rider split-rail fence is to cut the rails. Delphine Hinze, a native of the Winedale community on the Washington-Fayette County line and the descendant of German settlers who came to the area in the 1850's, explained how this was done: "You look for trees, either cedar [Eastern red cedar, or *juniperus Virginiana*] or post oak, that are tall and straight and about eight to ten inches across at the stump. A tree that size will give you at least four twelve-foot rails, and eight if its tall enough. After you cut the trees and cut the branches off right at the trunk, there are two ways to split the rails. If it's cedar and you have two men, they can do it with axes, working towards each other from opposite ends of the tree, each one striking his axe on the same line. If you are by yourself, or if you

have a knotty post oak, you have to use a wedge and maul with your axe. You drive the axe in, then drive a wedge in the split with your maul, then pull the axe out and drive it in ahead of the wedge." Mr. Hinze went on to say that cutting trees and splitting rails was always winter work, partially because post oak had to be cut in the winter when the sap was down and partially because it was too hot to work in the woods in the summer. He did not estimate how many rails a man could make in one day, but a correspondent to the *Southern Cultivator* in the late 1850's estimated that a good hand could make a hundred and twenty-five rails a day.[4]

Once the rails are cut, they are stacked until used in piles of about fifty, with the rails within each pile arranged against each other somewhat in the manner of a collapsed row of dominos, so that only the two or three on the bottom are in full-length contact with the damp ground.

The path of the fence is kept in a straight line by stretching a string or cord between two stakes, usually a hundred feet apart. If twelve-foot rails are used, stakes are driven along this line at eight-foot intervals. At this point a homemade gauge, consisting of a pole with a sharp point and a horizontal arm two-and-a-half feet long projecting at right angles from it about a foot above the point, is employed to set the fence corners. The pointed end of the pole is stuck in the ground next to each eight-foot stake, a right angle to the cord is turned, and a flat piece of sandstone is placed at the end of the horizontal projection. These pieces of sandstone will support the fence corners and protect them from dampness. The bottom rails are then brought up and laid on the sandstone blocks for the entire course of the fence, with the end of the first rail under the end of the second, the end of the second over the end of the third, and so on. The second layer of rails was then laid on the first, and the third on the second, up to the sixth layer. The thinnest rails are used at the bottom of the fence, so that the cracks there will be the smallest, and the thickest rails on top. The result so far will be a split-rail fence without stakes and rider. To add these, the stakes, sharpened at one end, are driven into the ground at an angle, with the bottoms about two feet from the bottom rails and the tops crossing over the lapping ends of the top rails. Finally the riders are then laid in the forks of the stakes. The result is a hog-proof fence with a bed about five feet wide.

This type of fence, of course, was wasteful of both timber and land, two items that were fortunately plentiful in nineteenth-century Texas. The timber was obtained when the field was cleared; a common estimate was that it required 5040 rails to build a seven-rail fence around thirty-six acres. At the same time, a rail fence that enclosed a forty-acre field was estimated to occupy about one acre of that field. For many farmers, the rail fence was their greatest capital investment, and the cost of rail fencing was much discussed in the journals of the late 1850's. A writer in the *Southern Cultivator* estimated the cost of a rail fence around a thirty-six acre field to be $176.[5] This was a considerable sum when a hired man earned $1.00 per day and a log house could be built for $40. The rail fence also required constant maintenance. The corners had to be kept clean and the entire fence had to be kept free of overhanging branches, which would cause water to drip on the fence and rot to set in.

In the German Hill Country of Texas, where timber was scanty and limestone plentiful, many rock field fences survive. These are dry-stacked fences; that is, the rocks are stacked together without mortar. They were usually built by the farmer and his family as the field was cleared of rock

before the initial plowing, and there are many stories of fences built by wives and daughters. If men were hired to lay a fence using the farmer's stones, the cost was $.10 to $.12 a yard, according to a letter written from Comal County in 1870. If the hired men provided the stones, the cost was $.35 a yard.[6] An ox-drawn sledge was used to haul the rock to the edge of the field, where it was piled along a shallow trench, usually about two feet wide and a foot deep. This trench was the foundation for the wall. The largest flat rocks were bedded in it, then the next largest laid crosswise on the top of them, and so on until a height of between three and four feet was reached, which is about as high as a man can conveniently lift a heavy rock from ground level. The wall was finished out with a layer of flat stones along the top to shed water, and additional loose stones were sometimes laid on these flat stones for added weight. Two things were desirable in a good stone field fence: a smooth face, which made it difficult for animals to clamber over it; and interlocking stones, that is, some stones going all the way through the fence, which gave it strength. There was always a tendency for fence-builders to build two smooth faces and then fill the space in between with rubble, but this technique did not provide the stability given by interlocking stones. Spaces between the larger stones were filled with smaller stones and chips, until a smooth surface was achieved.

Fencing for the cowpen and horsepen presented an entirely different problem to the farmer from the field fence: that of confining large and powerful animals in a small space. Strength and stability were needed, and the solution was usually a "pole fence," made of solid panels of cedar rails laid up horizontally between stoutly set pairs of posts. A good pole fence is between five and six feet high, and many are still in use today. The posts are between four

Details of pole fence (*Williamson Co.*)

Mortised rail fence (*Denton Co.*)

183

Pole fence and Longhorns (*Goliad Co.*)

Pole Fence (*Williamson Co.*)

Ornamental picket yard fence (*Winedale*)

Cow pen made of cedar pickets and poles (*Bell Co.*)

Picket and hog-wire lot fenced and stile (*Brazos Co.*)

Pine picket fence at Miss Ludell's (*Nacogdoches Co.*)

184

and six inches in diameter, and are set two to three feet in the ground in pairs, with about six feet between each pair of posts. The space between the two posts in each pair is not more than four inches. The poles, seven feet long and three to four inches in diameter, cut from cedar saplings, are then dropped between the pairs of posts with their ends overlapping, forming a wall of alternate posts and cracks. The two posts are then lashed together at the top, in the early days with rawhide strips and later with smooth wire. The result is a cheap, almost impenetrable solid wooden wall that will not only restrain cattle and horses but could be a much more handsome ornament to the suburban backyard than the chain-link fence.

In Central Texas, horsepen gates are constructed on a simple but effective principle. The posts supporting the gates are extremely heavy and well set, and the gates themselves are made of flat boards mortised into heavy round poles. The gate is hinged to the gatepost by means of two iron rings slipped over the top and bottom of the gatepole and spiked into the gatepost, while the bottom of the gatepole revolves in a round depression scraped out of a flat piece of sandstone. In the Hill Country, perhaps due to the Mexican influence, palisade pens, corrals, and chutes are more common than the horizontal-pole variety. These are made from heavy, straight cedar posts, four to six inches in diameter, set in the ground side by side two to three feet deep. The tops of these poles are wired together for added strength.

Hill Country horse and cowpens were sometimes built from limestone in the same way that field fences were, although the walls were built up five or five-and-a-half feet high, with the builders working from the back of a wagon to add the last foot and a half. Gates and gateposts for these stone pens were constructed in the same way as those for

wooden pens in Central Texas. In both cases the two tall gateposts were sometimes braced apart by a board or rail of posts. This board, which is found on modern gateless "ranch" gates and cattleguards carrying a smaller board with the owner's name, or sometimes a cow skull, was far from ornamental where a working corral was involved. It braced the gateposts against the pull exerted by the weight of the gates and kept the gates themselves from sagging. Gateposts were also braced with rocks placed in the posthole, one at the base of the hole on the side of the post away from the gate, the other just under the surface of the ground on the side toward the gate. An old gatebuilder's trick, demonstrated to this writer by Delphine Hinze and Ronald Klump of Winedale, was to make a double gate as one solid panel, hang it, level it, then saw it in half and add the two endpoles to each half. This insured an even, matching hang that would be almost impossible to obtain if each half were hung separately.

The traditional garden fence, before the advent of chicken wire, was almost invariably a palisade fence of some type. Its purpose was to protect the tender young shoots of beans, cabbages, and turnips from varmints, especially rabbits, and it had to be a barrier that they could not squeeze through or tunnel under. Slender saplings, about four feet high, pointed at each end and driven into the ground side by side, usually served the purpose. Since the saplings were not strong enough to support a hanging gate, a stile gate, built on the same principle as a panel in a pole fence but set up so that the poles could be slipped out of the top, was used. A more substantial and higher fence could be made from sawmill waste—the rounded sides cut from logs in a sawmill—if it were available. The waste was pointed and driven into the ground, but since it was thin and flimsy, strips of it were woven through the pickets at the base and top of the fence.

The yard fence was the most ornamental of all farm fences. It was always a picket fence, with the pickets nailed to two parallel nailers (the boards onto which the pickets are nailed) which in turn were nailed to posts set about eight feet apart. A picket fence is laid out starting with the gates; the two front gateposts are set, then the rear and side gates, if any, are located, then the corner posts and then the intermediate posts. The posts are usually four feet above the ground, and the bottom and top nailers are set into mortises cut in the outer face of the posts. Frequently a dirt-board is nailed below the bottom nailer, on the outside of the post, and the bottom of the pickets rest on the dirt-board; this protects the pickets themselves from rotting. The sections of dirt-board can be easily and cheaply replaced as they deteriorate.

The earliest picket fences were made with pickets rived from logs and pointed with a saw, usually by having their top slashed at a forty-five degree angle. Occasionally, a spike or diamond-shaped point was cut into the top of each picket, probably in imitation of the ornamentation on cast-iron fences. Gateposts and cornerposts were frequently sheathed with boards capped with moulding to give them the appearance of masonry posts. By the 1870's, when the jigsaw came into general use in Texas, lumber mills and sash-and-door factories were turning out ornamental jigsawed pickets with elaborately curved points, and these began to supersede the homemade variety. Many of the latter are still in place on Texas farms, and are much in demand by restorationists, who have been known to pay as much as a dollar apiece for them.

Pickets were not always flat, and a popular picket fence of the 1890's incorporated square 1" x 1"'s of differing lengths to create panels with graceful arcs along the top. A variation of this type, which must have taken all winter to build, still fences the yard of the Wilbur Marburger farm near Warrenton, in Fayette County: instead of being nailed to the top and bottom nailers, each 1" x 1" is carefully and tightly mortised through them.

Changes in fence laws, in agricultural practices, and in manufacturing technology have rendered virtually all of these traditional fences obsolete. Barbed wire, chicken wire, hog wire, and electric fencing keep animals in their place now, and the price of wood has made picket fencing unavailable to anyone but Houston millionaires playing weekend farmer. But on some isolated farmsteads the old fence lines and patterns can still be traced by the hackberry trees that came up along them or by piles of rotting rails, and when they can they serve to remind us of the infinite variety and ingenuity that went into building these ubiquitous and necessary structures.

NOTES:

[1] Karl von Solms-Braunfels, *Texas, 1844-1845*, translator unnamed (Houston: The Anson-Jones Press, 1936), p. 112.

[2] *Southern Cultivator* 13:3 (March, 1855), 1-2.

[3] *Ibid.*

[4] *Southern Cultivator* 13:5 (May, 1855), 155.

[5] *Ibid.*

[6] Oscar Haas, *History of New Braunfels and Comal County, 1844-1946* (Austin: The Steck Company, 1968), p. 46.

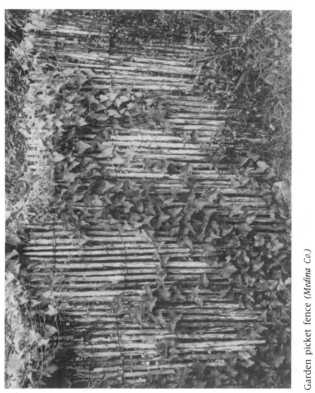

Garden picket fence (*Medina Co.*)

Pole fence (*Williamson Co.*)

Cedar Palisade corral fence (*Sutton Co.*)

187

Palisade corral fence tied with iron pipe (*McCulloch Co.*)

Rock fence (Blanco Co.)

188

Gates

C. W. Wimberley

Stopping and getting out to open and close a gate has always been a fretful chore to the country traveler. Today it's an impossible task. Nowadays when you can bank, eat, see a movie, or go to church without leaving the car's seat, who the devil is going to leave that seat to open a gate? That's how cattle-guards were born. Using the wreckage from several gates, an Edison-inclined owner devised a contraption a car could run over with only minor damage and a cow would have better sense than to walk into, and he called the thing a cattle-guard.

Over in the hills of San Saba County, Mack Yates had a means of slowing the speedsters on his ranch. Like many of the oilmen ranchers, Mack had his herds of cattle, horses, and buffalo, and many western innovations on his ranch, but he is most often remembered for his own brand of bump gates. The gate proper was made of two-inch timber and operated on three of the biggest cedar logs to be found. For years the cedar-cutters in that part of the country hauled all their "Yates Posts"—straight heart logs over twenty feet long and with tops measuring twelve or more inches in diameter—to Mack for a premium price. These gates operated well with the proper bump and a smooth followthrough, but, when hit too fast, they would retaliate by denting fenders and smashing lights fore and aft, and leaving deep scratches alongside for any who attempted quick escapes. And, if the gate was damaged in the incident, Mack rewarded the offender with a boot in the pants. His size twelve's were no idle threat.

Some fifty years ago, when most roads were caliche and cars were automobiles, people didn't have speed troubles. Back in my part of the hills, the "Dutchmans" kept drivers down to a reasonable gate-opening speed. "Dutchmans" were mounds of dirt the oldtime commissioners built across the roads at intervals on grades to divert water from the roadbed. After your Model T had hit one of these "Dutchmans" while your foot was hung in the carburetor, it was always a good idea to stop and count the kids before leaving the scene.

Along these old county roads each property line was usually marked by some sort of gate. Perhaps as old as barbed wire itself, the wire gap was the most worrisome of the lot. With an old harness hame or bowed stick to lever it shut with taunt wires, it remains picturesque Old West. As late as the 1930's, by using these "saddle gaps," you could ride from Lone Grove to Tow Valley along the old wagon road to Lampasas. But, as people began to be more concerned about deer leases than neighboring, these gaps were closed. Now that travel in the area is restricted to county roads, deer are more abundant, and old neighbors continue to speak to one another, if they happen to meet in town.

Along about that time, an old saddle gap on the divide between Falls Creek and the Little Llano River was closed under different circumstances. For forty years, Jim Tow had courted a lady who lived across the hills; at least, he seemed to have figured it that way. The lady lived on the

Little Llano and Jim lived at the headwater of Falls Creek, and theirs was the last link of an old party-line telephone. After each weather spell, Jim would phone over to compare rainfall and temperature changes in the two locations. Over the years, the affair had advanced to the stage where Jim saved his grease and rancid lard for her to render into soap on the halves. Every month or three, he would ride over with a bundle of clothes to be patched or have buttons replaced and a Sunday shirt to be ironed for a reasonable fee.

For several days following a rain storm, Jim had been unable to raise an answer on the phone, so he saddled up to see if the line was down. He found the trouble not too far from the lady's house. The line was not only down but it had also been rolled up most of the way across his pasture.

At the saddle gap he found "a fellar a-tyin' up the gap good and tight with telegraph wire that was half mine."

As Jim told it, "He looks up but don't stop workin' an' says: 'Be Jim Tow, I reckon, an' me, I'm the man of the house on this side of the fence now, an' I allow my woman won't be washin' er sewin' for anybody except me from now on—so's we won't be needin' this gate er phone anymore.' An' I don't say nothin' an' he keeps on tyin' wire."

"You know, he was the ugliest kind of a lookin' little cuss. If'n she wanted to get married, why didn't she say so to me. I could of beat that for her. He shore don't look like much to me."

During the depression years, my brother-in-law, Guy Alexander, built some gates that would be a worthy reminder of those moneyless days. Guy was the kind of fellow that could do more with a double-bit ax than most jack-legged carpenters could with a whole box full of tools. One blade of his ax was dressed thin from the eye to the edge with a file, then honed smooth with a wet-stone. The handle was scraped with glass until it had the proper spring-in-the-hand when used. Then it was soaked in linseed oil with a washer used to wedge it properly in the eye. No one but Guy used this ax or so much as laid their hands on it. In a tight, I have seen him field dress an old doe with his ax. With a short blow he could sink it to the eye in green cedar. For dry cedar or other timber, he carried another blunt-edged ax.

For his gate Guy selected a cedar with a heavy branch extending at an angle from the body. This tree was cut several inches below the fork and topped at about ten feet. Small cedar poles were used as gate panels with the forked branch serving as a cross brace supporting the panels. The butt end of the tree was set in a hole beside the gate post and the top was wired loosely to the post allowing the gate to swing, after a fashion.

Blacksmith and tinker of sorts, Great-Grandpa Adare found time in his old age to build gates on his place to suit his taste. Fashioned from slab lumber and hewn cedar, they were something to see. Wagon axles with hub spindles fixed to the gate post served as hinges. This post was tenoned at the top and a long bowed log with a hole in it was placed atop it. The small end of this log was attached by a chain to the end of the gate and a trough on the butt end of this log held enough rocks to balance the weight of the cumbersome gate, making it swing quite easily. Each time these gates were opened or closed, the tenon at the top of the gate post moaned and groaned like a tom cat with his tail caught under a rocking chair.

Sitting beside Grandpa Lawrence in his hack and being his gate-opener as we rode from his place on Pin Oak down the old road to Wimberley and on to San Marcos is one of my fondest memories. Grandpa had a way of always

Bump Gate
(Crockett Co.)

Cattle guard

making a boy feel right big. He let me open the gates that were easy to handle, and, on the mean ones, he would allow me to drive the team through. The fact that Grandpa could talk old Mox and Bill through a gate from start to stop at a distance of forty feet had no bearing on this matter.

The gate at the old Decker place was my favorite and a standard for that era. The lumber used in making these old gates was of a grade that seemed only to weather gray with age, and hardware was usually made from worn wagon tires by some local blacksmith. The hinges consisted of two long strips bolted to the gate and hung by the eye on male spikes driven into the gate post and a figure "4" latch held it shut. At the Decker gate, the top male spike was slightly right of center, causing it to swing open in a rising arc and, therefore, close on its own weight. By hanging on, a six-year-old boy could get a free ride on this gate while it swung shut, and a teeth-rattling jar if he failed to step off before it slammed against the post.

During Great-Grandpa's earlier days, travelers going up the Blanco from Wimberley entertained another shade of memories for Bill Adare's pole gate. This antiquated contraption of inconvenience consisted of a series of small poles held parallel to the ground by a series of holes augered through a large gate post standing on either side of the road. After climbing down from his wagon, the traveler had to remove each of these poles by sliding it through one of the gate posts and stacking it beside the fence, one by one, before leading his team through the opening. By the time he had replaced each of these poles to its proper position and had regained his seat in the wagon, the traveler was certain to feel that he had had his dose of self-control for the day.

Being sticklers to the code of leaving a gate as you found it, most people closed Grandpa's gate, with the exception of

an occasional Saturday nighter returning from Fischer's Store. Sometimes one of these riders would try to jump the poles with splintering effects, or would merely leave them scattered about in the dark. Either event could add substance to sermons on the evil of drink preached at Wayside Schoolhouse and in Wimberley on second Sundays.

According to my Dad's memories, the first attempt to devise a cattle-guard in this area took place at a site some two miles from San Marcos on the Old Wimberley road during the late, late 1890's. As is often the case, the name of this creative genius has been lost to time and it is just as well.

From logic that only he could fathom, he figured that a steep barrier in the middle of the road would serve to stop and turn livestock. So, he set about to fill one side of the road with a long slope gradually rising from ground level to the height of three or four feet, then dropping back to ground level within a distance of about four feet. Parallel to and at opposite hand, he filled the other side of the road with another slope.

Needless to say, cattle paid no heed to this cattle-guard, but a short-fused teamster did. One run through this cattle-guard and on his return trip, he skirted it, and cut a hole in the fence to create a new bend in the Wimberley road that remained intact long after the reason for its existence had been forgotten.

The first cattle-guard I can remember seeing was in the Wimberley area. This guard consisted of an open pit four feet wide and three feet deep, extending across the road bed with the fence anchored to posts at either end. Two flat-bottomed trough-like affairs made of two-inch lumber bridged this pit. With a careful, well-aimed approach, this cattle-guard was a surmountable obstacle. Get a bit reckless and you could very well end up with one of your Model T's front wheels hanging in the pit while the other tried to climb an anchor post. In any event, the old milk cows or savvy brood sows soon learned to trot these cattle-guards with more ease than most drivers.

In time this type of cattle-guard was revised to be bridged with a lateral framework of poles or two-inch lumber stood on edge, secured at two- to four-inch intervals across the width of the guard. With that improvement you could zip your Model A across this guard at a fair rate of speed without losing the muffler or having a blow-out, that is, if it was a relatively new structure. Heavy traffic and age could turn a cattle-guard into a booby trap.

After prosperity began to smile on Texas, the cattle-guard blossomed in all sorts of elaborate forms and fashions. The proven standard and most practical of the lot consisted of a concrete walled pit of various dimensions bridged with two-inch parallel piping set at four-inch intervals. Old tubing from boilers which had seen service in the Texas oilfield drilling rigs often did its final service imbedded in cattle-guards of this area. The fence anchor posts were often set three or four feet from the end of the guards with sloped concrete piers or metal grill-work closing these ends to discourage goats and other animals from attempting to skirt these guards.

Cattle-guards were a relatively new innovation in my corner of Llano County when my brother-in-law, Herman, rode old Blue down to one of the shindigs held in Lone Grove. During the course of the evening he must have visited the jug of moonshine the boys had hid in the bushes a mite too often for, with a hoot and a holler, Herman jumped in the saddle and headed home in a high lope. Recent rains had left the road in proper condition to record each hoofprint for all the neighbors to see just how old Blue had loped up the center of the road, clearing each cattle-guard with the ease of an English jumper—all the way home.

The Devil's Hatband in the Lone Star State: The Introduction of Barbed Wire in Texas

Robert J. Duncan

They say that heaven is a free range land,
Goodbye, goodbye, O fare you well;
But it's barbed wire for the devil's hat band;
And barbed wire blankets down in hell.
(Cowboy song)

A nostalgia lingers yet for that unfenced world of long ago. Few, if any, can personally remember it, but it's in our collective memory, our literature and our songs. The theme threads through some of J. Frank Dobie's early works. In fact, one of his books was entitled *On the Open Range.* In an early Texas Folklore Society volume, edited by Dobie, Jovita Gonzalez tells of an old vaquero to whom paradise was the open prairie. The vaquero said, "*Cuando vino el alambre, vino el hambre.* (With the coming of wire, hunger came.)"¹ Surely many ranchers and cowboys have yearned for the life of the open range to return. One cowman put it this way: "If I knew a country where it would, I'd go there if I had to go in a canoe."²

Until the late nineteenth century, the open range was the *status quo* in West Texas and the Panhandle, as it was all over the western United States. Many cattlemen owned little or no land. They grazed and watered their stock on public land or on other people's land. There were few fences because of the dearth of wood and stone. By the 1870's the boundary lines between cattle territories in West Texas had been pretty well agreed on, and it was up to the cowboys to see that the stock stayed on their own home range. Cattle did drift around, but were sorted out each spring at the big round-up.

The Federal Homestead Law was enacted in 1862. It gave homesteaders 160 acres of land for a nominal fee if they would live on the property and cultivate it for at least five years. As farmers (and civilization) moved westward across the continent, they were stymied when they emerged from the timberland of the East. There was nothing to build fences with, and they had to have fences to protect their fields from roaming cattle and buffalo.

Some farmers experimented with different thorn bushes and hedges, but these took several years to grow, were susceptible to fire and locust, and were not movable. Many types were not well suited to the western climate or soil. For a while there was a thriving business in bois d'arc seed, which sold for as much as five dollars a pound. The term *nester* was applied to the farmer because his homeplace, with its surrounding hedge fence to retain his livestock, when viewed from a distant ridge, resembled a bird nest.³ Smooth wire was used to some extent, but livestock experienced no pain when they pushed against it and would, therefore, often break the fences down. Some newcomers tried to make do with a fence consisting of "one wire and a dog" to protect their property. Dobie says that Captain Mifflin Kenedy used smooth wire in 1872 to fence the first big pasture in Texas, and that Richard King followed his example the next year. Planks from Florida were shipped in and used for some fencing in the 1870's.⁴

At least two Texans had experimented with wire fencing

197

materials in the 1850's. William Meriwether, in New Braunfels, was issued a patent in November, 1853, for a fence consisting of undulating single strand plain wires and a wooden rail. The wire was made in a wavy shape to compensate for expansion and contraction caused by temperature changes.

John Grenninger, a Swiss who worked in an iron foundry in Austin, owned an orchard and garden about the size of half a city block. The board fence that enclosed the garden was sometimes broken through by stray cattle. Some say there were occasionally human trespassers, too. In 1857, Grenninger added a wire or two to the fence and attached some hoop iron and jagged metal pieces, perhaps some broken glass. Grenninger was not well liked, and his neighbors resented the fence. He never tried to patent his fence; the idea of doing so probably never occurred to him. He was murdered in 1862.[5]

Several people around the country were experimenting with barbed wire ideas. In 1867, a patent was issued to Alphonso Dabb for a picket strip of spikes to be attached to a fence, but his application did not mention animal trespassers. The same year, patents were issued to Lucien B. Smith for a single strand wire with barbed spools attached and to William Hunt for wire with a rotating spur. Not much, if anything, was done commercially with either of these ideas, although they became important later in patent litigation.

Henry M. Rose was granted a patent in May, 1873, for a wooden strip with metal points driven into it, to be used as a fence attachment to control "breachy" cows. His invention was displayed at the De Kalb, Illinois, county fair in 1873. Three local men who were later to become major figures in the barb wire industry—Joseph Glidden, Jacob Haish and Isaac Ellwood—studied the exhibit, then each

went home and began experimenting with barbed wire. Ellwood soon realized that Glidden's version was superior to his, so he paid Glidden $265 to become his partner. They called their venture the Barb Fence Company. Haish continued his work independently.

Joseph Glidden is known as the inventor of barbed wire because he developed the first practical commercially produced wire and established the first factory. Glidden, himself a farmer, knew firsthand the problems of fencing. In experimenting with ways to lock barbs in a lateral position on a single strand of wire, he hit upon the idea of twisting a second smooth wire around the one with the barbs. This not only locked the barbs in place, it also allowed the finished wire to compensate for thermal expansion and contraction by twisting tighter or looser rather than by expanding or contracting horizontally.

Glidden made the first strips of barbed wire in his kitchen, using a coffee grinder to twist the wire. With the help of three boys, he could produce fifty pounds a day. He established his factory a few months later; in 1874, ten thousand pounds of barbed wire were made and sold. By 1876, production of barbed wire had jumped to nearly three million pounds a year. By 1880, production was to exceed eighty million pounds per year. The huge growth was almost unbelievable. One day Glidden received an order for a hundred tons of wire. "He was dumfounded and telegraphed to the purchaser asking if his order should not read one hundred pounds.[6]

The De Kalb wire factories began buying so much plain wire that, in 1876, Charles Washburn of the Washburn and Moen Company, smooth wire producers in Worchester, Massachusetts, decided to investigate. He visited De Kalb and later bought Glidden's interest for $60,000 and a twenty-five cent royalty for every hundred pounds of

Crandal's Champion, or Zigzag

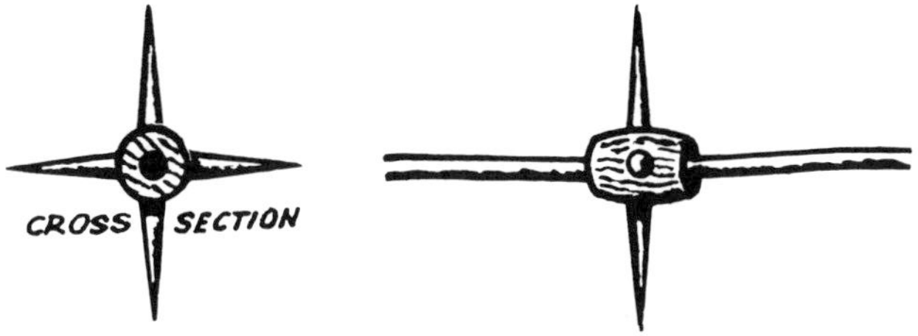

Smith's Spool and Spurs

Glidden's The Winner

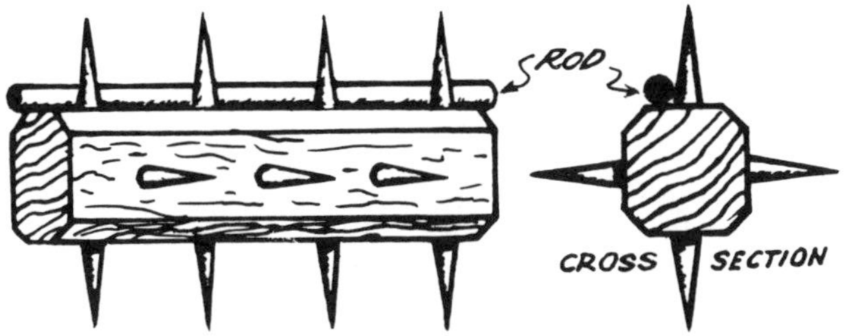

Rose's Wooden Rail

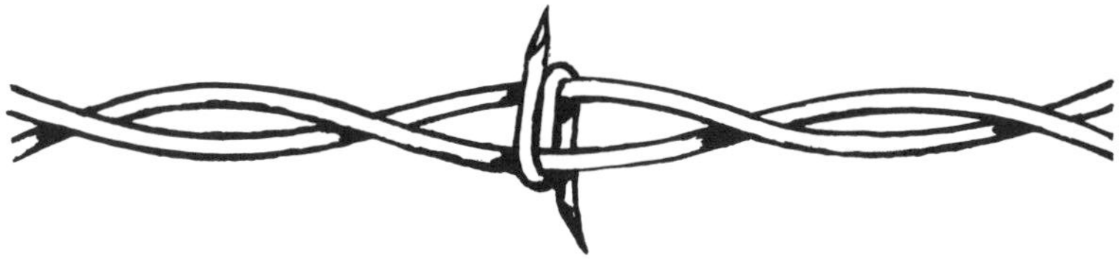

Hunt's Spur Wheel

Haish's "S" Barb

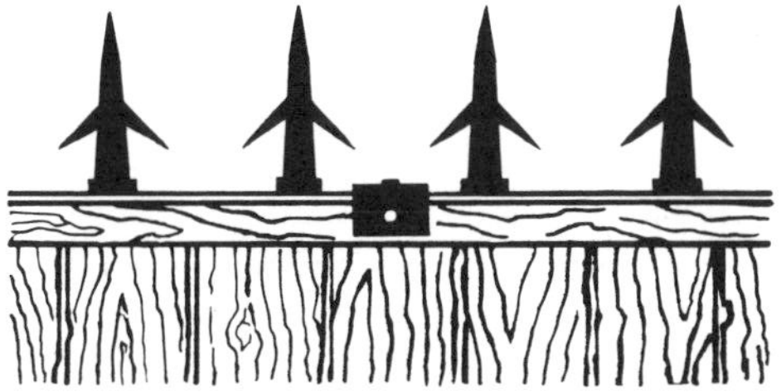

Dabb's Picketed Strip

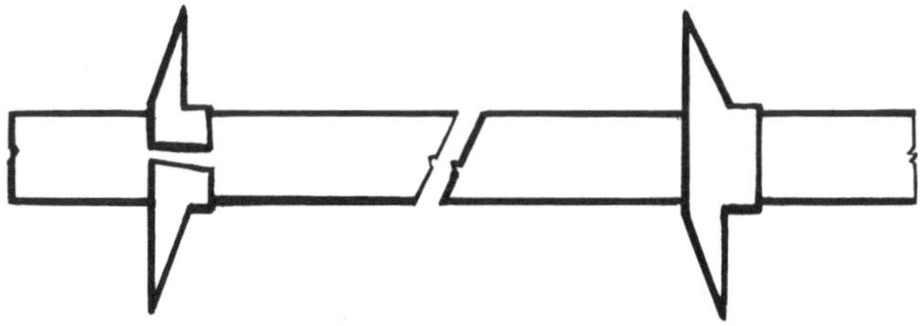

Brink Flat or Brink's Buckle

Fence drawings *by Ben Carlton Mead*

199

barbed wire made.

Glidden and Ellwood considered Texas their major potential market. In 1875, they sent Henry Sanborn to Texas. "At Gainsville, he sold the first spool of barbed wire ever sold in the state."7 He sold about thirty more spools in north central Texas. Soon he and J. P. Warner, the other general agent, were selling wire by the carload in Texas. Warner sold a carload to the Webb brothers in Austin and Sanborn sold one to Coleman, Mathis and Fulton, at Rockport, to be used in enclosing a huge pasture. They established a sales office in Houston and were very successful.

John W. Gates was a "go getter." He was born in Turner Junction, Illinois, in 1855. He took a six-month commercial college course, and, at age nineteen, he bought half-interest in a hardware store. He saw the market for barbed wire, so he went to De Kalb and brashly offered to become Ellwood's partner. Ellwood must have been amused, but he was apparently also impressed, because he hired Gates to sell barbed wire in Texas.

There was much resistance to the use of barbed wire in Texas. Many merchants would not sell it and most cattlemen thought it was too vicious. Shanghai Pierce was a prominent eccentric cattleman who was very outspoken, but he voiced the sentiments of many when he said, "It may keep 'em in, by God! But my cattle would cut themselves and die from screwworms, and I'll be damned if I treat my critters that way."8 Many cattlemen didn't think horses or cattle would ever get used to barbed wire fences.

When John Gates arrived in Texas, he went directly to San Antonio, the gathering place of many old-time cattlemen. John, later nicknamed "Bet-a-Million" Gates, was a good talker. It has been speculated that he spent his days telling farmers and hardware merchants about the

advantages of barbed wire, and his evenings in card games with the cattlemen. Soon Gates realized that a demonstration would be necessary to sell much wire, so, showman that he was, he got permission to build a fence in the Military Plaza. He kept his plans secret. When the fence was completed, he announced that this fence could hold the wildest cattle in Texas, and he got the ranchers to bring in their roughest old longhorn steers. The cattlemen could not believe that this flimsy-looking fence could hold their steers, and neither could the steers. Gates made some wagers with the ranchers, then had the steers put in the pen. They made two or three wild dashes at the wire, then started milling around, having learned their lesson. A couple of men were sent in with flaming torches to stir them up. The steers charged again, but, of course, retreated. One fence post had been broken, but the wire had held. Gates won the bets and sold many miles of wire that night.

W. H. Richardson's father, a hardware merchant in Mexia, bought a carload of wire from Gates. The wire was four-pronged, coated with a sticky black paint and unevenly wound on wooden spools. Richardson junior says:

(At first) no one would unload the wire ... no one knew how to handle it. But Gates and my father arranged demonstrations and showed them how. My father built a chute up to the car door and secured the services of several more venturesome cowboys, some of whom were put in the car and the others at the end of the incline, and the unloading started. I remember one of the spools got away, or jumped the chute, struck one of the cowboys on the leg and tore half of his boot off. They all struck and went to a near-by saloon and were only persuaded to return when their spirits were attuned. ... But Gates got the job done. ... He certainly was a good talker, because my father got only five cents a spool for handling the stuff.9

Gates was selling lots of wire on this end of the line, and

Brace to support king posts

in De Kalb he was trying to renegotiate for a better commission. He was jealous of Sanborn and Warner's contract, which Ellwood renewed in January, 1877. Ellwood and Washburn refused to meet Gates' terms, so he angrily resigned. He went to St. Louis and formed the Southern Wire Company, to compete with Ellwood and Washburn. He kept in contact with most of his Texas customers and retained much of their business. Gates became the foremost of the "moonshine wire" makers, manufacturing without patents or license agreement. There were many wire patent cases in the courts and the very lucrative industry was in a great flux. Ellwood got an injunction against Gates, but before the papers could be served, Gates put his equipment on a barge and crossed the Mississippi River from the Missouri side to the Illinois side. Ellwood proceeded to have injunction papers drawn up and issued to Gates in Illinois, but he floated back across the river first. While this maneuver was just a showy delaying tactic, it inspired the other "moonshine wire" makers to make Gates their leader.

Ellwood and Washburn had been buying patent rights and increasing their position gradually. There were cases in the courts for many years, but in December, 1880, Ellwood and Washburn won a major case which established their rights to license other barbed wire makers and to collect damages for wire already produced. Finally, in 1881, Jacob Haish took out a license with them to continue producing his famous "S" Barb wire.

Ellwood and Washburn and Moen hired "Expostulators" to educate dealers to recognize the types of barbed wire that they made and licensed. These agents also discouraged the purchase of "moonshine wire" by reminding merchants that they could be held legally responsible for selling unlicensed wire. They also hired J. W. Millington to track

down "moonshiners," obtain proof against them and threaten to bring suit. Millington caused over a hundred "moonshiners" to stop operations "voluntarily." Suits were brought against many others.

Colonel Charles Goodnight told of his first jolting realization of how barbed wire was changing the country. In 1879, he rode over to meet the people at the Christian Colony. When he arrived, he discovered that because of language difficulties, the settlers were about to execute some peaceful Pueblo Indians, thinking they were Comanches. Goodnight explained their mistake, rescuing the grateful Pueblos. He went on to say:

I asked the old chief where they had been, and he said they had gone down by way of the Canadian River to the Reservation to trade with the Kiowas and had decided to take a short cut back to Taos. Then the old chief asked me a question that dumfounded me. "How do you get back to Taos?" I said, "You surely know the way back to Taos. Haven't you lived in this country all your life?" To which the old chief replied, "*Alambre! Alambre! Alambre! todas partes—Wire! Wire! Wire! everywhere.*"10

The Frying Pan ranch in the Panhandle, owned by Sanborn and Glidden, put up a barbed wire fence in 1882 around a 250,000 acre pasture. The XIT ranch was so huge it ordered the wire for its northern and its southern pastures from sources in two different states. Its northern pasture was fenced with Brinkerhoff flat ribbon barbed wire brought in by wagon from Trinidad, Colorado. Goodnight's JA ranch put up some fence in 1882. The Quitaque ranch was fenced in 1883, and the Tule ranch in 1883-84. Fences were springing up all over the cattle country. Many ranchers who had previously owned no land, bought land next to streams, homesteaded their headquarters and got their cowboys to homestead surrounding land. Some of them fenced land they didn't own yet, but planned to buy eventually.

A terrible drought hit West Texas in the summer of 1883. It was so dry many prairie fires broke out. As a result, cattle were starved for both water and grass. Fences made it difficult, and usually impossible, to move herds to the little water and grass that were available.

Many cattlemen still owned no land at all, just cattle. They were, of course, strongly in favor of the open range. Ranchers who owned large tracts were in favor of privately owned big fenced pastures. Most cowboys were against fencing because they saw it as a threat to their jobs. Farmers, who had been first to use barbed wire to fence out range cattle, now sometimes found that ranchers had fenced *them* in and that to get to town they had to cut fences from across public roads. The Texas Greenback Party came out against fences, seeing them as a symbol of monopoly.

The drought got worse, and by late summer the Fence Cutting War was on. One of the first fence cutting incidents reported in newspapers was in southwest Texas in early 1883. The fence cutters called themselves by such names as Javelinas, Owls, Mob No. 1, and Blue Devils. R. D. Holt says:

When once begun the trouble spread at an alarming rate. The offense was new in its character, extensive and rapid in development, secret in its methods yet found open support in many communities. Fence cutting was peculiarly a Texas craze. It began in the summer of 1883 as a regular, organized movement and spread like wildfire.[11]

Big Foot Wallace was right when he said, "'Bob' wire is startin' to play hell with Texas."[12] The fence cutters often posted armed guards and did their snipping in "broad open daylight." L. B. Harris in Tom Green County found nineteen miles of his fence cut—the wire had been clipped between each pair of posts. Often notes were left warning against rebuilding. Sometimes not-so-subtle hints were made by leaving a dangling hangman's noose, a freshly dug grave, or a coffin next to the cut fence. Five hundred miles of fence were destroyed at one time in Coleman County. In Brownwood, a mob of fence cutters took over the courthouse for one day.[13]

As Walter Prescott Webb has pointed out, it was difficult to tie the criminal to the crime. Since he had stolen nothing, he carried no incriminating evidence with him. The possession of a pair of wire clippers could make people suspicious, but, after all, they were also a legitimate tool used by the cowboys to maintain fences.

In January, 1884, Governor Ireland called a special session of the legislature because of the Fence Cutting War. They passed laws making fence cutting a felony and the fencing of public lands a misdemeanor. Generally, the fence builders had been victorious over the fence cutters. Before it came to an end, fence cutting had been reported in more than half of the counties of Texas and tens of millions of dollars worth of property had been destroyed.

There were outbreaks of fence cutting for the next several years. When it flared up in Navarro County in 1888, two undercover Texas Rangers, Ira Aten and Jim King, were sent there. They posed as farm laborers and got jobs picking cotton. Soon they learned who was doing the fence cutting. In a letter to a Ranger captain, Sergeant Aten said, "The fence-cutters themselves have told me that while a man was putting up his fence one day in a hollow a crowd of wire-cutters was cutting it back behind him in another hollow back over the hill."[14] Using dynamite, Aten "booby-trapped" some fences with bombs. Orders came from Austin to stop this activity and return to headquarters, but, by this time rumors about the bombs had put the quietus on the fence cutting. Webb notes that Aten was an unusual man, fearless, and with a fine wit. He says that when Aten was sent to arrest cattle thieves he recorded in his diary that he had increased his life insurance, but also oiled his six-shooter.

In some instances, kindness prevailed. In 1892, some farmers settled on the JA ranch. The ranch manager was trying to keep the settlers out, but he found himself furnishing them with milk cows and giving them work. During the drought of 1883, Doc Burnet at Gonzales couldn't stand the sight of his neighbors' cattle looking through the fence at the water in his pasture. He opened his gate to the cattle and then offered to roll up his fence for the duration of the drought.[15]

J. L. Vaughn, whose fences had been cut repeatedly, probably expressed the sentiments of many when he said he wished that "the man who invented barbed wire had it all wound around him in a ball and the ball rolled into hell."[16]

Many of the fences put up in the Panhandle and West Texas were not enclosures, but drift fences, usually running for many miles east and west to prevent the mingling of large herds from the north in winter.

The winters of 1885-86 and 1886-87 were severe, with repeated blizzards. Cattle from the north, trying to avoid the cold north wind, walked right into the drift fences in the Panhandle. The cattle would not turn and face the north wind, or try to go around the drift fences, which stretched for miles. They bunched up and were found later, smothered, starved or frozen, with "icicles hanging from their muzzles, eyes and ears."[17] One account says:

> They (had) gathered in bunches reaching as much as four hundred yards back from the fence.... At the storm's end their bodies were found piled against the wire, some of them standing stiffly upright, others looking as if they had bedded down in a swath of snow.[18]

A ranch foreman said, "There are big mounds of cattle, nothing visible but horns, for the snow had drifted over them and you are spared meantime the horrible sight of ... piles of carcasses."[19] One man from the LX ranch reportedly skinned 250 head per mile for thirty-five miles along a drift fence.[20]

The drift fence and the pasture fence were seen as part of the problem, along with the weather, contributing to the "big die-ups." There were renewed outcries against barbed wire. Some said it was inhumane and unnatural. People talked about how sharp the barbs were and how hard it was for livestock to see the wire before they were against it. The argument about screwworms was voiced again.

There was such an outcry against barbed wire that the manufacturers found it necessary to quickly modify designs to increase the visibility of the wire and to decrease its ability to inflict pain and do damage. Shorter barbs were introduced. In retrospect, much of the early wire was categorized as "vicious" and the later wire, which was designed to be seen rather than felt, was categorized as "obvious." Barbed wire collectors use this terminology still in their classification and identification of samples.

Ross's Four-Point, Scutt's Clip, and Underwood's Tack are good examples of the "vicious" type; Stubbe Plate, Brink-Martelle, and Champion Zigzag typify the "obvious" wires.

Wire sales continued slowly for a while and then, as tensions eased and ranchers saw that they could never return to the open range system, sales of "obvious" wire began to boom. Shanghai Pierce was even converted from an open range spokesman to a "big pasture" cattleman as he turned to barbed wire fencing. The development of the windmill made it possible to fence pastures that had no natural water holes or streams.

As the country settled, the barbed wire fence presented a

Stubbe-Plate

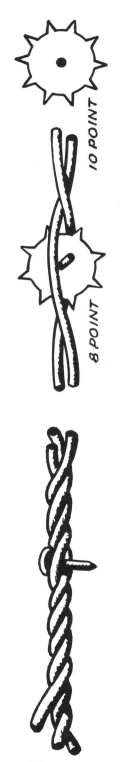

Brink-Martelle

10 POINT

8 POINT

Hodge's Spur-Rowel or Spur Wheel

Ross's Four-Point

Scutt's Clip

Underwood's Tack

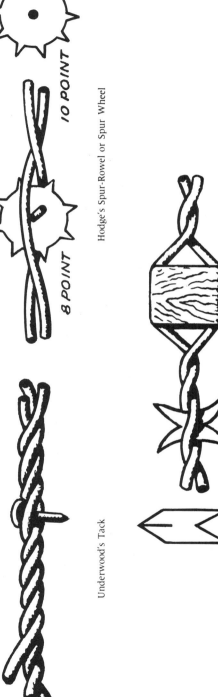

Scutt's Wooden Block

Fence drawings by Ben Carlton Mead

205

serious obstacle to raiding Indians. Fencing brought an end to cattle drives, forcing ranchers to depend upon the railroads to get their beef to market. It also allowed cattlemen to control breeding and develop blooded stock to replace the longhorn. It made winter feeding possible. High tensile strength wires have been developed in the last few years, and plastic coated barbed wire can be bought in any color.

In recent years the collecting of barbed wire has become a popular hobby. Patent records provide a means of identification of the more than 700 types. Some are, of course, very rare. The "barb-arians," as the collectors sometimes call themselves, appreciate the prominent role that barbed wire played, along with the six-shooter, the windmill, the railroad, and the Winchester, in the settling of the West.

After contemplating all this, one's thoughts return, with empathy, to that lonesome, nameless cowboy who yearned for a return to the simple, hard life of the open range and who said, "If I knew a country where it would, I'd go there if I had to go in a canoe."

NOTES:

[1]"Folklore of the Texas-Mexican Vaquero," *Texas and Southwestern Lore* (Austin: Texas Folk-Lore Society, 1927), PTFS Number VI, p. 8.

[2]Louis Pelzer, *The Cattlemen's Frontier* (Glendale: Arthur H. Clark, 1936), p. 248.

[3]Ramon F. Adams, *Western Words* (Norman: University of Oklahoma Press, 1944), p. 104.

[4]J. Frank Dobie, *A Vaquero of the Brush Country* (Dallas: The Southwest Press, 1929), p. 117.

[5]Jack Maguire, *Talk of Texas* (Austin: Shoal Creek Publishers, 1973), p. 39, and R. D. Holt, "The Introduction of Barbed Wire Into Texas and the Fence Cutting War," *West Texas Historical Association Year Book,* Vol. VI (June, 1930), p. 65. The name has been spelled, alternately, Grinninger and Grenniger.

[6]C. Boone McClure, "History of the Manufacture of Barbed Wire," *Panhandle-Plains Historical Review,* Vol. XXXI (1958), pp. 37-38. The whole issue is devoted to this article.

[7]Holt, p. 66. The rest of the information in this paragraph came from this same source.

[8]Chris Emmett, *Shanghai Pierce, A Fair Likeness* (Norman: University of Oklahoma Press, 1953), p. 137.

[9]This quotation has been reconstructed from parts quoted in Henry D. McCallum and Frances T. McCallum's *The Wire That Fenced the West* (Norman: University of Oklahoma Press, 1965), pp. 73-74, and Walter Prescott Webb, *The Great Plains* (Boston: Ginn and Company, 1931), p. 311.

NOTES (Continued)

[10]Harley True Burton, *A History of the J A Ranch* (New York: Argonaut Press Ltd., 1966), p. 93.

[11]Holt, p. 75.

[12]McCallum, p. 154, quoting an article from the *Austin American Statesman*, June 13, 1937.

[13]Wayne Gard, *Frontier Justice* (Norman: University of Oklahoma Press, 1949), Chapter 6: "The Fence Cutters," pp. 104-119. Virtually all of the information in this paragraph came from this source.

[14]Webb, *The Great Plains*, p. 314. Also see Gard, p. 115.

[15]See Burton, p. 96, for first incident; see Gard, pp. 113-114 for second.

[16]Webb, *The Great Plains*, p. 315.

[17]Lewis Nordyke, *Cattle Empire* (New York: William Morrow and Company, 1949), p. 69.

[18]McCallum, pp. 132-133.

[19]John Clay, *My Life on the Range* (Chicago: privately printed, 1924), p. 291.

[20]McCallum, pp. 133-134. Paul Patterson told me that his father, J. D. Patterson, took down the last drift fence in West Texas in about 1898. It was one hundred miles long and ran east and west, from north of Seminole into New Mexico.

Holding Water

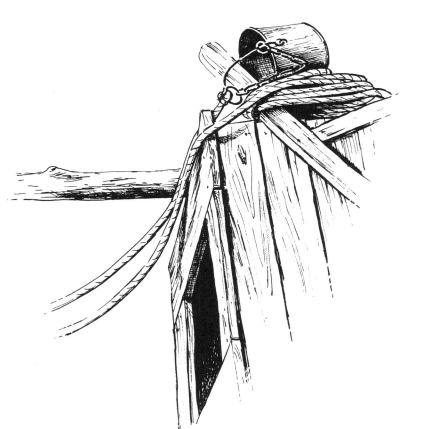

The most satisfying sound on the Plains was a smooth pumping windmill and the surge of a full pipe of water. The pipe ran from the windmill into the damp cool of the milk house, filled the deep concrete tank that held the drinking water, then poured out into the milk trough. Lard cans with rocks on their lids stood waist deep in the flowing water and cooled the milk and buttermilk and clabber and the butter wrapped in an old dishtowel. A small crack in the trough allowed just enough water to get to the floor to keep a damp spot for the dirt-dobbers.

The water then flowed out of the milk house into the horse trough, leaking enough water into a big concave disk blade for a few chickens and small cats. You could put a horse hair in that water and in a few days it would turn into a worm! Children swam in the horse trough, you could test leaky innertubes in it, and it was the favorite gathering place for the hands after supper. They sat around on the curbs rolling cigarettes and talking, and during thrashing time they would splash each other off with buckets of water.

Water ran out of the horse trough into a shallow calf trough that was about a foot deep and had some big rocks for the rescue of any small animals or chickens that might topple in. Late one hot summer afternoon a large bull snake stretched out across the entire width of the curb to cool his stomach and let a boy watch him. In good times the water ran out of the calf trough and down a little furrow toward the chicken house until somebody noticed and cut off the windmill. In bad times the windmill sucked air, and the green coated layer of mud in the bottom of the tanks caked, cracked, and curled up, and the people had to haul water in barrels from the river.

Vanes in the Wind: Art and Custom in Texas Windmills

James M. Day

"The windmills were spinning like bright dimes," wrote Allan Bosworth as his family approached Ozona in a covered wagon. The year was 1907 and Bosworth was five years old. Yet the image imbedded itself in his mind, and as the years passed he came to know that its meaning was life in that water-starved Southwest Texas country. He continued: "The windmills offered a point of reference, as lighthouses do for a ship at sea. . . . except for the windmill and a barbed-wire fence beside the road, there was no sign of human habitation."[1] Such scenes were repetitive in Texas in the century that began in 1860, and their meaning saturated many a lonesome mind and sank deep into the fiber of the people.

Though the earliest remembered existence of a windmill in Texas was in 1848 near Indianola, the great impetus for them came after 1860 when the Houston Tap and Brazoria Railroad started using them to help stay the thirst of their giant steam engines. By 1874 railroads across the state were popular consumers, as were towns and farms. Beginning in 1882 in Schleicher County, the windmill found its most consistent user, the ranch. At that point its stock went up. The windmills were all of wood at first, but in 1887 the manufacturers turned to an all-steel construction as demand increased. No one has estimated the number of windmills that dotted the Texas landscape at any one time, but their numbers grew substantially after 1915 when Aermotor started selling its self-oiling version of the pumper, and in 1928 some 36,500 windmill heads were

marketed in the Lone Star state. After 1930, with the advent of gasoline and electricity, the use of windmills declined to the point that only 3,000 were sold in the state in 1963.[2]

The first windmills in Texas were either of the Dutch or the German varieties with the difference being that the Dutch mill was on a stationary base and had a top section that rotated to meet the wind, while the German mill was constructed so the entire structure moved to meet the wind. Both mills had either four or six long arms that formed a wheel some fifty to one hundred feet in diameter.[3] Probably the Bullard windmill at Indianola belonged to one type or the other. That was the windmill which created such a "buzz of interest" in March, 1848, because it offered hope of providing a dependable flow of water from the shallow sands along the coast. The effort proved a failure when experimental digging revealed that salt polluted the water to the point that it was not usable.[4]

In *Mills of Yesteryear*, A. T. Jackson notes that the Dutch windmills spread from the port of Indianola to a restricted area where the Germans settled. The most notable of these Dutch windmills was the one built by Randolph Witte in 1856. Using millstones and mechanical parts shipped from Germany, Witte constructed his mill beside a creek about one mile out of Goliad. It was simply a case of old world construction on the American frontier. This windmill, used for grinding corn, was considered dependable as it operated throughout the Civil War. Afterward, Louis Albrecht purchased it and moved it to Coletto Creek. In 1870 Fred Meiss, Sr., became its owner and relocated it on Spring Creek in Victoria County where it operated for several decades. Appropriately it sat in the middle of a corn field.

Its main shaft was hewn from a tree twenty feet tall and fifteen inches in diameter. On the outer end of this shaft was attached the wind wings, while the inner end operated the two wheels used to turn the millstones. The two wheels, which were approximately twenty-one feet in diameter, had cogs and spokes made of oak, while green boards some twelve inches thick were selected, bent and fastened to make the outer rims. On the outside, logs were shaved and fastened together with wooden pegs. The mill was divided into two levels, each of which contained one of the gigantic wheels. The top floor was used for grinding the corn, while the bottom level was for sifting and storage. A detailed description of the mill's parts and operation is pertinent:

The two grinding rocks, nine inches thick and four feet in diameter, used to crush the corn to meal were on the top floor. The corn was fed into a 12-inch hole in the center of the top rock by a hopper. A crude elevator lifted the grain into the hopper, from which receptacle it fell into the millstone cavity. The top rock revolved on the bottom stationary one to grind the corn. The ¼-inch-deep grinding grooves in the stone carried the cornmeal to the outer edge of the millstone, where it fell into felt cups that carried it to a sifter. The power for the wheels, to run the stones and the sifter, came solely from the wind rotating the wings.

The whole top of the mill, where the wings were attached, turned. The four posts in the ground at intervals around the mill each had a frame with a spool attached. Rope connected with the top was wound around the spools from post to post, always from left to right, until the top turned the wings into the wind.'

Outside, the wooden framed wings, which were some forty feet long, had canvas sails stretched over them. The sails were adjusted to catch sufficient wind to turn the shaft

while the mill was operating. When the wind became too strong the sails were hauled in and tied, and ropes were fastened to the wings to keep them from twirling. But when the wind was right, this Dutch windmill could grind out some five hundred pounds of corn meal in six days. It became an important institution in the community.

Its preservation was not always easy though, for storms sometimes lashed at the structure. Notable were those of September, 1875, and August, 1886, the first of which blew off one of the wings and carried it some two miles away, while the latter blew it down completely. Fred Meiss and Otto Fink rebuilt the mill, but shortened the wings to increase its chances of survival during future hurricanes. This Witte-Albrecht-Meiss Dutch windmill survived, and in 1935 the Meiss heirs donated it to the Morning Study Club of Victoria for preservation. It now rests in Memorial Square in Victoria, a monument to the windmilling lore of Texas.[6]

In De Witt County, Moses Rankin built a Dutch windmill in 1869 near his home on the Victoria-Gonzales road, and at Yorktown a man named Huff did the same thing. Huff became such an institution in his community that he was known as "Windmiller Huff." Both mills were used for grinding of corn into meal, and there is no reason to think that their appearance differed substantially from the Witte-Albrecht-Meiss windmill.[7] Though Dutch windmills would pump water, most of those built in Texas were designed for grinding. Since West Texas needed a machine to pump water, and since it had a sparsity of wood materials used in Dutch windmills, an adaptation was needed.

The change came in 1854 when David Halliday of Ellington, Connecticut, registered a patent for a light-weight streamlined wooden windmill, one which called for a skeleton of a tower when compared to the Dutch

windmills. Manufacture began shortly afterward and only a short time elapsed before windmills of this sort began to dot the Texas horizon. Railroads were the first users. On March 30, 1860, the Houston Tap and Brazoria Railroad contracted with James Mitchell of Galesburg, Illinois, for the use of his patented "wind wheel" on their line from Houston to Wharton. Mitchell received $375 for relinquishing the rights for the company to "manufacture and use" his patent. This experiment was short-lived owing to the intrusion of the Civil War, which caused abandonment of the railroad.[8]

Windmills did not become popular in Texas until 1880. During those two intervening decades several Texans constructed their own homemade versions of the windmill. One consisted of an old wagon wheel and axles. Boards were nailed on the spokes of the wheel to form sails, and a spike was driven into the hub to serve as a pin for the connecting rod to the pump. The wheel with its axle was nailed to the top of a tree, and with the first puff of wind the sails went to work. It was not a thing of beauty, but it was cheap, and it pumped good water.[9]

Between 1854 and 1881 many changes occurred in the construction and manufacture of windmills and there were many companies to produce the varieties. Halladay's invention was sold by the U.S. Wind Engine Company and marketed under the brand name "Standard." Fairbanks, Morse and Company first offered the Wheeler-Eclipse in 1867, and it became the most popular Texas model. Then in 1884 came the Aermotor. Other varieties used in Texas were the Flint, Walling, Walpole, Star, Air King, Monitor, Samson, Jim Dandy, Axtell, Baker, Air Royal, Challenge, Bird, and Iron Turbine. Later came the Dempster, a machine geared to compensate for variations in wind speed.[10]

The biggest single advancement was the all-metal windmill first patented in 1872 by Mast, Foos and Company, but made popular in the late 1880's by Aermotor. Shortly after Aermotor appeared on the market, the same company offered an all-steel galvanized tower which could be tilted for ease in servicing the wind wheel. In 1915 Aermotor also introduced the other innovation that was significant. Prior to that time the mills had to be greased often, but Aermotor introduced automatic oiling by encasing the gears so that they could run in oil and would have to be greased only one time a year.[11]

Windmills found immediate acceptance in the towns and on the ranches and farms. Sterling City, northeast of San Angelo, laid claim to having more windmills per acre than any other town in the world. In town, and it was not a large community, there were some three hundred windmills in operation at one time, while an expert, Sam Simmons, the windmiller, estimated that Sterling County had one windmill per 640 acres. Simmons likes to tell about the woman tourist, an easterner, who stopped by Sterling City, and after seeing the windmills, asked, "Where do you get all the wind for all those fans?"[12]

Many West Texas towns laid claim to being the windmill capital of the world, and Midland was no exception. It was larger in population than Sterling City and it had more windmills, an estimated three thousand at its peak. Paul Patterson was just a youngster when he first saw these windmills at Midland. In a Rock Island wagon loaded with six people, the Pattersons approached the town and saw the windmills. It was a marvelous sight until an older brother, Sog, called Paul off to one side to warn him that they might all smother to death. He argued that there were so many windmills in town that there "won't be air enough left for us to breathe." Paul went into a panic and did not want to believe the impending doom. He hoped Sog had overestimated the situation, but the closer they came to town, the more windmills they saw. These breath robbers were there, "bunches of them, herds of them. All busy wheeling up precious air."

Patterson decided to save what wind he had, so he slammed his eyelids shut to close out the terrifying picture only to find the image clearer than ever. He was thankful when they camped overnight about a mile out of town and he again was grateful next morning when he saw a "high, rolling cloud, red and boiling" at the top edge of the horizon. It turned out to be a sandstorm rolling in off the Staked Plains. Since the sandstorm hit Midland before the Pattersons got there, young Paul noted with relief that the storm provided enough air for windmills and humans alike. As they passed through town, Patterson had great delight in watching the wildly wheeling windmills. "I took a sadistic pleasure in seeing them wheel into the wind like bulls on the prod only to have to turn away with their tails tucked, to escape being wheeled to pieces," he later wrote. No youngster was ever more appreciative of a sandstorm than Paul Patterson that day he wagoned through the windmills of Midland.[13]

Every town had at least one public windmill and some had more. Ozona had a windmill that worked atop a magnificent seventy-five foot tower. It was one of those that Allan Bosworth saw shining in the sun like bright dimes. The waterworks systems of many Texas communities evolved from these public windmills. Rankin did it by private enterprise. In 1922 Ira Yates drilled two wells in Rankin over which he erected windmills used in putting in a water system for the south side of town. R. C. Harlan did the same thing with three windmills for the north side. With the passage of years they added other wells

and windmills, even though the water was alkali and never palatable. But it was all the people had until the city of Rankin purchased both systems in 1939 and introduced refinements in filtration that gave the water a better taste.[14]

When the Texas and Pacific Railroad built between Fort Worth and El Paso in 1881, it brought windmills to West Texas. In the wake of the development, the windmills found their natural habitat on the ranches, where they were soon in great demand. The first ones were built near San Angelo in 1881 and in Schleicher County in the following year. By 1884 Major W. V. Johnson had four of them at work on his ranch in Lubbock County. In 1886 the manager of the Matador Land and Cattle Company stated that he had not seen a windmill, but concluded that it came "more nearly answering the purposes of cattlemen than anything that has yet been introduced." Other cattlemen shared the same view. David Boaz of the IOA Ranch drilled ten wells and erected windmills over them in the mid-1880's, and between 1886 and 1900 the famed XIT provided use for 335 windmills on their property.[15] Other successful ranches were in tune with the times, but the Espuela Land and Cattle Company of London, owned by some Scots, refused to invest in windmills. They lost money and eventually had to rid themselves of their property. "The principal error," wrote one observer, "was in not allowing funds for the drilling of wells, erecting of windmills, and building of tanks after the ranch was fenced."[16] Fenced ranges demanded windmills for successful cattle raising, a requirement which made the Dallas branch office of Aermotor the largest of its five branch offices. In some years this one office alone sold more windmills than all the other four combined.[17]

Wind wheel sizes varied with the depth of the well and

they ranged from ten to thirty feet in diameter. A large wheel required more wind to turn, but it had more power to pull water from greater depth. A ten-foot wheel was usually sufficient for a well one hundred feet deep, while an eighteen-foot wheel would pull from about four hundred feet.[18] The number of blades also had something to do with power. Bill Oden discovered this in 1887 when a Bird windmill would not pump sufficient water for the cattle. He was in Crockett County working for Frank Divers and they were having a tough time watering the cattle even though water was later found to be only six feet below the earth's surface. After experimentation born of despair, Oden lengthened the mill's stroke from four to six inches and removed alternate slats on the wind wheel. This adaptation slowed the wheel speed and provided more pumping power so that the mill pumped thirty gallons of water per minute. The water problem for that range was solved, but Oden wryly observed: "The manufacturers did not know as much about design of windmills as they learned later."[19]

Well drilling was very expensive, but necessary. The first hundred feet cost $.75 per foot and each foot after that cost $1.00. This was a running average by 1900, but when casing, piping, and sucker rods were added, a 375 foot well could cost about $1,000. Add to that the cost of the mill, some $250 to $300, and the price of the tower, and a windmill proved to be no cheap item. It could be done for less, though. Cliff Newland, a windmill man out of Crane, tells of the time he mounted a mill on top of a twelve foot tower and "the whole damned thing, mill and all, just cost $140."[20]

Even after steel towers were available, many Texans still preferred wooden ones, which ranged from ten to seventy-five feet in height. Using 8" x 8" or 6" x 6" pine lumber for the beams, the tower man put them together on the ground. Belts, or braces, were of 2" x 6" or 2" x 8" pine, while the ladder and platform called for 2" x 4" planks. Many times the windmill head was installed while the tower lay prone. When all was ready, a gin pole was fastened to the tower, the feet of which were braced, and the tower was winched upright by a team of horses or mules. Beside each foot a hole 4 to 4½ feet deep was dug for the anchor posts which were bolted to the feet. Cedar was used for anchor posts because it rotted slower than pine. Each tower was constructed a little differently according to the art and craft of the maker, but Cliff Newland explained the process when he said, "Damned few windmills towers are built right, I'll tell you that!"[21]

To the ranch folk the windmill became a way of life. While at work they made sounds that became natural to those who live around them. Ed Syers said it best perhaps when he wrote: "I loved few sounds like a country windmill's—a remote, magic one at twilight, a call-to-work at morning, and—in between, one to sleep by. It just repeated the wonderful song of nature—all's right with the world."[22] D. D. Stallings, a windmiller for the XIT Ranch, deplored the coming of the metal mills in the 1890's because "they were too busy and noisy to do a respectable job of pumping water."[23] Mrs. David Price, who lived near Castle Gap in Upton County, recalled that "loneliness engulfed her" when her husband was away to Midland on his mail run. At such times, as she looked for his return, she "would go to the windmill and climb to the top just to see if her husband was in sight. Then she would watch for the dust, for that would be someone coming."[24] One old-timer dressed his own beef and hung it on the windmill struts beyond the reach of coyotes and lobo wolves. When he wanted beef, he went to the windmill to cut off what he

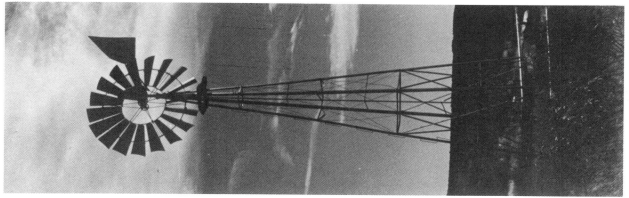

219

needed.[25] When winter came to the plains, the windmill was the first harbinger of a variation in the weather, for a sudden gust of wind changed its sound. Many ranchers declared they could predict a change in the weather by the creaking of their windmills in the morning just before sunrise.[26]

One of the first cattlemen to use windmills in the Big Spring country was C. C. Slaughter, but tradition has it that he did not accept them readily. Before he bought one, Slaughter sent a foreman over to the railroad to look at the windmill to be sure it would not harm the cows. Once committed, however, Slaughter was proud of his contraptions. One day he appeared at one of the windmills where his men were working a herd. When the cowboys went to the windmill for a drink, Slaughter started philosophizing on how the windmill would revolutionize the cattle business. After a pause, one cowboy who had been drinking, raised up and shouted: "That windmill reverlutionize anything! Hell, I can drink water faster than that thing can ever pump it." Slaughter asked: "How long could you keep drinking before the mill got ahead of you?" To which the cowboy replied: "Until I starved to death for water."[27]

Windmills and barbed wire changed the life of the cowboy as nothing else did. They brought the industrial revolution to the range. At first the cowboys had to learn to oil the mills and that was about all they could do. A windmill crying for grease issued a screeching sound across the pasture like no other, and it led the cowboy and his bottle of oil to the source of trouble. He rapidly scaled the ladder to drench the sucker rods and gears till they quit making noise. If the "mill rider" or "windmill monkey" found a wind wheel racing and no water running, he knew a sucker rod had been severed and additional help was needed to fix it. And if there was no wind and the trough or tank was dry, the cowboy had to climb the tower to turn the wheel by hand until the cattle were watered.[28]

Many a cowboy has been knocked off a tower and seriously injured by a sudden gust of wind. They also have had to fight yellow jackets and rotten timbers. Though often serious, such incidents sometimes were a source of humor, bringing forth some of the cowboy's best witticisms. One time two hands were working on a windmill when the tower man accidentally dropped a monkey wrench. Just as it glanced from the head of the unsuspecting cowboy on the ground the tower man hollered, "Look Out!" The acid reply from the man on the ground was: "What the hell you gonna do? Tho'w another'n?" Then there was the time Rhome Shields and a friend were getting ready to repair a windmill over in the San Angelo country. The friend was a good way up the ladder with Shields just starting. The former lost his grip and came hurtling down upon the latter, causing both men to hit the ground with considerable impact. Once Shields regained his wits, and air enough to put them into words, he berated his *compadre*: "You crazy son-of-a-bitch, don't you know you can kill a man falling off a windmill on him?"[29]

As time passed and "windmill man" became a part of Western speech,[30] a pattern emerged on the ranches. The smaller outfits had one man who rode the mill line to keep them in working order. For major repairs he called for additional help. The larger ranches hired themselves a windmiller. While cowboys got $45 per month in pay, the windmiller received about $75, making him the best paid man on the ranch with the exception of the boss. His status was alongside the straw bosses and the cook. The windmiller's wagon was equipped with the tools he needed: a chain wrench, Stillsons, blowtorch, vise, pipecutters, hammers, pliers, threaders, and hacksaws. He also carried spare parts: pitmans, joints of sucker rod, pipe, bolts, nuts, nails, pieces of lumber for tower repair, an extra cylinder, check valves, and a good supply of leather for the valves. He could make every repair needed except pull a mill head to replace the bearing. At such times he called on one of the regular hands to help him.[31]

In time the ranch windmiller moved to town to become an independent entrepreneur. His wagon became a pickup, but his constancy never flagged. The belief is that the "windmill's rhythmical dependability" inspired the windmill men to loyalty, integrity, and hard work.[32] For years they served their communities loyally and faithfully,

being in great demand until electricity and gasoline diminished their importance. But many a windmill still dots the Texas landscape and does the job it was designed to do, and there is harmony in that.

And the belief is still there, particularly among some ranchers. Two cowboys were talking about their boss, a rancher who was continually drilling new wells. One of the hands remarked: "When that old man dies and goes to hell, he's sure gonna try to drill hisself a windmill first thing." The other answered: "Yeah, and if he hits water, he'll start running cattle in hell too."[33] Like bright dimes glimmering in the sun, the windmills still turn in the minds of many old-time Texans, and some young ones, too.

NOTES:

3.

[1] Allan R. Bosworth, *Ozona Country* (New York: Harper and Row, 1964) pp. 2-

[2] Brownson Malsch, *Indianola: The Mother of Western Texas* (Austin: Shoal Creek Publishers, 1977), p. 26; Daniel B. Welborn, "Windmills in Texas," in *The Handbook of Texas A Supplement Vol. III*, Elden Stephen Branda, ed. (Austin: Texas State Historical Association, 1976), 1119; Terry G. Jordan, "Windmills in Texas," *Agricultural History*, XXXVII (April, 1963), 83.

[3] Jordan, "Windmills in Texas," p. 80; Joe M. Carmichael, "Water From the Wind," *The Cattleman*, XXXVI (October, 1949), 23.

[4] Malsch, *Indianola*, p. 26.

[5] A. T. Jackson, *Mills of Yesteryear* (El Paso: Texas Western Press, 1971), p. 38.

[6] *Ibid.*, pp. 37, 39; Stewart Davis, Jr., "Old Dutch Windmill," *Texas Parade* (February, 1960), p. 41.

NOTES (Continued)

[7] Jackson, *Mills of Yesteryear*, p. 37.

[8] "Texas Collection," *Southwestern Historical Quarterly*, XLV (January, 1942), 278; Jordan, "Windmills in Texas," p. 81.

[9] Lewis Nordyke, *Great Roundup: The Story of Texas and Southwestern Cowmen* (New York: William Morrow and Company, 1955), p. 92.

[10] Jordan, "Windmills in Texas," p. 83; *King County: Windmills and Barbed Wire*, King County Historical Society, comp. and ed. (Quanah, Texas: Nortex Press, 1976), p. v; Nancy Fowlkes, "Windmills: 'Sentinels of the Plains'," *The Texas Historian*, XXXI (September, 1970), 22; Fred Frank Blalock, "Wind, Water and Wheels," *The Cattleman*, LX (May, 1974), 70, 72, 74; Carmichael, "Water From the Wind," 24.

[11] Blalock, "Wind, Water and Wheels," p. 72; Carmichael, "Water From the Wind," p. 70.

[12] Beverly Daniels (ed.), *Milling Around in Sterling County: A History of Sterling County* [Texas] (Canyon, Texas: Staked Plains Press, 1976), pp. 125-126.

[13] Paul Patterson, *Crazy Women in the Rafters: Memories of a Texas Boyhood* (Norman: University of Oklahoma Press, 1976), pp. 41-44.

[14] N. Ethie Eagleton, *On the Last Frontier: A History of Upton County, Texas* (El Paso: Texas Western Press, 1971), p. 23.

[15] Jordan, "Windmills in Texas," p. 81; J. W. Williams, *The Big Ranch Country* (Wichita Falls, Texas: Terry Brothers, 1954), pp. 72-73.

[16] John Hendrix, *If I Can Do It Horseback: A Cow-Country Sketch* (Austin: University of Texas Press, 1964), pp. 108-109.

[17] Jordan, "Windmills in Texas," p. 83.

[18] Fowlkes, "Windmills: 'Sentinels of the Plains'," pp. 19, 23.

[19] Bill Oden, *Early Days on the Texas-New Mexico Plains*. J. Evetts Haley, ed. (Canyon, Texas: Palo Duro Press, 1965), p. 21.

[20] Cliff Newland, Crane, Texas to Paul Patterson, March 15, 1978 (cassette recording in possession of the writer).

[21] Newland to Crane, March 15, 1978; Fowlkes, "Windmills: 'Sentinels of the Plains'," p. 22; Margaret A. Elliott, "History of D. B. Gardner's Pitchfork Ranch," *Panhandle Plains Historical Review*, XXVIII (1945), 57.

[22] Blalock, "Wind, Water and Wheels," p. 74.

[23] Jerry and Mickey Hodge, "Singing Wheels of the Plains," *Texas Parade* (June, 1969), p. 33.

[24] Eagleton, *On the Last Frontier*, p. 16.

[25] John Howard Griffin, *Land of the High Sky* (Midland, Texas: First National Bank of Midland, 1959), p. 102.

[26] Nordyke, *Great Roundup*, p. 92.

[27] J. Frank Dobie, *A Vaquero of the Brush Country* (New York: Grosset and Dunlap, 1929), p. 260.

[28] Ramon F. Adams, *The Old-Time Cowhand* (New York: Collier Books, 1961), pp. 211-213.

[29] Paul Patterson, *Pecos Tales* (Austin: Encino Press, 1967), p. 19.

[30] Lewis Nordyke, *Cattle Empire* (New York: William Morrow and Company, 1949), p. 144.

[31] William Curry Holden, *A Ranching Saga: The Lives of William Electious Halsell and Ewing Halsell* (San Antonio: Trinity University Press, 1976), II, 301-303.

[32] Bryan Wildenthal, "Windmill Schmidt," *Publication of the West Texas Historical and Scientific Society, Number Twenty* (Sul Ross State College Bulletin, XLIV, No. 3, September 1, 1964), 129.

[33] Jack Walker, "Wind and Water," *Texas Parade* (May, 1964), p. 25.

Tank, Tub, and Cistern

Ernest B. Speck

When man and animal are in the symbiotic relationship that has existed throughout all of recorded time, a primary factor is water. On farms and ranches in Texas from the Trans-Sabine, where water is generally plentiful, to the Trans-Pecos, where water is treasured, means of containing and dispensing water have long been a concern.

The simplest form of holding water for stock is the dirt tank, or farm pond, to use the United States Department of Agriculture designation. The dirt tank has, of course, an earthen dam across a draw or branch which impounds water during rainy periods to be available when rain does not fall. These little reservoirs were built at first by farmers and ranchers using a slip or a Fresno scraper. The slip was a dirt scraper about two-and-a-half feet square with sides some ten inches high and was pulled by a two-mule team. The average slip could hold about four cubic feet of earth. There were handles on each side extending out behind, similar to those on an old-fashioned wheelbarrow. The operator controlled the bite of the slip into the earth by lowering and raising the handles. In front of the handles on each side were pins around which a flat steel bar was wrapped at each of its ends. The center of the bar formed a U in front of the scraper where there was a clevis for attaching the double-tree. If the handles of the scraper were raised high enough for the lip to hang on the ground, the scraper rotated with the handles falling forward and the contents were dumped. Since the handles were very close to the ground, a limber back was needed to operate a slip.

The Fresno was much larger than a slip and required a three-horse team. Instead of two handles, it had one long bar (the Johnson Bar) that came out from the back of the scraper. The bar had a drag rope attached to it to pull the Fresno back in scraping position after it had been dumped.

The construction of a dirt tank began with the selection of a draw which could be dammed with relative ease but which would impound a considerable amount of water. Too deep a draw would require a dam larger than a farmer could build with simple tools. In country where there was a convenient supply of loose rocks, rock was laid across on the line of the dam. The mound of the dam was generally crescent shaped with the dirt piled a foot or more above the level the water would reach when the dam was full. Weeds and grass were encouraged on the dam to prevent washing. At each end of the dam were overflow areas, lined with rock or concrete, where excess water was channeled around the dam when rains were heavy.

The typical stock tank ranged from a few hundred square feet in area to over half an acre. Larger ones that were later built on large farms and ranches were properly small lakes. Obviously something more than a slip or a Fresno and a team of mules is needed to build a dam large enough to impound a tank of several acres. The average country man could eyeball his work on a small tank to get the top level and the proper height; a larger one required someone, such as the county agent, to use a transit.

More prevalent in some areas were watering troughs of

225

various kinds. The standard wooden trough was constructed of heavy boards, two by twelve or wider. Six to eight feet long or more, the troughs were in a square-bottomed U shape. The ends were pieces of similar plank, fitted inside the U of the body of the trough. Assembled on the ground, using ten or twelve penny box nails, the tank was then put at a level convenient for the animals that were to use it. Stanchions made of short posts with a cross piece under the trough supported the trough. These pairs of stanchions were at two- to three-foot intervals for the length of the trough. Since virtually every countryman could do any sort of rough carpentry, building a wooden trough posed no problems. If he did not have a carpenter's level, he could determine that his cross pieces were on a level either by sight or by setting a vessel of water on a board laid across them. No caulking was needed because the wood swelled as soon as it was saturated with water and sealed all the cracks.

Troughs were filled from a hand pump, from a tank fed by a windmill, or directly from a windmill. The latter two methods utilized float valves. On some places, a series of troughs, each successive one at a lower level, was arranged in various pens and fed water from one trough to the next to provide water for various kinds of stock. Running pipelines, whether from trough to trough or from windmill tank to the house, was easily done. A couple of Stillson wrenches and some pipe dope were all that was needed. Proper lengths of pipe, with nipples, elbows, and faucets, were purchased and assembled.

The troughs in smaller pig pens were of another design. Two boards, usually one by tens, were nailed in a V-shape. They were generally five or six feet long. The ends were pieces of the same size boards nailed across the V. They served both to close the ends and to form braces to hold the

V upright. Smaller ones of the same design were used in chicken yards. Water was poured into both of these sorts of troughs from buckets.

Another type of trough which was built on the farm or ranch was one made of rock or concrete, or, as we said, "see-ment." Such troughs are more often round, taking advantage of the inherent strength of circular structures, although rectangular ones were more frequently used, in part because forms for them were more easily made. First a base for the trough was built. A round area, five feet or more in diameter, was cleared, leveled, and covered with sand. A form for the base was made, often of corrugated sheet metal. Tie steel, more likely lengths of criss-crossed barbed or smooth wire than the usual concrete mesh, was laid to reduce the chances of major cracks in the concrete. The wire was bent upward near the outer edges to help tie the sides to the base. All concrete structures were cured by preventing them from drying too quickly by shielding them from the bright sun and by keeping them moist for a couple of days.

After the base had dried, the sides were added. Two methods could be used. If the builder were something of a mason, he could build the circular sides of rock and mortar. It did not have to be a master job; it required only that all cracks between the rocks be well filled with mortar and that the top have a relatively smooth surface. A concrete wall around the trough was constructed by building a form of sheet metal, braced on the outside with stakes driven in the ground and on the inside with cross-pieces in an intricate pattern of braces. Again, wire of any sort available was used for tie steel.

Concrete for this and other farm and ranch structures was mixed either in a trough built for the purpose or a mixer, hand turned in early days, electrically or gasoline

Rocked-in spring with milk trough *(Cherokee Co.)*

Water tank with shower room and milk house *(Hamilton Co.)*

High pressure water tank *(Mason Co.)*

227

Gutter for catching rain water (*Tyler Co.*)

Cypress horse trough (*Tyler Co.*)

Well shed (*Panola Co.*)

228

Front porch wash stand (*Tyler Co.*)

driven later. A trough for mixing concrete could be made by nailing a piece of sheet iron, three feet wide and six or eight feet long to two pieces of eight-by-ten planking which had been trimmed to a quarter circle at each end. Cement, sand, rock, and water were put into the trough and kept agitated with either a proper mixing hoe, which had a large blade with holes on each side, or an ordinary corn hoe. Concrete was fed from the trough with buckets.

Metal water troughs were also used, but they were either built by the local tinner or ordered from mail order houses. Later hardware stores began carrying them. The farmer had only to prepare a level place for the trough. However, because even a heavily galvanized trough would eventually rust, it was often put on a low platform to hold it a few inches off the damp earth. Such platforms were made either of concrete or of pieces of one-by-fours nailed across two-by-fours.

Round wooden troughs, usually of cypress, could also be bought and were usually placed directly on the ground. More expensive than metal troughs, they had the advantage of never rusting and required less preparation to put in place.

The most prevalent of water containers before water was piped wherever it was needed was the ten- or twelve-quart galvanized bucket. The homemade oaken or cedar bucket was pretty rare. Sometimes enameled buckets were used for drinking water to avoid the metalic taste, as were enameled dippers. Homemade gourd dippers, however, were much more common. Dipper gourds, like most gourd plants, are easy to grow, and the dippers are easy to make. All that is needed is to cut away about a third of the side of the ball at the end of the gourd and then clean out the seed and dried fibers on the inside. One important function of the bucket in earlier times was filling the five-to-eight-

gallon copper reservoir on the wood cookstove. Even when there were faucets at two or three places in the house, hot water heaters were not in evidence on most farms until quite late. A cooper could also make wooden tubs for washing clothes and people, but most people used galvanized ones.

One water container that could not be homemade but was indispensable was the iron washpot needed for boiling the dirt out of the clothes, heating water for the washtub, and for scalding hogs, rendering lard, and making soap. Its importance was evidenced by the fact that a black washpot with a bleached out poke stick sat in every farmer's yard, not far from the wood pile.

The stone jug carried to the field by the farmer was bought in a store, but two additions he made were not. The cork or "stopper" was a piece of corn cob, trimmed to fit tightly into the neck of the jug. And the jug was covered with either tow sacking or cotton sacking stitched together with binder twine. The sacking was well dampened when the jug was filled, and each time the farmer took a drink he sloshed a little more water on it, and evaporation provided at least enough cooling to prevent the water from getting hot.

Another important water container which was usually purchased but had important additions made by the landholder was the water tank mounted beside the windmill. These tanks, ranging in size from one thousand to five thousand gallons, were most often made of sheet iron or wood. As with metal troughs, sheet iron tanks would eventually rust. Wooden tanks had one other advantage: because of seeping dampness they did not heat up as much as metal ones. Though the tank was bought, the farmer built the tower or platform on which it was mounted. The tower had to be only high enough that the bottom was as high as the highest point to which water was to be piped, but a higher tower would provide more pressure.

The towers were made of wood almost entirely. A smaller tank of one or two thousand gallons was mounted on a platform which had heavy posts of pine or cedar at each corner. The posts were tied together at the top by bridge timbers and were so spaced that they fit just inside the circumference of the tank. Since the edges of wooden water tanks extended below the bottom of the tank, two by fours were placed edgewise on the bridge timbers to support the bottom of the tank. When the wooden tank was placed on the tower, the boards forming the bottom of the tank were placed at right angles to the supporting two by fours. The space beneath the tank was frequently walled in to provide a small room which could be used as a milk room, cooled by the evaporation of water, or, with a drained concrete floor, as a shower room.

Water tanks were also made of rock or concrete. The method of construction was similar to that used for concrete and rock water troughs, except that there was a lower section some six or eight feet high. Heavy timbers were then laid across the top and sheet iron or wood was used to build a form for the bottom of the tank. After the bottom of the tank had cured, the sides of the tanks were then added, either of concrete or rock. A variation was a masonry or concrete tower to support a metal tank.

There was one other major water container which the farmer bought or constructed himself, sometimes with the help of a neighbor or two. Cisterns were of two sorts. The sheet metal tanks were similar to those for windmills, but they had to be built close to the ground to be below the rain gutters on the house. There was a faucet at the bottom to drain water into buckets.

The other type was the underground cistern. Such cisterns resembled dug wells in several ways. They had a curbing and well posts and pulley. And they were constructed much as a dug well was, in that a hole was dug in the ground. They differed, however, in that they were cone or bell shaped and were wider at the bottom than at the top. A hole eight or ten feet wide was dug ten or twelve feet deep. It was then floored and walled with rock or concrete, with the walls narrowing until the surface of the ground was reached. When the walls were well set, dirt was filled in around them and the curbing was added.

Cisterns were used when there was no ground water close to the house. In dry years, however, they would go dry. This called for two actions. Even though the water was clean enough when it fell on the roof, there were impurities on the roof—dust, botanical chaff, and barnyard debris borne on the wind—so the cistern had to be cleaned. The cleaning usually consisted of a thorough sweeping. The second action was replenishing the water by hauling in a new supply from a well or creek. Barrels holding thirty to forty gallons contained about a day's supply each for a family of five or six, and bathing was at a minimum. Thus eight or more barrels a week had to be hauled for the average household.

Where there was no cistern, rain water was often caught in barrels or number-three wash tubs placed under a valley in the roof. The soft rain water was highly prized by the women especially for washing hair in areas where Kirk's hard water soap was needed for the usual water supply.

There were other means of handling and holding water, but most of them, such as self-feeding troughs for chickens, were not constructed by the farmer or rancher. In some areas there was irrigation, which required ditches, gates, weirs, and sluices, some of which were made by those on

Miss Ludell's well *(Nacogdoches Co.)*

231

Water tank over milk house (*Montague Co.*)

232

Rock curbed well (*Bosque Co.*)

Water tank *(Blanco Co.)*

233

Tank foundation *(Blanco Co.)*

234

the scene. But whatever the containers or methods, the characteristics most in evidence were tradition and ingenuity. The traditional way was followed until a new situation arose when ingenuity came into play. (Example, a masonry water tower was built when no large timber was available.) The coming of REA obviated much of this equipment and practice when electric pumps were installed. Only the dirt tanks and the troughs, still fed by windmills on the big spreads, are still very much in evidence.

Guenther's Live Oak Mill at Fredericksburg
(Courtesy of Pioneer Flour Mills)

236

When the Creeks Run Dry: Water Milling in the German Hill Country

Glen Lich and Lera Tyler

"I am busy building. We cut the wood in this vicinity, which is open country, and with the help of five men have been building on the dam for eight days. Then we must dig the millrace and then the mill. I hope to be grinding in four months. I cannot delay because there is no mill within sixty miles from here. The farmers sell their corn to the government and buy their flour seventy to eighty miles from here."[1]

C. H. Guenther, 1851

A water mill in a frontier German settlement, like a bank and the railroad a generation later, signified stability and prosperity to the inhabitants. Mills made life easier and attracted other business, so that when a millwright arrived in a community, neighbors saw the promise of a better life. But building a European water mill and then keeping it running in western Texas was difficult. Although German millers brought skill and experience to the Hill Country, their dependence upon the cantankerous environment required quite untraditional adaptations to the Texas terrain and weather in order to keep a traditional mill in operation. Most of them served a second, some even a third, apprenticeship on the frontier. The mills they built, though now no longer standing, were tests while they worked of how well these old builders learned their lessons.

One hot August afternoon, we stopped at the hillside west of Fredericksburg where Carl Hilmar Guenther built his first Texas mill. It did not seem a likely place for

perhaps the most important of the early Hill Country mills built by Germans. The creek was wide, shallow, and slow-moving; the creek bed was full of gravel and sand. In 1851, however, when Guenther's Live Oak Mill was erected, Hill Country streams flowed through narrow and deep beds and grass grew to the water's edge.[2]

Guenther, the son of a prosperous cloth merchant in Saxony, was apprenticed in Germany to a millwright. In 1848 he arrived in America, and, after traveling through New York and the Midwest, the young Guenther journeyed down the Mississippi to New Orleans and finally to Texas where he selected a mill site near Fredericksburg, a five-year-old German town without a mill.[3]

Walking along the creek bank on that day, we saw no evidence of the old mill. One local resident, Mr. Bruno Fritz, who as a boy herded livestock for his uncle by the Live Oak Creek, remembered playing on the site sixty or more years ago. Even back then, he told us, all that remained was a remnant of the foundation and part of the millrace. Guenther operated the Live Oak Mill for eight years before moving to San Antonio, and the letters he wrote to his family in Saxony tell that building, rebuilding, and improving the mill was a continuous undertaking. Construction of the Live Oak Mill took over six months. "The minute I appear in town," Guenther wrote to Germany, "everyone cries, 'Will the mill be running soon?' These people find it very tedious to do their grinding with hand mills."[4] Shortly after the mill began operating, the

237

millwright sent another letter home. "The mill is running excellently," he wrote. "The machinery runs like a clock. Up to now I have not needed a milling engineer, for everything was built by carpenters and cabinetmakers who worked by my drawings. The people around here are all surprised that I have succeeded in this project with so little money and in so short a time. The mill is run by a waterwheel that is 16½ feet high and 3½ feet wide. The shaft is 2½ feet thick, and the iron trunnion is 6 inches. You may well imagine that this generates a lot of power; moreover, it moves very slowly, for the stone moves 45 times while the waterwheel revolves once. There is a cogwheel 20 inches in diameter with 16 teeth. This is fastened onto a vertical shaft which is geared to a cogwheel 20 inches in diameter with 16 teeth. This is fastened onto a vertical shaft at the top of which is a gearwheel 8 feet in diameter with 84 teeth. This is geared to the millstone."[5] The millrace was dug with picks and shovels; the waterwheel and the driving gears were fashioned from native woods. The buhrstones, or millstones, were imported from Europe, for only in southern France and the Canary Islands was located the special siliceous formation preferred by millers. They were durable enough to withstand constant grinding and known not to adversely affect the meal or flour.[6]

The mill had been operating only a few weeks when the first flood water tore away the dam. "I thought of you—especially of Father! I had hoped that the dam would last for a few years, until I would be in a position to afford a more massive one. The Lord had other plans!... Without a dam I could not grind. There was no escape for me, I had to start building again!

"I started in again and contracted to have 200 stones cleared away. While tearing down part of the framework which was still standing, I dropped my ax and saw into the swirling waters and to this day have never seen them again. In hunting for them I discovered how deeply the water had torn into the dam. That horrible hole in the dam frightened me.

"Stunned and disgusted I walked up along the Live Oak Creek. My morning's desire to work was gone. I walked for more than an hour. By that time I had made my decision. I would move my dam and lengthen the canal so that the dam need not be so high!

"That very afternoon we started in.... The dam needed to be only two feet high. The old one had been seven feet. The next day I went to town and engaged men for $1.12½ a day.

"After one month the mill was working again.... I am determined to make this little dam so strong that I will never have to think of its being torn down again. That is the only danger. The mill itself is as solid as your own house. It is not near the water."[7]

His second dam did hold up. Within two years Guenther had survived several floods, added a sawmill, strengthened the dam again, and increased the water's speed.[8] In June 1856 he wrote home, "I am still busy building. Now my mill is getting eight feet more fall. This millrace is 3,000 paces long and is cut out of hard rock.... The new waterwheel is 22 feet high; it is placed up to the other wheels.... We are just waiting for the digging to be completed. Stones, lime, and sand, everything is ready and a pair of the best French millstones are on the way from Indianola to here."[9] These new stones were specifically cut for grinding flour, for the German farmers had begun cultivating wheat, as well as corn, by 1856.

On that still summer afternoon, we tried to imagine the activity which once surrounded Guenther's mill. "Often,"

(*Left*) Carl Hilmar Guenther
(*Courtesy of Pioneer Flour Mills*)

(*Below, left*) Guenther's first mill in San Antonio (1859)
(*Courtesy of Pioneer Flour Mills*)

LIVEOAK MILL, C.H. GUENTHER FREDERICKSBURG.

GRINDING WORKS

84 TEETH

8 GEARWHEEL

BEAM

BEAM

BEVELED AND PEGGED
COGWHEEL 20"
16 TEETH

BEAM

FLUME

WATER

16 ½'

WALNUT
OR
HICKORY SHAFT

2 ½'

METAL
REINFORCEMENT

3 ½'
OVERSHOT WATERWHEEL
OF CYPRESS WOOD

BEARINGS

1 REVOLUTION OF WATERWHEEL = 45 REVOLUTIONS OF GRINDINGSTONE

DRAWN BY AN INTERVIEW WITH C.W. GUENTHER, SAN MARCOS

The Perseverance Mill at Comfort. From a lithograph by Hermann Lungkwitz.
(Courtesy of the Comfort Museum)

Christian Dietert
(Courtesy of Mr. Harry Dietert)

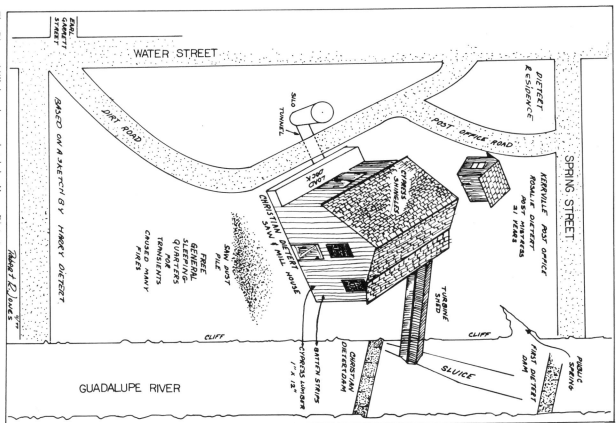

The Dietert Mill, based on a sketch by Harry Dietert
(Drawing by Robert R. Jones)

EARL GARRETT STREET

WATER STREET

DIRT ROAD

BASED ON A SKETCH BY HARRY DIETERT

SILO

TUNNEL

DIETERT RESIDENCE

POST OFFICE ROAD

SPRING STREET

KERRVILLE POST OFFICE ROSALIE DIETERT POST MISTRESS 31 YEARS

LOAD DECK

CYPRESS SHINGLES

CHRISTIAN DIETERT SAW & MILL HOUSE

SAW DUST PILE

FREE GENERAL SLEEPING QUARTERS FOR TRANSIENTS CAUSED MANY FIRES

TURBINE SHED

Robert R. Jones '77

CLIFF

CLIFF

CYPRESS LUMBER 1" X 12"

BATTEN STRIPS

CHRISTIAN DIETERT DAM

SLUICE

FIRST DIETERT DAM

PUBLIC SPRING

GUADALUPE RIVER

he wrote to his father, "this place looks like a market place with three to five wagons drawn by two or four yoke oxen and driven by a man on horseback. They arrive any time between eight and ten o'clock. Mules and horses come and go constantly, carrying bags of cornmeal and flour. Even after the customers have been attended to they often stay as long as an hour or two for a sociable visit as this is the place where all the farmers get together."[10]

For us on that August day, the busy scene contrasted altogether with the present site. The heat and stillness predominated. Across the creek, toward the place where the stream trickles into the Pedernales, a whirlwind zigzagged through a harvested field. There was no sign of other movement except the sound of trucks and cars on Texas 16, a quarter mile behind us. Drought was not difficult to understand. To the Germans back then, it was still another unaccustomed hardship. Business would slow down almost to a standstill. At these times, Guenther explained to his parents, not only was there little water to turn the wheel, but there were no crops, no grain to grind. During the good years, though, Guenther prospered, and his business was secure enough to pull through the dry years. Yet after eight years on the frontier, Guenther astutely decided to leave Fredericksburg. "My business is middling. But soon I will have strong competition," he told his mother. "The merchants in Fredericksburg are building a mill to be run by steam. This will hurt my mill during these first years. I had already made inquires about buying a steam engine and mentioned it in public to interest the farmers in planting more wheat next year. Immediately these merchants who had pledged themselves not to build a mill now agreed to combine and together buy a steam mill and the building has begun.

"I will not compete with this steam mill," Guenther continued, "as I figure there is only enough business here for one such mill. So I have decided to travel to San Antonio in two days and find a better location for my steam and waterpowered mill. San Antonio has now 10,000 inhabitants, and only one very meager water mill. I have been to San Antonio once or twice every year and have often remarked that there is real need for a good mill which could do a marvelous business."[11]

By 1859, when Guenther moved to San Antonio and relocated on a river site south of the center of town, the population of the Hill Country had increased considerably, and several other conventional water mills had been built in the new German towns. In Fredericksburg itself, another mill had been started in 1853 on Baron's Creek by a Hanoverian named Bierschwale, who, Guenther claimed, spent $3,000 in drinking and building with only a half-completed mill to show for it a year later.[12] This operation was finished eventually in 1856 by Nikolas Zink, a Bavarian engineer who had built roads in Greece during the revolution, immigrated to Texas in the 1840's, laid out the streets of New Braunfels for Prince Solms, and planned the construction of two or three Hill Country mills.[13]

Prior to buying this Bierschwale mill, Zink and Christian Dietert, another German millwright, had built Perseverance Mill at Comfort for Ernst Altgelt. The wealthy Altgelt had carefully laid plans for the founding of a new German community twenty miles southeast of Fredericksburg, at the confluence of the Cypress Creek and Guadalupe River. The township was surveyed in 1854, and town lots were laid. As settlers came, the town's most immediate need in Altgelt's mind was for a saw- and gristmill.[14] In 1855 he brought in Zink and Dietert to plan the Perseverance Mill and hired thirty men to help with the building.[15]

A painting by Lungkwitz shows this Comfort mill as a typical three-story mill building. An open basement contained the waterwheel works; the second story was the millroom proper where meal was ground and timber cut; and an attic housed the upper main shaft and storage facilities.

Altgelt and his builders saw in the Cypress Creek a promising place to locate a milling venture, and as we climbed the bluff outside of Comfort where this mill once stood, we would have agreed with them. Below us, water from spring rains flowed around cypress trunks through a narrow creek bed, and above us cypress boughs formed tall arches. What we could not see, but knew nonetheless, was that the Cypress Creek is a fitful stream, and Altgelt quickly discovered that milling in Texas could be a "thankless undertaking."[16] His wife later recalled the lesson. "Hardly had a dam been completed which was considered indestructible, along came a cloudburst and tore away the work of man's labor by hand. . . . With renewed effort, a deeper channel was excavated and a more massive dam was built that could defy the worst of floods. What was anticipated did not happen, for the following summer barely a trickle of water was visible and the mill was kept idle. The elements seemed equally determined. . . . The mill operated only a few years and had to be discontinued, but not until a fortune was lost."[17] The cause of the failure was their unfamiliarity with the new land. However attractive the Cypress Creek might have appeared to newcomers, especially in rainy seasons, the area it drained was not sufficient in a prevailingly semi-arid climate to provide year-round water power.

Christian Dietert stayed with the Comfort operation for not quite two years before moving to Fredericksburg. Misfortune followed the young miller there, too, for in the

next year a flood washed away his second Texas mill. After this Fredericksburg disaster, Dietert was drawn by an abundance of giant cypress trees along the Guadalupe River about twenty miles southwest of Fredericksburg to the lumbering and shingle making camp of "Kerrsville." He scouted the headwaters of the river to insure that the drainage was ample for continuous operation, and in 1857 he moved his family to Kerrville, as it came to be called, where he chose a protected mill site above the broad river. Since the river at this point was wide, shallow, and carried mud and gravel, Dietert compensated by designing a diagonal dam across the river which would step up the rate of flow through the millrace and keep the dam free of sediment. The saw- and gristmill which he built on a bluff thirty feet above the river was safe from flood waters, and the waterwheel was placed inside an edge of the cliff for protection. This German millwright was learning to deal with his Texas environment.

We visited Harry Dietert, a grandson of Christian Dietert and an engineer himself,[18] and discussed the old Kerrville mill with him. It was he who explained the purpose of the diagonal dam. The dam was built six or seven feet high, and a sluice five feet wide and three feet deep was cut into the limestone river bed. The site of the dam and millstream are still easily recognized. We waded in the river, following the row of 14-16 inch square cypress posts which were sunk into holes cut in the river bed to support the dam. Christian Dietert's waterwheel, like the one at Perseverance Mill, was an undershot wheel.[19] It turned a series of gears on a shaft, and this shaft climbed up the bluff to the mill house. With the wheel and gears in this location, the need for a basement was eliminated; and the mill at the top of the cliff was a two-story wooden structure, 30 x 55 feet. Inside the millroom on the ground floor, Dietert's millstone was designed to be a toprunner, for a square oaken shaft drove the top stone, while the bottom one remained stationary. Since Christian Dietert's fine French millstones were lost in the Fredericksburg flood, he had to make a second pair himself, twenty inches in diameter and four inches in thickness, from native granite according to a pattern he knew from his homeland. Grain dropped into an eye in the center of the top stone; then, channeled by grooves cut into the grinding face and carried outward by centrifugal force, the ground meal emerged at the edges of the stones and fell into a square hopper below. It then funneled down into a one-bushel wooden bin from which Dietert poured the cornmeal into his customers' canvas bags. In accordance with European milling and the bartering system prevalent on the frontier, the miller was paid with a tithe of grain.

The business succeeded because of the constantly increasing demands of a growing community for its services—grinding corn and barley, sawing lumber, and making shingles. The mill was also a popular place. Standing next to it was the post office, a 12 x 12 foot, one-door building where Mrs. Dietert served as postmistress of the town for over twenty years. The mill and post office naturally drew townspeople, ranchers, and farmers during the daytime. In the evenings, young people congregated in the Dietert home, where, to the music of the fiddle and accordion, Rosalie Dietert held dances for Kerrville and introduced the waltz to the settlement.

Mill work was hard, though, and Christian Dietert employed several men to help with the operation. Lumber milling was especially difficult, since the crew cut down and hauled cypress trees sometimes as wide as six feet in diameter. Harry Dietert explained to us how after the tree was cut with an ax, his grandfather placed two inclined logs against his wagon. A rope was wrapped around the fallen tree, and with his team of oxen Dietert hoisted the cut timber up onto the wagon bed. Once, while Christian Dietert was cutting logs alone, he was caught in a flash flood on the Guadalupe. A four-foot rise came rolling down the river bed, and he shinnied up a cypress tree, where he slept all night. Dietert spared that tree, and we saw where it still stands.

At the sawmill, Dietert and his crew winched the trunks, one at a time, onto a carriage inside the millhouse. A circle saw over this carriage was attached by a metal shaft to the gearwheel which was driven, in turn, by the waterwheel. The millstones and the saw operated off the same main gearwheel, but a series of small cogwheels which turned the metal shaft of the circle saw stepped up its revolutions per minute. The saw first squared up the timber on the carriage in four passes and then sliced the cypress into planks of rough, green lumber.

Travelers brought the only news into Kerrville before a newspaper was started in the town. They would hang around one of the major businesses, and for a long time Dietert's mill was the stopping place for these wanderers. They usually could get a meal at the Dietert table, and the sawdust pile outside the mill house was made available as a sleeping place for them. These transients would smoke at night and invariably catch the sawdust on fire. The mill house itself was damaged and rebuilt at least a dozen times during Dietert's ownership. Not floods nor drought, but these fires eventually convinced Christian Dietert to quit milling. Harry Dietert told us, "One day while my grandfather was walking west along Water Street towards Charles Schreiner's store, he met Captain Schreiner who told him, 'Christian, you should sell that mill, because it's just going to burn down again.' And Grandfather felt that that was a warning and agreed to sell it."[20]

The Kerrville mill changed its face after Schreiner purchased it. Just as efficiently as he had built the town, Captain Schreiner modernized the operation by adding steel rollers and then he expanded the mill complex to include a cotton gin, ice plant, and light plant. These advances of technology were fairly standard at that time, and in his last years Dietert had failed to keep pace with them. Basically the same improvements were made in San Antonio with C. H. Guenther's milling business, where an increasingly industrialized operation developed into one of the major milling firms of the Southwest.

Everywhere in the 'eighties and 'nineties the era of the traditional water mill was drawing to a close. Whether the design had come from Mexico with Spanish padres, migrated through eastern America with Anglo frontiersmen, or crossed the Atlantic with immigrant German millwrights, European mills had provided the basic, centuries-old pattern for building mills in Texas until the 1850's. Beginning after the Civil War, however, mills started to take on a different appearance. First, the big waterwheel disappeared from the side of the mill house, to be replaced by the smaller and more efficient water turbine. Then, in the 1880's and 1890's, steel rollers replaced the millstones. Meanwhile, the power source changed from water to steam. Parts were ordered rather than made, as mills now grew more complex and machinery more standardized. By the turn of the century, building a mill was altogether a different business. Millwrights and mill engineers no longer worried about creeks and rivers, droughts and floods, native materials and imported buhrstones. The sound of the waterwheel was gone, stone-ground meal and flour were gone, and the old mill builders were gone from the Texas Hill Country.

NOTES:

[1] C. H. Guenther, *Literal Translation of Diary and Letters of Carl Hilmar Guenther*, trans. Regina Beckmann Hurst (San Antonio: Clegg, 1952), 16 March 1851.

[2] Based on Department of Agriculture, Soil Conservation Service studies for Kerr, Kendall, and Gillespie counties; photographs (ca. 1870-90), and nineteenth-century paintings.

[3] Ernst Schuchard, comp., *100th Anniversary Pioneer Flour Mills, San Antonio, Texas, 1851-1951* (San Antonio: Naylor, [1951]), pp. 1-2.

[4] Guenther, 25 September 1851.

NOTES (Continued)

[5] Guenther, n.d.

[6] Schuchard, p. 2.

[7] Guenther, 6 February 1853.

[8] Guenther, 20 February 1855.

[9] Guenther, 8 September 1856.

[10] Guenther, 9 June 1853.

[11] Guenther, 22 August 1859.

[12] Guenther, 8 September 1856.

[13] Guido Ernst Ransleben. *A Hundred Years of Comfort in Texas: A Centennial History* (San Antonio: Naylor, 1954), p. 208. See also Oscar Haas, *History of New Braunfels and Comal County, Texas: 1844-1946* (Austin: Hart Graphics, 1968), p. 24.

[14] Ransleben, p. 19.

[15] Emma Murck Altgelt, *Beobachtungen und Erinnerungen*, manuscript translation by Guido Ernst Ransleben, Comfort, Texas.

[16] Altgelt.

[17] Altgelt. Furthermore, in the Comfort centennial history Ransleben gives an account of the technical problems involved with the second Perseverance dam. Zink and Dietert moved the second dam upstream where it did not have to be as high. A new canal was dug, this time along the west bank of the Cypress Creek, and a viaduct was built across the creek into the millstream which led to the mill house on the east bank. After Perseverance Mill was abandoned, flood waters eventually tore down the second dam and the viaduct, and subsequent rises cut deeper and deeper into the mill canal, until the stream was permanently diverted and now flows next to the original bed.

[18] Harry Dietert grew up on his grandfather's farm across the Guadalupe River from the old Kerrville Mill. An internationally recognized foundryman, he taught briefly at Rice Institute, registered 97 patents, and was chairman of the board of directors of Dietert Detroit (Michigan). He resided in Kerrville.

[19] In an undershot operation, water flows under the wheel, pushing paddles or buckets on the rim of the wheel by the force of its current. An overshot wheel turns when water is fed by a flume to the top of the wheel, filling the buckets and rotating the wheel. The undershot is less efficient and requires a greater volume of water, but is necessary where a site has less water fall.

[20] After this efficacious purchase, Captain Schreiner converted the corn meal operation into a flour mill, because white flour from Guenther's mill in San Antonio was in such demand in Schreiner's store. People were disappointed, though, in the quality of Schreiner's flour. Mrs. Rosalie Dietert claimed that the captain ground undried grain into heavy, damp flour which made very heavy bread. The customers complained in general that they were paying for moisture.

Restoration & Preservation

Much that remains of early Texas building is going the way of all things built by man and is succumbing to time and termites. Some is being leveled to make way for progress in the form of super-highways, shopping centers, and improved pastures. The old styles are giving way to concrete blocks, asbestos shingles, and the omnipresent trailer house. Ways of life that are tied up in dugouts and windmills and dog trots are fast fading past us, and we would do well to capture the sight and sound of them before they go.

A sign of a culture's affluence and stability is its willingness to preserve the forms of the past, its ability to afford to collect and maintain antiques. The poor might preserve the old things by necessity. The rich keep them by choice, realizing and recognizing the history inherent in these things, their debts to the past, and their ties with the pioneers who first came to the land and prepared it for our generation. Our society is now prosperous enough to keep old houses and barns and other outbuildings because of the pleasure we get from looking at them and learning from them, and perhaps because their charm and simplicity provides a pleasing contrast to the complications brought on by the prosperity that permits their preservation.

Rice home soon after it was moved
(Courtesy of Texas Parks and Wildlife Department)

248

The Restoration of the Rice Family Log Home

Steve Whiston

The first time I saw the Rice family log home was in January, 1975. Years of abandonment and exposure had left the cabins in ruins. Its weathered, decayed log walls were laced and tied with steel cable, and its sagging beams were propped with poles. The house had been cut into three sections, each separated and lifted from its former setting and moved to a cleared site among the pines of the Mission Tejas State Historical Park. What was left of the Rice log home stood awaiting restoration by the Texas Parks and Wildlife Department.

The structure's original site was approximately eighteen miles southwest of the park near Crockett on State Highway 21. The three-room, hand-hewn log home was built by Joseph Redmond Rice, who was born in Tennessee in 1805. Rice built his home on the Old San Antonio Road in what is now Houston County. Known as the King's Highway or the El Camino Real, the deeply rutted but well-traveled road served as an important artery into Texas.

Joseph and his wife, Willie Masters Rice, began construction of their home sometime around 1828. The first cabin was built using hand-hewn pine logs squared on two sides and joined at the corners with a V-notch. Discouraged by marauding Indians, the Rices were forced to abandon their home before it was finished and move to Louisiana. Within a few years they were able to return to Houston County and take up where they had left off. The half-story loft of the first cabin was finished using larger logs, squared on four sides and joined with a square or quarter notch.

By 1838 the Rice log home was complete. Two other log rooms had been added, built with large timbers, squared on four sides and joined at the corners with a more sophisticated half-dovetail notch. An open hall or dogtrot connected the original cabin with the second, and a double fireplace and exterior loft stair connected the second to the third cabin. An open front porch and possibly three shed rooms at the rear ran the full length of the structure at one time. Joseph Rice died in 1866. Willie continued to reside in their home until her death in 1886, and succeeding generations of the Rice family occupied the structure until 1923. During that time, the Rice log home was adapted and modified to meet the changing needs of the family. Between 1923 and 1928 the Rice family moved the structure twice. Finally it was used as a garage and barn until 1963. The history of these changes could be vaguely traced by the marks, shadows, scars, nail and auger holes, layers of paint, and bits of wallpaper that could be found throughout the rooms.

Even within the crumbling walls of this pre-Republic of Texas home it was not difficult to see the evidence of the remarkable craftsmanship and to sense the hard work that fashioned the native pine timbers into a home. Portions of the roof had collapsed. The porches had long since vanished but the original form of the three-room structure survived. Hay, dirt, discarded lumber, and debris were scattered on the loft and ground level floors.

The term restoration is often used broadly to encompass any work that is accomplished on a historic building. Restoration, in a strict sense, is the process of accurately returning a structure in form and detail to a particular period in time. The restoration of the Rice home would involve the authentic reconstruction of many parts of the building and the preservation of those features that survived.

Restoration work began in late March. The original crew consisted of three craftsmen from Nacogdoches: Kurt Keul, David Smith, and myself[1]. Our first few days were spent cleaning and sorting through the debris for salvageable materials, missing parts, or anything that belonged to the building that could be retrieved, stored, and later reinstalled. It was necessary that the maximum amount of original material be protected and retained.

We began by dismantling collapsed roof sections and trying to secure and stabilize the structure in order to make it as safe as possible for us to work there. We emptied each room, uncovered the walls, and began to record, sketch, and photograph what was there and make an accurate inventory of deteriorated logs and materials that would require repair or replacement.

As with any restoration project, it was absolutely necessary to begin ordering and locating materials from the very start. The integrity of the work depended upon the use of authentic, traditional building techniques and materials that matched the kind and character of those available to Joseph Rice in the 1830's. We continually called on small lumber mills scattered in East Texas. We searched out abandoned, derelict buildings for useable parts. In time we were able to locate or have custom cut most of the materials that our work would require.

Since round wire nails were not introduced into Texas

until 1880, square cut nails had to be obtained. We also had to acquire rough-sawn, full dimension pine lumber for porch steps, stairs and rails; 1" tongue-and-groove flooring; board lumber for trim, doors, shutters, and mantles; window sash; flat sheet window glass with waves and seeds; and appropriate hardware, hinges, and rimlocks. Unlike many log structures whose logs were chinked with mud or plaster, the walls in the Rice home were sealed with ⅜" to ½" thick horizontal boards, most of which were missing and had to be replaced. Much time and effort was spent collecting materials because each new piece had to match the original as closely as possible in size, shape, texture, and configuration.

After the rooms were swept and the materials ordered, the time had come to sharpen our axes and begin the task of hewing the new timbers for the restoration. Our attention shifted from the building to the sea of logs that surrounded the structure. The Parks and Wildlife Department had furnished us with 150 pine timbers ranging from seven to twenty-eight inches in diameter to be used for the structural restoration. For twelve days the ringing of axes could be heard from early morning, when the chill kept us wrapped in long sleeved shirts, until late afternoon, when we stood exhausted and barechested to the heat of the work and sun. It took about a week for the blisters on our hands to turn to calluses.

Each log became a piece of sculpture to us. Each was selected for a specific use. The log was rolled and sized to take advantage of its contours. Chalklines were stretched over its length to mark the line; the timber was scored and then hewed square with a board axe and foot adze into a 4" x 10" wall log, 6" x 6" joist, or an 8" x 8" sill. Three of the larger logs were hewn into long 4" x 10" timbers to be used as girts that ran across the width of each cabin and

Rice home soon after it was moved
(Courtesy of Texas Parks and Wildlife Department)

Rice home after restoration
(Courtesy of Texas Parks and Wildlife Department)

251

Steve Whiston using foot adze
(Courtesy of Texas Parks and Wildlife Department)

Rice home after restoration
(Courtesy of Texas Parks and Wildlife Department)

Hewing a log
(Photograph by David Smith)

252

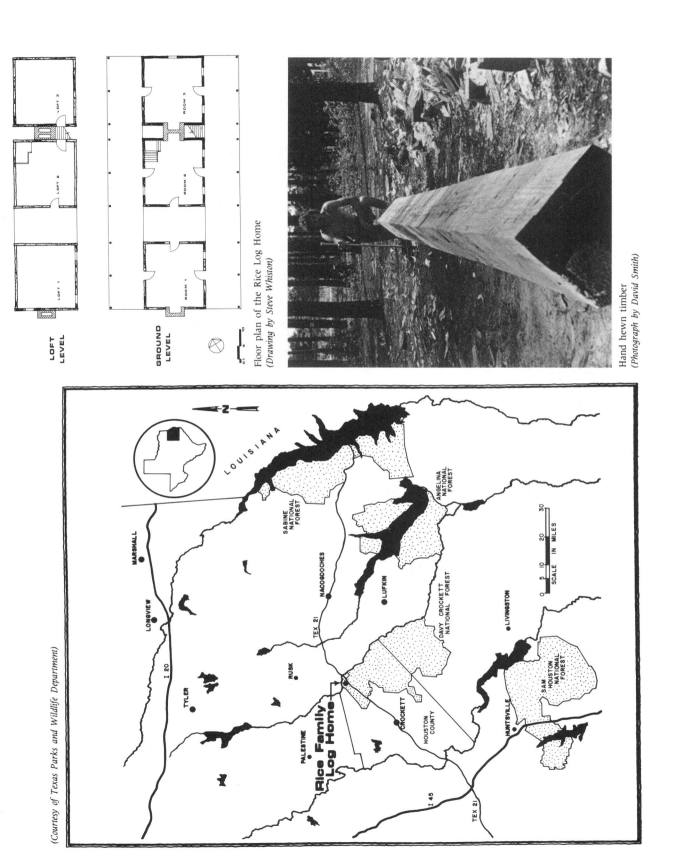

(Courtesy of Texas Parks and Wildlife Department)

LOFT
LEVEL

GROUND
LEVEL

LOFT 1

LOFT 2

LOFT 3

ROOM 1

ROOM 2

ROOM 3

Floor plan of the Rice Log Home
(Drawing by Steve Whiston)

Hand hewn timber
(Photograph by David Smith)

LOUISIANA

SABINE
NATIONAL
FOREST

ANGELINA
NATIONAL
FOREST

DAVY CROCKETT
NATIONAL FOREST

SAM
HOUSTON
NATIONAL
FOREST

MARSHALL

LONGVIEW

TYLER

RUSK

NACOGDOCHES

TEX 21

LUFKIN

Rice Family
Log Home

PALESTINE

CROCKETT

HOUSTON
COUNTY

LIVINGSTON

HUNTSVILLE

TEX 21

I 45

I 20

0   5   10   20   30

SCALE IN MILES

253

V-notch
(Photograph by Steve Whiston)

Half-dovetail notch
(Photograph by Steve Whiston)

254

extended ten feet beyond the eaves in each direction to support the porch roofs. The longest of these timbers measured forty-two feet. Two were required for room #1 and one for room #3.

For days the fires burned the pine chips and shavings from our hewing. Many of the chips were shared with campers who occasionally passed close by to watch and talk and sometimes recommend perhaps an easier way to go about what we were doing. To those interested we would explain that our methods were simple and that every tool leaves a particular, distinguishable mark on the surface of the material. Traditional tools—the broadaxe, adze, drawknife, chisel, plane, hand auger, and crosscut saw—all leave very characteristic marks that are quite different from the impressions left by modern and perhaps more convenient tools.

When the hewing was complete we were back at work again on the house. Years of settling and shifting, and the move from its former location, had left the three rooms misaligned. All were to be leveled, realigned, and set upon new, treated, hewn sills and round wooden piers. Some careful planning, a few strategically located trees, a system of steel cables, jacks, and wenches, and frequent shoving, kicking, and cussing enabled us to bring each section in line so that they all could be properly tied and spliced together at the sills and the eaves.

Of the three rooms, the original one was the most badly deteriorated and had sustained the most changes. The floor had been totally removed and the ceiling and loft floor had been raised. The fireplace and chimney on the south endwall had been dismantled and a large opening had been cut in the logs so the room could serve as a garage. Most of the logs of room #1 required repair and splicing or replacement. A decision was made to take the entire cabin

apart and reconstruct it, using as many of the original logs as possible. Logs were taken from the cabin one at a time and marked and laid out in sequence onto wood supports on the ground. It took two days to disassemble the cabin and eleven days to restack it. We duplicated the original corner joints of each log using a V-notch on the ground level and a square notch on the half-story loft. Auger holes found in the original wall logs were faithfully reproduced in the new logs. New hewn logs were introduced to close the garage opening so that a brick fireplace could be reconstructed. Two new thirty-eight-foot girts were inched slowly into place on two inclined log skids that reached from the ground to the top of the wall at each corner.

Room #2 had survived the years in good condition and required few structural repairs. It was leveled and set upon new sills, and two sections of hewn pine were spliced onto the rotted ends of two girts. Room #3 was then leveled and brought into alignment with the second room.

The north endwall of room #3 also had to be dismantled and rebuilt because so many of the logs were rotted due to the years of exposure to the weather. New ends were spliced onto some of the logs where the notches were badly decayed and unable to support the weight of the logs above. Our splices were glued and pinned with wood pegs. We were able to save and reinstall only a few of the upper logs at the loft. Most of the wall was replaced with new timbers. Each new log, like its original counterpart, was joined at the corners with a half-dovetail notch. Each notch was custom cut to fit tightly onto the previous log, locking it into place.

After the walls of the three rooms were complete, work began on the porches, columns, and porch beams so that in time the roof could be installed and the structure "dried in." Porch columns were rough-sawn 6" x 6" pine that we planed smooth by hand. The columns supported a hewn 6" x 6" beam that ran the entire length of the structure and upon which rested the porch rafters. We had earlier spent almost four days cutting, hauling, peeling, and stacking approximately 150 twelve-foot pine poles to be used as rafters. We spent another three days picking, pulling, and scratching the ticks that came with the rafters. One-inch, wane-edge or bark-edge boards of random width were nailed to the pole rafters for sheathing. A cedar shake roof was then installed with a weather ridge that extended the last course of shakes toward the east in the direction of the prevailing winds.

The fireplace and chimneys of the Rice log home were to be reconstructed using brick that matched an early brick sample that was uncovered during an archaeological investigation by Parks and Wildlife at the original site. Measuring 9¾" x 4½" x 2¼", the brick was made of local red-orange clay and hand-pressed in wooden molds. Suitable bricks were the most difficult material to find. We were finally able to locate an acceptable, used brick in Nacogdoches that was somewhat lighter in color but of the approximate size. We employed three brick masons to rebuild the fireplaces and set the brick hearths.

The next six weeks were spent restoring the pine floors, building board-and-batten doors, repairing and installing window sash and shutters, and building new wooden mantles for each of the three fireplaces. A new interior stairway was constructed to the loft in room #2, and an exterior stair was added between rooms #2 and #3 at the chimney.

The weathered and neglected log structure had been restored, and our work was finished 180 days after we began. Its rough features had been renewed. The history and heritage that was held in its hand-hewn log walls was preserved.

In our eyes, the Rice family log home is a monument, not because of what we did there, but because it is an outstanding example of our early material culture and folk architecture. After 180 days, we understood the investment Joseph Rice made there. The labor and craft that is required to carve by hand a triple-pen log structure enlarged its scale, in our eyes, beyond its actual proportions.

Many times throughout the project when we faced what seemed to be an unsurmountable problem we would ask ourselves, "How would Joseph Rice have done this?" He taught us a great deal. Not only did he share his knowledge of historic building technology, but he made us better understand the lifestyle of early Texas settlers and how they related to their environment. He taught us about climate, design, and orientation, and about deterioration and decay. Most importantly, Rice taught us to be tolerant, practical, to trust our feelings, and to appreciate simple things. He gave us respect for what we could do with our own hands.

NOTES:

[1] Other craftsmen who worked on the Rice home were David George, John Daniel, David Mohundro, Eric Keul, Ralph Fulton, Bill Mangham, Paul Engelmeier, Bill Edelbrock, Scott Goerlich. The following people contributed in their own way to its successful completion: Karl Lovett, Fred Crist, Jim Jongeward, Plev Cutler, Olden Dee, Severn Rogers, and the little Pentacostal lady who operated a grocery store in Weches and supplied us with RC Colas.

The restoration of Fort Leaton in Presidio County
(Courtesy of Texas Parks and Wildlife Department)

257

The University of Texas Winedale Historical Center
(Courtesy of Gloria Jaster and the Center)

Outdoor Museums in Texas

Willard B. Robinson

A strong interest in folk buildings was developed during the twentieth century. The rustic charm of indigenous buildings and their organic unity with their environment has generated much appreciation among historians, artists, and people generally. This, along with the desire to preserve and present the history of particular social groups and the way they lived, has led to the development of several outdoor museums in Texas where folk buildings have been moved in, restored, and are now being preserved. At several locations attempts are being made to develop living museums. These are house museums with people assigned to re-create old-time living conditions by practicing the crafts of the time—quilt making, blacksmithing, and spinning and weaving, to mention a few.

Perhaps the most serious criticism of many outdoor museums is that the buildings are moved from original, sometimes widely dispersed, sites to a common location, like bringing animals to a zoo. Since the original settings of historic structures are considered to be an integral attribute related to the structure, some preservationists believe that displacing a building is an undesirable procedure. Nonetheless, there are several conditions that justify moving old buildings to a new location. First, due to isolation and inaccessibility, many historically important buildings left without maintenance would be completely lost through deterioration. Moreover, most folk buildings are inaccessible to visitors, thus limiting their educational

potential. In some instances, cities and industry have moved in and engulfed the old structures and would destroy them if they were not moved. Old buildings moved to a special location as part of an outdoor museum can be maintained and visited, and their original historical atmosphere can be re-created through accurate landscaping.

The successful house museum includes the same kind of utensils, equipment, and decorations that were a part of them originally. The well-planned outdoor museum also involves the visitor. Rather than viewing exhibits from outside, the visitor is encouraged to imagine himself as a part of the atmosphere and to develop an appreciation of historical environments. With authentically restored buildings in accurately landscaped settings, the sights, sounds, smells, and materials associated with historical times illustrate the qualities of life in eras past. Basic to several, if not all, folk museums in Texas is the use and preservation of traditional methods. At the Institute of Texan Cultures, opened in 1968, crafts and building techniques are preserved and demonstrated. A log cabin, located on the grounds, represents some aspects of the complex Texas log culture. During the Institute's annual Texas Folklife Festival, folk building techniques—log hewing and notching, chimney building, shingle riving— are regularly demonstrated in the building of model log houses.

The concept of the outdoor museum, as a collection of

buildings preserving folk techniques, originated in the Scandinavian countries during the last quarter of the nineteenth century. In the beginning outdoor museums collected and displayed native costumes and agricultural implements. The next step was to demonstrate the items in actual use. Perhaps the most influential European institution is Skansen, founded by Artur Hazelius in 1891 in Stockholm, Sweden. Among the objectives of this museum were the preservation and interpretation of the rural culture, including craftsmanship.

In the United States, outdoor museums which preserved buildings and re-created traditional building practices were not developed until the early part of the twentieth century. Efforts to preserve Old Economy Village, Pennsylvania, a Utopian community established by the Harmony Society, were commenced in 1919. Old Sturbridge Village in Massachusetts has been among the most influential institutions providing direction for living outdoor museums which preserve and present folk architecture and crafts in action. Its focus is early New England farming, and numerous outdoor museums apparently have been influenced by this fine institution. While Old Economy is comprised of structures preserved on their original sites, Old Sturbridge Village is comprised of buildings moved in from their original locations.

In Texas, outdoor museums have been established and supported in various ways: by individuals and foundations, and by city, state, and national park services, to mention the main contributors. Interested, dedicated, and wealthy individuals concerned with their state's heritage have been responsible for most of the restorations. Many structures have been restored for their beauty's sake and for the sake of history, but some houses and museums have been restored with particular emphases. Some restorations are associated with important personalities, such as Anson Jones' Barrington at Washington-on-the-Brazos, Sam Houston's home in Huntsville, and the boyhood home of Lyndon Johnson in Johnson City. The Sauer Homestead in LBJ State Park emphasizes the German farming settlement, and the Ranching Heritage Center at Lubbock emphasizes Texas ranching. The missions of San Antonio illustrate the ethnic focus, as does the Navarro House in San Antonio and Henkel Square in the German area of Round Top.

While not specifically classed as folk architecture, buildings at several restorations of nineteenth-century forts provide insight into another phase of frontier life. Both National Park Service and Texas State Parks and Wildlife Department maintain outdoor museums with excellent restorations. Fort Davis National Historical site in Jeff Davis County and Fort McKavett State Historical Park in Menard County are excellent representations portraying military life in buildings that were originally erected utilizing folk techniques. Both were built near the mid-nineteenth century.

Early efforts in developing interest in Texas pioneer arts and crafts were made by Ima Hogg and Mrs. Charles Bybee. Both of these Texas philanthropists were interested in the assembling and collecting of early Texas furnishings and equipment, and both have been responsible for the restoration and preservation of folk structures. Miss Hogg's at Winedale and Mrs. Bybee's at nearby Round Top.

In 1963, Miss Ima, as she was affectionately known, purchased and restored historic properties at Winedale in Fayette County, which two years later she donated to The University of Texas at Austin. Emphasizing regional decorative arts, the Winedale Museum displays both Anglo-American and German traditions. Included in this

Dallas Heritage Park

261

Sam Houston Park bandstand
(*Houston*)

262

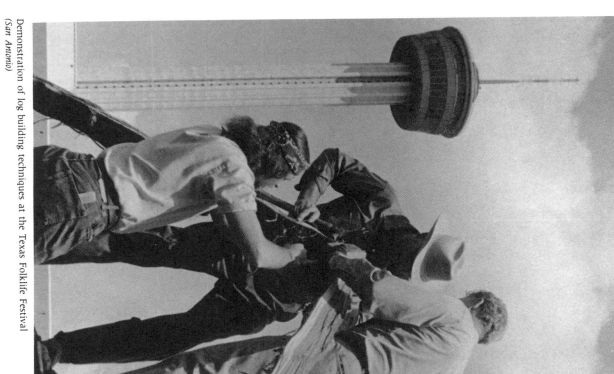

Demonstration of log building techniques at the Texas Folklife Festival
(*San Antonio*)

Sam Houston Park
(*Houston*)

263

Millard's Crossing *(Nacogdoches)*

Henkel Square *(Round Top)*

complex is the Sam Lewis house, a two-story frame dwelling, with a central breezeway, or dog-trot. An Anglo type, apparently built in stages, the house was begun as a one-room dwelling by William S. Townsend in 1834. Other sections were later added by another owner, Samuel K. Lewis, to create the present form. The style of building was brought to Texas from the Southeast United States. The framework was of sawed cedar. Although the form is Anglo, the elaborate interior wall and ceiling stenciling and painting was German. This was done by Rudolf Melchior, a talented German decorative painter. Nearby are two restored out buildings, one of which is a kitchen, the other a smokehouse. Also included on the 190-acre site of the outdoor museum are two large, restored barns. One is an oak log barn consisting of four cribs, covered by a single roof. The other barn, similar in structure, was altered to contain a stage and small auditorium which is now being used in the Museum's educational program.

After the Winedale properties were donated to The University of Texas, several other dwellings were moved to the site. A dog-trot house, Hazel's Lone Oak, dating from the 1850's, now contains offices. Lauderdale House (1858), serves as a dormitory for visitors participating in programs. The McGregor-Grimm House (1861) has been restored as museum piece. The McGregor-Grimm dwelling, originally located on a Washington County farm near Wesley, displays handsome Greek Revival form with central hall plan and fine German wall and ceiling paintings, also by Melchoir. The painted decorations include floral border ceiling patterns, floral friezes of morning glories, marbleized fireplace framework and freehand and stenciled decoration. In addition, wood graining was employed on doors and hall wainscots to further enhance the interiors.

Among the significant outdoor museums with log houses is Henkel Square at Round Top, with structures moved in and restored under the sponsorship of Mr. and Mrs. Charles Bybee. Henkel Square is now administered by the Texas Pioneer Arts Foundation, founded for that purpose by Mrs. Bybee. Included are houses of nineteenth century German design and an early church. Several log structures have been authentically restored, using materials obtained in the vicinity of the original sites. Authentic restoration work here also includes a mud cat chimney of clay, built by an East Texas family which retained knowledge of this craft. Also noteworthy are dwellings exhibiting fine interior wall stenciling. An excellent collection of early Texas furnishings is displayed within the structures.

The Harris County Heritage Society, which was incorporated in 1954 as a non-profit organization supported by contributions, also has developed an outdoor museum with buildings moved from the surrounding region. Included among the folk buildings in Sam Houston State Park, located adjacent to the Houston central business district, are The Old Place and the Kellum-Noble House. The style of both, which are in authentic restored form, expresses the times in which they were built, a desirable characteristic of any outdoor museum. Erected around 1825 by John R. Williams on a site some fifteen miles from Houston, The Old Place was a single dwelling with hewn-cedar frame walls, now covered with clapboards. It reflected the primitive conditions of the frontier on which it was built through the rough framework that originally might have been covered with pit-sawed lumber. Since stone was unavailable the chimney was built with "mudcats," a technique that was common in East Texas.

The Kellum-Noble House, built in 1847 and restored in 1955 on its original site, expresses a refinement of adopted folk building techniques that developed with the civilizing of the frontier. In response to the hot climate, the builder, Nathaniel Kelly Kellum, surrounded his house with a broad two-story porch which was covered by a projecting hip roof, a building form imported by French settlers to Louisiana and thence to Texas.

The furnishings of both these Southeast Texas dwellings express the life styles of the occupants. The frame cabin is furnished with primitive hand-made tables and chairs. The brick walls of the Kellum-Noble House contain elegant furniture of the type that would have been brought to Texas by the successful entrepreneur who built the house.

Also included in Harris County Heritage Society's restorations is St. John, an Evangelical Lutheran country church, originally built in Northwestern Harris County in 1891. In this simple frame building with its cypress plank pews, the simplicity and directness of religious services in the rural regions of Texas is preserved.

Dallas Heritage Park in Old City Park, a living history museum with regular demonstrations of spinning and weaving, includes several houses which have been moved from an area around Dallas. Buildings and furnishings have been obtained and restored by the Dallas County Heritage Society and maintained by the city's Park Department. The Miller cabin is the oldest folk building included on the site. This log structure was built in 1847 and is located near Millermore, an elegant mid-century house moved to the park in 1966. The Gano house was built in the 1850's by a physician, rancher, and businessman. Typical of many nineteenth-century folk dwellings, this is a double log cabin which had been covered with weatherboards, thereby disguising the exteriors of the logs. The rooms open into the dogrun where family activities were centered during the hot months.

Log cabins are popular restorations in Texas' outdoor museums. That type of structure played an important role on the frontier and is still a popular symbol of early Texas. The Log Cabin Village in Fort Worth includes several structures moved to the site from the surrounding region. The Fort Worth museum emphasizes log cabin building techniques and demonstrates the arts and crafts that went with the period. Interestingly, no outdoor museum apparently is interpreting the origins, development, and evolution of log construction in the state.

The best collection of East Texas houses in the Anglo style is at Millard's Crossing, just north of Nacogdoches. The project began in 1966 when Lera Millard Thomas (Mrs. Albert Thomas) restored a fine old Victorian home for her own use. Her interest in restoration and preservation continued, and she began rescuing other nineteenth century buildings from the wheels of progress and time's decay. At the present time the collection of buildings at Millard's Crossing includes ten structures, ranging from the simplest sort of log crib to the elaborations of the Victorian period. All of the houses are well furnished with pieces carefully selected to illustrate the household of the period. The Millard's Crossing museum is important for the historical interest of the buildings as well as for its illustration of nearly a century and a half of East Texas building styles.

The Ranching Heritage Center of Texas Tech University in Lubbock is an outdoor exhibit consisting of some twenty-five restored structures situated on a twelve-acre site. The chronological history and the geographical development of ranch life and range operations are interpreted through the buildings which have been moved to the Center from various places in the state. Funds for the moving and restoration are raised by the Ranching Heritage

Interior sotol house at Ranching Heritage Center
(Courtesy of Ranching Heritage Center)

Ranching Heritage Center of Texas Tech University (Lubbock)
(Courtesy of the Ranching Heritage Center)

267

Picket-and-sotol House at Ranching Heritage Center
(Courtesy of Ranching Heritage Center)

Association, a non-profit organization, and most of the work has been done since 1970.

To provide a sense of history that only the patina of time can communicate, as much original material as possible was retained in each historic structure at the Center. In many instances material weakened from deterioration was simply reinforced as unobtrusively as possible rather than replaced. Whenever new material was required the original type of material was employed. Then, insofar as today's skills allowed, the original building techniques were utilized. Thus, in the restoration of the El Capote cabin, a log shelter from the era of the Republic, the froe and mallet were used to split the shakes for the roof, and the shaving horse was used to refine them in the same manner that would have been used nearly a century and a half ago. In the same spirit, the adze was employed to hew the puncheons for the floor.

While every effort was made to minimize the visual incompatibility of new materials, it was considered essential that reconstructed details be discernible from historic forms. No attempt was made to "antique" materials to make them appear old. Careful notes relating to the installation of new materials, as well as to steps taken to conserve historic work, were recorded on drawings to aid future curators in conservation work. Characteristic of work at this and other authentic outdoor museums in Texas, the buildings at the Ranching Heritage Center were carefully researched. Before restoration was begun on any structure, the history of construction was documented as thoroughly as possible. Whenever they were available, the occupants of the various buildings as well as early visitors were interviewed, and their recollections of colors, furnishings, remodelings, etc. were recorded on tape. Then textual sources were studied to obtain additional

information. Various archival sources, courthouse documents, bills of sale, and family records were searched for official information. In addition, such other sources as travelers' journals and historic photos and paintings were studied to glean details of architecture considered to be typical to assist decisions where documentation of a detail was missing.

Basic to the philosophy followed was the recognition that taste and methodologies change and that decisions on restoration should be made only with adequate evidence and without the prejudice of 1970's taste. Moreover, every effort was made to avoid "over" restoration. With the exception of work necessary for public safety, care was exercised to avoid improving any structure beyond its original condition. This approach was also used in selecting plants in recreating the natural setting.

As has been done at several other outdoor museums, archaeological excavations were made at the original building sites in search of architectural artifacts that would provide patterns for parts and features to be reconstructed. At the site of the historic Jowell House (built ca. 1870) in Palo Pinto County, the archaeologists excavated the remains of a stone outbuilding believed to have been a springhouse, or cooler, along with a large cistern and filter system.

Among the interesting dwellings exhibiting indigenous building techniques at the Ranching Heritage Center is the Picket-and-Sotol House, a thatched-roofed structure originally located in Crockett County. This was authentically restored with roofs of sacahuiste and walls of sotol obtained from the vicinity of the original site.

Authentic restoration of primitive techniques, of course, presents significant maintenance problems. At the Ranching Heritage Center this maintenance is accepted as another part of the living museum concept. Periodic repair of chinking and adobe and the replacement of thatching is an interpretable aspect of life on the frontier that improvements made possible by twentieth-century technology would fail to convey. Moreover, continual restoration work assures that knowledge of certain actual indigenous building techniques that might otherwise be lost will be maintained for the appreciation of future generations.

The Ranching Heritage Center and other outdoor museums face many problems. Although technology has made available numerous materials which assist conservation, deterioration continues. Authentic techniques require constant maintenance and occasional rehabilitation. However, perhaps the most difficult problems evolve around the outdoor settings. The authentic exhibit requires numerous trappings, animals, and landscape features. Due to vandalism and theft these are difficult to maintain and are often neglected by other museums.

Nonetheless, in these Texas outdoor museums the visitor may develop an appreciation for folklife and art. Conducted tours at most of the museums, and open visitation at some, provide opportunities to view authentic settings similar to those known by Texas pioneers. Moreover, the folk activities sponsored by the outdoor institutions reveal further insight into life during by-gone eras. The qualities and experiences thus preserved will fortunately continue to be enjoyed and understood by future generations.

TEXAS HOUSE MUSEUMS

The following list and description of house museums is taken from the 1978 revised edition of the *Texas Museum Directory*, edited by Kit Fontaine and Vincent Scanio, compiled by Nancy Gayle, and published by the Texas Historical Commission. The list is selective and emphasizes collections of restored buildings rather than single buildings and does not include restored or reconstructed forts and missions. This listing includes the best of the state's outdoor museums as well as a representative collection of building methods and styles.

Pioneer Village: 913 West Park Avenue, Corsicana—Seven log buildings show different facets of pioneer or pre-pioneer life. Indian trading post, barn, slave cabin, blacksmith shop, and general store.

Old City Park: 1717 Gano Street, Dallas—Buildings include Millermore, 1855-1862; Gano House, 1856; Lively Cabin, 1856; Becut Place, 1876; Miller Cabin, 1847; Alut Grove Church, 1894; depot, 1886; section house, 1890; hotel, 1898; dr.'s office, 1890; general store, 1904; McCall's store, 1904.

Annie Riggs Memorial Museum: 301 S. Main Street, Fort Stockton—Museum presents area-related displays of life at the turn of the century. Pioneer rooms, cowboy room, kitchen. Rock and mineral display. House in adobe building constructed in 1899 as a hotel.

Log Cabin Village: 2121 Log Cabin Village Lane, Fort Worth—Six log cabins, all more than 100 years old, are furnished in keeping with their 19th Century construction. Restored well, working grist mill. Founded 1965.

Harris County Heritage Society: Sam Houston Park, Houston—Series of historic buildings including decorative arts of the 19th Century. Site includes four restored houses built by notable Houstonians: San Felipe Cottage, ca. 1840; Kellum-Noble House, 1847; Nicholas-Rice-Cherry House, 1850; Pillot House, 1868. Also includes reconstructed "Long Row" (originally built 1837) containing 19th

Century barber shop, general store, first "Circulating Library, Book, Stationery & Fancy Store." Restored St. John Church built by German-speaking Harris County farmers in 1891. Founded 1954.

Sam Houston Memorial Museum: 1804 Sam Houston Avenue, Huntsville—The Sam Houston Memorial Museum is the operational center for 15 acres of homestead that General Houston established in 1847. His home and log law office built that same year remain on their original locations. The Steamboat House, where he died in 1863, has been moved to the site. The museum houses the world's largest collection of Houston memorabilia.

Kermit's Medallion House Museum: North Side of Winkler County Park, Kermit—The Baird-Mosley Home, built in 1910 and relocated in "Pioneer Park" in 1969, is furnished in keeping with 1900-1910 period. Homesteader's one-room shack which was originally built 12 miles northwest of the town. The park also includes standard cable tool derrick with walking beam, last active equipment of its type in Texas. Founded 1974.

Ranch Headquarters: The Museum of Texas Tech University Complex, Lubbock—When completed, the Ranch Headquarters will consist of approximately 25 buildings representing the ranching industry from early Spanish era to the "elegant ranch house" of the early 1900's. Authentically restored interiors. Founded 1969.

Millard's Crossing Antiques and Texana Museum: 6020 North Street, Nacogdoches—Restored 1837 house, moved to site in 1971, was the first of ten traditional East Texas houses and buildings brought in and restored by Mrs. Albert Thomas. All buildings are equipped with the furniture and fixtures of their times.

Carson County Square House Museum: Fifth and Elsie Streets, Panhandle—Museum, part of a complex of restored buildings typical of the plains, shows the complete history of the area from the Indians through the Oil Boom. Restored dug-out home with furnishings used by Plains pioneers, farm and ranch building, Santa Fe Railroad caboose and windmill. Other exhibits include natural history and art. Accredited by AAM. Texas Historical Marker. Registered National Historical Site. Founded 1965.

Magdalene Charlton Memorial Museum: North Pine Street, Tomball—Complex of restored buildings including the Griffin House, circa 1858, which houses the Magdalene Charlton collection of furnishings and decorative arts; old Trinity Lutheran Church; and the farm museum depicting the rural and cultural development of the area. Founded 1964.

Pioneer Town: One mile S. of Wimberley, 7A Ranch Resort, Wimberley—Restoration and reproduction of a 19th Century Texas village. Buildings include a cafe serving pioneer menus, gunshop, printing shop, bank, barber shop, jail, ice cream parlor, emporium, hotel, arcade, opera house with melodrama and vaudeville shows, blacksmith shop. Founded 1956.

Heritage Garden Village: U.S. 190, one mile W. of town, Woodville—Recreated pioneer village—a "living museum of pioneer life"—included furnished home (Texas Historical Marker), blacksmith shop, operating grist mill, whiskey still, 1906 school, and 26 other furnished buildings. Collections of pioneer memorabilia, art and handicrafts of early Texas. Founded 1965.

Henkel Square: Round Top—Henkel Square contains restored frame houses, log cabins, and a church built in the 19th Century by German settlers of that area.

University of Texas Winedale Historical Center: 4 miles east of Round Top on F.M. 1457—Built circa 1834 and enlarged in 1848 to become "Sam Lewis' Stopping Place," the Inn now houses Pennsylvania Dutch, early Texas furniture, and other period furnishings. One room features an early ceiling mural. Also, a log cabin kitchen, smokehouse, a barn comprising four log cabins, theatre barn and the "Hazel's

Lone Oak" house which contains three exhibit rooms. Restored in 1964 by Miss Ima Hogg, and presented to the University of Texas in 1967.

Second hand log barn (*Medina Co.*)

Rock bridge abutment built in 1870's (*Hamilton Co.*)

273

Contributors

FRANCIS EDWARD ABERNETHY is a professor of English at Stephen F. Austin State University and Secretary-Editor of the Texas Folklore Society.

T. LINDSAY BAKER is Program Manager of the History of Engineering Program at Texas Tech University and the Associate Curator of History at the Panhandle-Plains Historical Museum in Canyon. His latest book is *The First Polish Americans: Silesian Settlements in Texas* (Texas A&M Press).

ANN CARPENTER is a professor of English at Angelo State University in San Angelo and is a regular contributor to the Society's publications.

G. LOYD COLLIER is professor of geography at Stephen F. Austin State University.

JAMES M. DAY is past-president of the Texas Folklore Society and is a professor of English at The University of Texas at El Paso.

ROBERT J. DUNCAN is the current president of the Texas Folklore Society and works in the research department of St. Regis Paper Company in Dallas.

THOMAS A. GREEN, who spent two years in grant-supported research on the Pueblo of Ysleta del Sur, is a professor of English at Texas A&M University.

SYLVIA GRIDER is a professor of English at Texas A&M University and is presently conducting research on the Texas Wends.

CONNIE HALL is a former instructor of English at Stephen F. Austin State University, now working on her doctorate at Texas A&M University.

TERRY G. JORDAN is Chairman of the Geography Department at North Texas State University. He is a specialist in folk-geography and recently published *Texas Log Buildings* (University of Texas Press).

274

REESMAN S. KENNEDY is a professional artist, the owner of Gallery 107 in Nacogdoches, and is a professor of art at Stephen F. Austin State University.

GLEN LICH AND LERA TYLER are a husband-and-wife research and writing team, formerly of Southwest Texas State University, now of the English department at the University of New Orleans.

HOWARD N. MARTIN is the manager of the Research Department of the Houston Chamber of Commerce. He is the author of *Myths & Folktakes of the Alabama-Coushatta Indians of Texas* (Encino Press) and serves as the reservation's historical consultant.

WILLARD B. ROBINSON, the author of *Texas Public Buildings of the Nineteenth Century*, is a professor of architecture at Texas Tech University.

TERRI ROSS, formerly of McMurry College in Abilene, is a recent mother and Ph.D. and is an instructor of English at The University of Texas.

ERNEST B. SPECK, the editor of *Mody Boatright, Folklorist* (University of Texas Press), is a professor of English at Sul Ross State University.

THOMAS J. STANLY is Head of the Department of Agriculture at Stephen F. Austin State University.

LONN TAYLOR is the Curator of History for the Dallas Historical Society at the Hall of State and is the author of *Texas Furniture: The Cabinetmakers and Their Work, 1840–1880.*

PAT ELLIS TAYLOR of Edgewood and other points is a free-lance writer and editor of the *Hot Springs Information Network.*

JOHN O. WEST, the recent editor of the *American Folklore Newsletter*, is a professor of English at The University of Texas at El Paso.

STEVE WHISTON is a first-class carpenter and log-house builder who presently is working as a restoration architect in the Historic Sites and Restoration Branch of Texas Parks and Wildlife Department.

C. W. WIMBERLEY of Wimberley is a free-lance writer and author of *Wimberley Hills: A Pioneer Heritage* (Von Boeckman-Jones, Printers).

Index

Page numbers in italics indicate a photograph or illustration on that page.

286

Speck, Ernest B., 275
spider's web, 5
spikes, 85
split rail fences, 156, 189
    mortised, 183
    stake-and-rider style, 179, 181, 182, 261
    varieties of, 175, 178–182
split slabs, 150
splitting wood, 101
spool and spurs barbed wire, 199
springs, 227. See also water
Spur Ranch, 53
Spur Wheel barbed wire, 199, 205
square notching, 78, 79–80, 82, 249
St. John Lutheran Church, 266
stables, 133, 154–161
stairs, outdoor, 16, 116
stake and rider fences, 179, 181, 182, 261
Stallings, D. D., 218
stalls, 133, 154–161
Standiford, Les, 91
Stanly, Thomas J., 275
steam power, 241, 244
steel's effect on construction techniques, 103
Stephen F. Austin State University, viii
Sterling City, Texas, 215
stile gates, 185
stock tanks, 214
stone jugs, 229
stone structures. See rock structures
stonemasons, 132
storage structures, 100, 102, 112
storm cellars, 163
stoves, vii, 57
straw binder in mud, 118
Stubb-Plate barbed wire, 205
stucco, 43 n. 22
Sunday houses, 39
sweat houses, 103

Sweetwater, Texas, 54
Syers, Ed, 218
syrup-making, 164, 166

T
Taos, New Mexico, 61
tarantulas, 58, 162
Taylor, Lonn, 275
Taylor, Pat Ellis, 275
telephone poles used in buildings, 7
Temple, Buddy and Ellen, viii
tepees, 53, 95
Texas and Pacific Railroad, 216
Texas Folklife Festival, 259, 262
Texas Folklore Society, viii, 41, 197
Texas Greenback Party, 203
Texas Museum Directory, 270
Texas Parks and Wildlife Department, 249, 250, 256, 260
Texas Pioneer Arts Foundation, 265
Texas Rangers, 203
Texas Tech University Ranching Heritage Center, 260, 266, 267–268, 269–270
thatch roofs, 121, 131
Thomas, Lera Millard, 266
Tidewater region's architectural influence, 21–22, 29
tie structures
    barns, 84, 87–89
    fences, 176, 190
    houses, 85, 90
Tigua Indians, 97–99
Time Inc., viii
tin roofs, 121, 150
tongue-and-groove floorboards, 142, 250
tool houses, 7
tools
    adze, 45, 252, 269
    drawknife, 45, 255
    foot adze, 252
    Fresno scraper, 225